STUDIO A

THE BOB DYLAN READER

STUDIO A

THE BOB DYLAN READER

EDITED BY BENJAMIN HEDIN

W. W. NORTON & COMPANY

NEW YORK   LONDON

Since this page cannot accommodate all the copyright notices, pages 317–21 constitute an
extension of the copyright page.

Manufacturing by The Haddon Craftsmen, Inc.
Book design by Dana Sloan
Production manager: Anna Oler

Library of Congress Cataloging-in-Publication Data
Hedin, Benjamin.
Studio A : the Bob Dylan reader / edited by Benjamin Hedin.
p. cm.
Includes bibliographical references and index.
ISBN 0-393-05844-1 (hardcover)
1. Dylan, Bob, 1941– I. Title.
ML420.D98H44 2004
782.42164'092—dc22

2004013616

ISBN 0-393-32742-6 pbk.

W. W. Norton & Company, Inc., 500 Fifth Avenue, New York, N.Y. 10110
www.wwnorton.com

W. W. Norton & Company Ltd., Castle House, 75/76 Wells Street, London W1T 3QT

1 2 3 4 5 6 7 8 9 0

For my brother, Alex

CONTENTS

INTRODUCTION

BOB DYLAN seems even more respected today than he was in the sixties, when he was a leading figure in folk and rock music as well as a talented lyricist whose writings aspired to the condition of poetry. This past decade could be the most exciting era of Dylan's life, since the most recent collections of original songs and live recordings—*Time Out of Mind, Love and Theft* and further installments of *The Bootleg Series*—are not just a "return to form," but the summing up and moving forward of an entire career. Besides, as Robert Christgau put it some years ago, there's really no place for Dylan to return *to*: his moment has long since passed. Or has it? The culture's answer is an emphatic no: lately, he has received a nomination for the Nobel Prize, a Kennedy Center Honor, several Grammys and an Oscar. Dylan, who now writes about forgotten relics, like Charley Patton or the horse and buggy, and plays more state fairs than arenas, is everywhere and nowhere at the same time; he is the retired candidate who gets elected once he stops running for office. So while in many ways the awards and headlines are unavoidable and feel like just recognition, they make it difficult to go back and find some sort of objective starting point.

But go back we must. In 1961, the year of Dylan's debut with Columbia, many of rock's central figures were at the margins: Elvis was at the movies, Buddy Holly was dead, Chuck Berry had been out of the Top 40 since 1959 and it would be three years before the Beatles landed at JFK. The top spots on the charts were held by groups like Dick & Deedee and Bobby Vee. Their songs were variations on the classic verse-chorus form, topped off with a little vocal harmony and the appropriate amount of orchestral embellishment. The emphasis was on polish, not design. "People didn't know who Leadbelly was," Dylan says. "They never heard Leadbelly, they didn't hear Blind Willie McTell, they didn't hear Woody Guthrie."* And, "Life is full of complexities and rock and roll didn't reflect that. It was just put on a happy face and ride Sally ride."† This explains his ambivalent embrace of the folk community; it is likely that had he waited a few years before coming to New York, during the reign of British rock and R&B, Dylan would have turned immediately to rock—skipping, in effect, his folkie debut and beginning with the likes of "Mixed-Up Confusion" or "She Belongs to Me."

Yet Dylan's passion for the sounds of Americana was no kind of youthful caprice or posturing, and he never turned his back to the folk ethos. Technique was always secondary to craft: the legends are plenty about studio faux pas, buttons scratching across guitars and vows to never record more than one take. In *The Recording Sessions*, his book-length study of Dylan's recording habits, Clinton Heylin points out that while many figures of the sixties were using the studio to come up with more elaborate pop arrangements, Dylan was suspicious of and antagonistic toward the technological novelties being explored inside Abbey Road and elsewhere. It took the Beatles 129 days to record *Sgt. Pepper*, and Heylin reminds us that "Dylan managed to record his entire studio output up to and including 1976's *Desire* in just 90 days!" Even with a dozen musicians behind him, Dylan valued primacy of spirit over production, and his songs still had more in common with Frank Hutchison than the Shirelles. *Don't mind me: I'm only singing the tradition*, he was saying, *one that goes back at least as far as Leadbelly and probably further* (see Greil Marcus), *one that will outlive me, the critics and tomorrow afternoon's opening act.*

What's more, by "going electric" Dylan had given the burgeoning rock idiom its poet laureate. In the development of contemporary pop, lyrics had always been important, but usually for the dramatic purpose of plot in musicals and operettas, or to showcase the singing talents of a Billie Holiday or Louis Armstrong. There were highly sophisticated lyrics, of course, in the nineteenth-century songs of Schubert, Schumann, and more recently, in the work of composers like Ives, Copland and Rorem. But these words, many of which were penned by Goethe, Heine, Dickinson and

---

* Bob Dylan, interview by Serge Kaganski, *Mojo* (February 1998): 64.

† Bob Dylan, interview by Cameron Crowe, liner notes to *Biograph*: 35.

Whitman, were preexisting texts of poetry to be appreciated and studied on their own terms—and unlikely to figure in on most commentaries of art song. Dylan turns this on its head: a common reaction to his early albums was something like "The guy can't sing or play the guitar, but I sure love the words. He's really a poet!" Here was a popular songwriter who didn't sing about blue skies or funny valentines or farmers and cowmen, but elicited comparisons—justifiably or not—to William Blake and T. S. Eliot. The theme and structure of "Desolation Row" and "Visions of Johanna" were endlessly debatable and provocative topics. Even his liner notes could be thought of as minor works of art. Later, the excited teenagers and college students who stayed up all night hoping to decipher "Maggie's Farm" became professors, journalists and other leaders of the educational hierarchy. I'm not sure when exactly the Academic Jazz Age began, but one of its more telling trends has been the proliferation of rock and popular music studies courses that can be taken alongside or instead of a seminar on Western music. Dylan 101, coming to a university near you.

In fact, this (almost certainly unconscious and unintentional) role in democratization seems like a more significant cultural effect than, say, social protest or Jewishness vis-à-vis Christianity. Dylan rose to popularity during the time when the distinction between "highbrow" and "lowbrow" became irrevocably confused. Reading lyrics and listening to rock and roll suddenly had something to do with more than drugs or dance—for some, it had turned into an intellectual exercise. The baby-boom era was marked by such ideas and events: Campbell's soup cans, the marriage of Marilyn Monroe and Arthur Miller, metafiction.

And then something happened: the sixties ended, and Dylan kept on writing songs. Longevity is normally not the property of rock stars. Starting around 1970, Dylan began to call his into question, while releasing an exception-tease of indisputable greatness every five years or so. Though he continued to experiment with a variety of strains of pop, some of these experiments—*Self Portrait, Saved, Down in the Groove*—were difficult to accept, and they put off more than a few listeners. His lyrical energy suffered. In the late seventies, of course, Dylan found God; personal convictions aside, this now looks like a desperate and confused method of solace to which he turned in the hopes of escaping fame and its attendant pressures.

Fans and critics had long since divided into camps; you were either for him or against him. As Alex Ross notes in "The Wanderer," no one could wait before mythologizing the earlier self: in this way, Dylan was the rarest of pop culture survivors—he had managed to both burn out *and* fade away. The specter of the sixties hung on his back. The highest praise any album could hope for was to be "the best since *Blood on the Tracks*." Certainly the market helped things somewhat (Bono: "If Bob Dylan walked into a record company in 1987 and played them 'Subterranean Homesick Blues' and told them it was a hit record, they would show him the door"*), and in many ways it seemed a happy break-up; as early as 1965 Dylan described his music as "historical-traditional," and if he wasn't allowed to sing "Talkin' John Birch" on *The Ed Sullivan Show*—well he couldn't really sing it on *Total Request Live*, either.

This opened something up in him: being forgotten, Dylan said a few years ago, "was the best thing that ever happened to me." Written off and on his own, so to speak, he was free to go about searching for the bottom line. Tom Piazza said it best when he wrote that instead of choosing one of his influences over the others, Dylan finally decided to make room for all of them. In other words, Dylan kept trying out new voices and styles— folk, blues, gospel, rock—until he realized that his true voice was all the voices at once. The various recording slumps can surely be attributed to the anxiety inherent in such a lesson—a lesson that is made possible, perhaps, only with age. In 1997 *Time Out of Mind* came out and he had returned to center stage, brought back from the dead, right there on the cover of *Newsweek*, saying, "the songs are my lexicon. I believe the songs." Dylan has demonstrated a willingness to learn in public, and we've all had to learn alongside him—about ourselves, certainly, but also about America and the literature of song. Most of all, song: in its ability to depict mature thought, or a set of images or as a tool of narrative expression, popular music has advanced significantly since 1961—and generous praise is owed Dylan for helping to make it a more accommodating and eclectic idiom.

---

* Holly George-Warren and Shawn Duhl, eds., *Rolling Stone: The Complete Covers* (New York: Harry N. Abrams, 1988), 115.

ALL OF THIS may or may not explain why writers have been so singularly drawn to Dylan's music. At one point it seemed that the unifying appeal between these pieces would be relatively easy to identify: his American-ness, I thought at first, the blending of indigenous poetry and oral musics. Surely that was the reason the literati had been following him around for forty-plus years. Then again, it could be the voice, that scratchy, unmistak-ably human timbre. Or the love songs; and so on. In the end, I realized that this was one man's opinion, and nothing more. People make of Dylan what they will, which I suppose is the point of this collection. "It may be the most purely American music for us," says Joyce Carol Oates, who also observes how Dylan's voice is "frankly nasal, as if sandpaper could sing." Camille Paglia insists, "His best work shows how the creative imagination operates—in a hallucinatory stream of sensations and emotions that per-haps even the embattled artist does not fully understand." Earlier, Rick Moody describes *Blood on the Tracks* as an "album of love only briefly found and then voluminously, expertly, incisively lost, album that proves that all love has something *lost* in it." Michael Chabon remembers sitting on the floor of his room, a lonely and confused thirteen-year-old, listening to *Desire* for the first time.

While hoping to preserve a more or less linear progression through the man's biography, I tried not to follow a rigid quota concerning the length of each section; that Part Three covers eighteen years in 90 or so pages is an unavoidable and somewhat regrettable consequence of the way the goods have been handed down over the years. With over 300 pages to work with, something had to give, and the reviews of *Knocked Out Loaded* seemed like a good place to start. Besides, with its emphasis on slumps and comebacks, the tone of Dylanology 1985–1990 is all but identical to that of 1970–1975. I did aspire for parity between critics on one hand and poets and novelists on the other; that was the best way, it seemed, to communi-cate as holistic a sense as possible of Dylan's legacy. Not everything on the wish list could be included here. Dylan's 1964 letter to Lawrence Fer-linghetti remains unpublished, and nothing from Joan Baez's memoir was allowed to be included. *Rolling Stone* also refused to grant permission for anything under their copyright, so I am unable to reprint David Fricke's wonderful review of *Live 1966*. When it became difficult to choose one entry over another, I often included the piece more germane to *Studio A*'s dominant theme—Dylan's indebtedness to and place in the folk/blues tradition. I think that even a cursory read over the table of contents will reveal that the selection concentrates on Dylan the singer-songwriter and excludes commentary on his lesser-known but worthy projects like *Tarantula*, *Renaldo and Clara* and *Masked and Anonymous*.

It might be said that the anthology moves in a single direction: just after Dylan went into his garage to record the public domain tracks on *Good as I Been to You*, critics began trying to definitively identify his proper context, in a more articulate manner than the Guthrie-Kerouac theory of earlier times. Greil Marcus chose the folk songs that were tied to the Great Depression and, before that, the entire American project; Sean Wilentz wisely points out that "of course, among the great old last-century songwriters whom Dylan recycles is himself." Alex Ross, at one point, compares Dylan's singing to seventeenth-century English opera. When it comes to context, everyone has a theory. In the early sixties, Duke Ellington described rock and roll—somewhat romantically—as "the most raucous form of jazz." Jazz came first, said Ellington, but it didn't matter, finally, since at the end of the day both should be considered folk music. All popular music had these same roots, so the future of music was beyond reproach—it couldn't outlast or escape its past, and would just go on citing its antecedents. This seems more and more convincing the longer Dylan stays on the road, and it is as good a reason as any for writers to keep on writing. Underlying the works that comprise *Studio A* is a set of simple but profound questions, which are not altogether different from those asked by the songwriter: What is the nature of our past, of our roots? And how must they affect our lives today?

Benjamin Hedin

PART ONE

I WAS YOUNG
WHEN I LEFT HOME
(1961–1969)

"Song is the reincarnation of a poem which
was destroyed in order to live again in music."

—*Ned Rorem*

My Life in a Stolen Moment

BOB DYLAN

Dylan's creation myth is elaborate and well publicized. Though he led a comfortable and stable childhood in Hibbing, Minnesota, Dylan began to reinvent his background when he moved to New York at the age of nineteen. Starting out as a musician, he hoped to earn a reputation similar to those of his heroes—Woody Guthrie, Lightnin' Sam Hopkins, and other blues and folk singers.

This prose-poem was included in the program for a concert at New York's Town Hall on April 12, 1963. A cross between a ballad and a poetic catalog, "My Life in a Stolen Moment" reveals a youthful awe of the blues lifestyle; abandonment and the open road are riffed on at length, and its colloquial syntax shows how Dylan thought hobos spoke. As far as his life story goes, some of its claims are false. Dylan never ran away from home, for instance, served time in jail or played gigs like the "Indian festivals in Gallup, New Mexico." But within this embellished exterior, many of the lines are informative. He chronicles his frustrating days as a college student, his first trip to New York and, toward the end of the piece, offers some mature thoughts on the pervasiveness of influence.

Duluth's an iron ore shipping town in Minnesota
It's built up on a rocky cliff that runs into Lake Superior
I was born there—my father was born there—
My mother's from the Iron Range Country up north
The iron range is a long line a mining towns
        that began in Grand Rapids and end at Eveleth

We moved up there to live with my mother's folks
     in Hibbing when I was young—
Hibbing's got the biggest open pit ore mine in the world
Hibbing's got schools, churches, grocery stores an' a jail
It's got high school football games an' a movie house
Hibbing's got souped-up cars runnin' full blast
     on a Friday night
Hibbing's got corner bars with polka bands
You can stand at one end of Hibbing on the main drag
     an' see clear past the city limits on the other end
Hibbing's a good ol' town
I ran away from it when I was 10, 12, 13, 15, $15\frac{1}{2}$, 17 an' 18
I been caught an' brought back all but once
I wrote my first song to my mother an' titled it "To Mother"
I wrote that in 5th grade an' the teacher gave me a B+
I started smoking at 11 years old an' only stopped once
     to catch my breath
I don't remember my parents singing too much
At least I don't remember swapping any songs with them
Later I sat in college at the University of Minnesota
     on a phony scholarship that I never had
I sat in science class an' flunked out for refusin' to watch
     a rabbit die
I got expelled from English class for using four-letter words
     in a paper describing the English teacher
I also failed out of communication class for callin' up
     every day and sayin' I couldn't come
I did OK in Spanish though but I knew it beforehand
I's kept around for kicks at a fraternity house
They let me live there an' I did until they wanted me to join
I moved in with two girls from South Dakota
     in a two-room apartment for two nights
I crossed the bridge to 14th Street an' moved in above
     a bookstore that also sold bad hamburgers
     basketball sweatshirts an' bulldog statues
I fell hard for an actress girl who kneed me in the guts

an' I ended up on the East Side a the Mississippi River
with about ten friends in a condemned house underneath
the Washington Avenue Bridge just south a Seven Corners
That's pretty well my college life
After that I thumbed my way to Galveston, Texas in four days
tryin' to find an ol' friend whose ma met me
at the screen door and said he's in the Army—
By the time the kitchen door closed
I was passin' California—almost in Oregon—
I met a waitress in the woods who picked me up
an' dropped me off in Washington someplace
I danced my way from the Indian festivals in Gallup, New Mexico
To the Madri Gras in New Orleans, Louisiana
With my thumb out, my eyes asleep, my hat turned up
an' my head turned on
I's driftin' an' learnin' new lessons
I was making my own depression
I rode freight trains for kicks
An' got beat up for laughs
Cut grass for quarters
An' sang for dimes
Hitchhiked on 61—51—75—169—37—66—22
Gopher Road—Route 40 an' Howard Johnson Turnpike
Got jailed for suspicion of armed robbery
Got held four hours on a murder rap
Got busted for looking like I do
An' I never done none a them things
Somewheres back I took the time to start playin' the guitar
Somewheres back I took time to start singin'
Somewheres back I took the time to start writin'
But I never ever did take the time to find out why
I took the time to do those things—when they ask
Me why an' where I got started, I gotta shake my head
an' weave my eyes an' walk away dumfounded
From Shreveport I landed in Madison, Wisconsin
From Madison we filled up a four-door Pontiac with five people

An' shot straight south an' sharp to the East an'
     in 24 hours was still hanging on through the Hudson
     Tunnel—
Gettin' out in a snowstorm an' wavin' goodbye
     to the three others, we swept on to MacDougal Street
     with five dollars between us—but we weren't poor
I had my guitar an' harmonica to play
An' he had his brother's clothes to pawn
In a week, he went back to Madison while I stayed behind an'
Walked a winter's line from the Lower East Side
     to Gerde's Folk City
In May, I thumbed west an' took the wrong highway in Florida
Mad as hell an' tired as well, I scrambled my way back to
South Dakota by keepin' a truck driver up all day an' singing'
One night in Cincinnati
I looked up a long time friend in Sioux Falls an' was let down,
     worried blind, and hit hard by seein' how little we had to say
I rolled back to Kansas, Iowa, Minnesota, lookin' up
     ol' time pals an' first-run gals an' I was beginnin'
     to find out that my road an' their road
     is two different kinds a roads
I found myself back in New York City in the middle part
     a summer staying on 28th Street with kind, honest
     hard-working people who were good to me
I got wrote up in the Times after playin' in the fall
     at Gerde's Folk City
I got recorded at Columbia after being wrote up in the Times
An' I still can't find the time to go back an' see why an' where
I started doing what I'm doing
I can't tell you the influences 'cause there's too many
     to mention an' I might leave one out
An' that wouldn't be fair
Woody Guthrie, sure
Big Joe Williams, yeah
It's easy to remember those names
But what about the faces you can't find again

What about the curves an' corners an' cut-offs
     that drop out a sight an' fall behind
What about the records you hear but one time
What about the coyote's call an' the bulldog's bark
What about the tomcat's meow an' milk cow's moo
An' the train whistle's moan
Open up yer eyes an' ears an' yer influenced
     an' there's nothing you can do about it
Hibbing's a good ol' town
I ran away from it when I was 10, 12, 13, 15, $15\frac{1}{2}$, 17 an' 18
I been caught and brought back all but once

Bob Dylan: A Distinctive Folk-Song Stylist

ROBERT SHELTON

During his first months in New York, Dylan expanded his repertoire, wrote a few original songs and began performing at clubs in Greenwich Village. Though the major folk labels—Folkways, Elektra, Vanguard—declined to record a debut album, he received a positive notice in the September 29, 1961, *New York Times* from Robert Shelton, the paper's folk-music critic. The first recognition of any kind to come from outside the Village circle of musicians, Shelton's review is often seen as the watershed moment of Dylan's career. (Though he later claimed that it played no part in his decision, John Hammond informally offered Dylan a contract with Columbia Records the day the piece ran.)

His observations on the singer's raw technique and grasp of the folk tradition are precise, and the description of a demure Huck Finn—"a cross between a choir boy and a beatnik"—became the standard portrait and was widely imitated over the years. The review is prefaced here by a full report of the evening, which Shelton published in his Dylan biography, *No Direction Home*. He elaborates on thoughts set forth in the *Times* piece, and describes Dylan's awkward but endearing stage presence. When interviewed after the set, Dylan is misleading about his past, although in so doing he credits several musical influences. (Dylan's true past would finally be revealed in "I Am My Words," a two-column write-up in the November 4, 1963, *Newsweek*. In addition to describing his middle-class background and rapport with his family, the article claimed that Dylan aped the melody of "Blowin' in the Wind" from a high school student. Dylan's guarded approach toward the media is widely attributed to this article.)

Shelton's memoir remains a first-rate account of Dylan's earliest performances in New York.

BOB STARTED a typical set with "I'm Gonna Get You, Sally Gal," in a lively tempo. He set up a three-way conversation between his voice, guitar, and mouth harp. Suddenly you saw how he could share the stage with as brilliant a trio as the Greenbriars. "Here's a song suitable to this occasion," Dylan said, as he retuned his guitar and changed his mouth harp. He sailed into a traditional blues dirge, "This Life Is Killing Me." His technique was everywhere, the covert technique of the folk idiom. It was antipolish, anticonscious of surface form, yet all those elements lay below. He gave the impression that he had started in music yesterday, not five years earlier. But one couldn't be sure.

Between songs, Dylan droned a soliloquy, formless yet very funny. He started to tell a story about a toad. It was an open-ended shaggy-toad story that didn't start anyplace, didn't go anywhere, and didn't end up anywhere, but it gave him a bit of fill-in patter while he tuned. His face was pouting and boyish. His slow delivery made him sound half-awake to optimists and half-asleep to pessimists. Next, he growled his way through "a train song," "900 Miles." To punctuate certain guitar breaks, he raised the body of his guitar to the microphone, an old country-music gambit that magnified the stringed sound.

In the background were the usual Folk City distractions. Bartenders clinked and poured as if starring in TV commercials. The cash register rang during soft passages. At the bar a few drunks were gabbing while others tried to silence them. Dylan was all concentration. "Here's a song outa my own head," he said, tuning his guitar for "Talking New York," a very old style of talking blues, in which three sparse chords support wry lyrics more spoken than sung. Dylan delivered his first protest song with a comic's timing.

Bob turned to other songs out of other people's heads. He moaned his way through "Dink's Song," long favored by Josh White and Cynthia Gooding; Dylan said he had picked it up on the Brazos River when he was down in Texas. Actually, the ballad hunter John A. Lomax had heard it in

1904 from a gin-drinking black woman who sang it as she wearily scrubbed her man's laundry. It is one of the most pathetic women's laments in American folk song. Bob did a variation on Van Ronk, with vamping guitar figures keeping the underlying pattern moving. At times his voice sounded like gravel being shoveled, at other times like a sob. He caught the original's tension, grit, and plaintiveness. "I was never a motherless child," folk singer Ed McCurdy used to say, "but I know what it feels like." Dylan was never a black laundress, but he knew what it felt like. Occasionally, Dylan threw his head back full as if he were scanning the ceiling for his next words.

From Texas, the twenty-year-old world traveler took his audience to a famous Chicago bar, Muddy Waters' Place, where he said he had picked up another blues song. He shuffled to the junk-heap upright piano and played primitive chords. Then he hit Woody's road again, with "Hard Travelin'," a lurching, careening road song, sticky with hot asphalt, aching with calloused feet. Then he did another couple of songs out of his own head, including "Bear Mountain" and "Talkin' Hava Negilah Blues," his little jape of international "stylists" like Harry Belafonte and Theo Bikel.

The audience responded more to Dylan's wit than to his slow, serious, intense material. Audience reaction led him to play Chaplinesque clown. He closed with his own "Song to Woody," suspensefully built to keep attention focused on each new line.

After the set, we went back to the Folk City kitchen for his first press interview. The answers came fast, but I had a feeling that he was improvising and concealing. It went like this: "I'm twenty years old, don't turn twenty-one until May. I've been singing all my life, since I was ten. I was born in Duluth, Minnesota, or maybe it was Superior, Wisconsin, right across the line. I started traveling with a carnival at the age of thirteen. I did odd jobs and sang with the carnival. I cleaned up ponies and ran steam shovels, in Minnesota, North Dakota, and then on south. I graduated from high school. For a while, Sioux Falls, South Dakota, was a home, and so was Gallup, New Mexico. I also lived in Fargo, North Dakota, and in a place called Hibbing, Minnesota. I went to the University of Minnesota for about eight months, but I didn't like it too much. I used to play piano with Bobby Vee and the Shadows, a country rockabilly band. I came east in February 1961, and it's just as hard as any town I've seen."

When he sang "Poor Girl," he had pulled out a kitchen table knife and used the back of the blade to fret his guitar. Where did he learn that old blues bottleneck guitar? "I learned to use a butcher knife," Bob replied, "from an old guy named Wigglefoot in Gallup, New Mexico. He was a beaten-down old bluesman who wore a patch on his eye. I do a lot of material I learned from Mance Lipscomb, but not in public. Mance was a big influence. I met him in Navasota, Texas, five years ago. I've been a farmhand too. I learned 'House of the Rising Sun' from Dave Von Ronk and 'See That My Grave Is Kept Clean' from Blind Lemon Jefferson. I like the recordings of Rabbit Brown a lot too.

"Jack Elliott and Dave Van Ronk are the two best folk singers in New York. I can only sing one way . . . in the way I like to hear it. I don't have a pretty voice. I can't sing pretty, and I don't want to sing pretty." Bob dropped the names of a lot of admired musicians, a mélange of those he had heard on recordings only and those he said he'd met and worked with. He appeared to have known them all. "Yes, I like Ray Charles very much. I picked up the harmonica after hearing Walter Jacobs—you know, Little Walter—of the Muddy Waters band. But I play my own style of harmonica. I played piano for dancers in the carnival."

Had he made any recordings? "The recordings I've made haven't been released. I played with Gene Vincent in Nashville, but I don't know if they have been released. . . . As to that bottleneck guitar, when I played a coffeehouse in Detroit I used a switchblade knife to get that sound. But when I pulled out the switchblade, six people in the audience walked out. They looked afraid. Now, I just use a kitchen knife so no one will walk out." Any other musical influences? "A lot, quite a lot. Woody Guthrie, of course. I have seen quite a lot of Woody since last winter. We can talk, even though he is sick. He likes my songs a lot. I met Jesse Fuller two years ago in Denver and studied with him."

Bob went on for another set. I told Carla* that it had been a good interview and that I really loved his work and manner. But, I told her, I had the strange feeling that he was putting me on. He seemed to have traveled so far and known so many famous and obscure musicians. He was evasive

---

* Carla Rotolo, the older sister of Suze, Dylan's girlfriend at the time. A regular at Gerde's Folk City, she worked as an assistant to Alan Lomax. —ED.

about his past. I told Carla to tell Bob there was a difference between kidding around with a Village guy and talking for publication. Minutes after Dylan's set Carla huddled with Bobby, and then we continued the interview at a table in between songs by the Greenbriar Boys.

"Listen," Bob told me, "I'm giving it to you straight. I wouldn't tell you anything that isn't true." Did he want me to call him Bobby Dylan or Bob Dylan? He thought that one out, as if he were about to sign a contract. Half aloud, he repeated the two names to himself: "Bob Dylan, Bobby Dylan, Bob Dylan, Bobby Dylan . . . Make it Bob Dylan! That's what I'm really known as," he declared confidently. I wrote the review, which appeared in *The Times* on Friday, September 29, 1961:

> *A bright new face in folk music is appearing at Gerde's Folk City. Although only twenty years old, Bob Dylan is one of the most distinctive stylists to play in a Manhattan cabaret in months.*
>
> *Resembling a cross between a choir boy and a beatnik, Mr. Dylan has a cherubic look and a mop of tousled hair he partly covers with a Huck Finn black corduroy cap. His clothes may need a bit of tailoring, but when he works his guitar, harmonica or piano and composes new songs faster than he can remember them, there is no doubt that he is bursting at the seams with talent.*
>
> *Mr. Dylan's voice is anything but pretty. He is consciously trying to recapture the rude beauty of a Southern field hand musing in melody on his porch. All the "husk" and "bark" are left on his notes and a searing intensity pervades his songs.*

Slow-Motion Mood

> *Mr. Dylan is both comedian and tragedian. Like a vaudeville actor on the rural circuit, he offers a variety of droll musical monologues: "Talking Bear Mountain" lampoons the overcrowding of an excursion boat, "Talking New York" satirizes his troubles in gaining recognition and "Talkin' Havah Nagilah" burlesques the folk-music craze and the singer himself.*
>
> *In his serious vein, Mr. Dylan seems to be performing in a slow-motion film. Elasticized phrases are drawn out until you think they may snap. He rocks his head and body, closes his eyes in reverie and*

seems to be groping for a word or a mood, then resolves the tension benevolently by finding the word and mood.

He may mumble the text of "House of the Rising Sun" in a scarcely understandable growl or sob, or clearly enunciate the poetic poignancy of a Blind Lemon Jefferson blues: "One kind favor I ask of you—See that my grave is kept clean."

Mr. Dylan's highly personalized approach toward the folk song is still evolving. He has been sopping up influences like a sponge. At times, the drama he aims at is off-target melodrama and his stylization threatens to topple over as a mannered excess.

But if not for every taste, his music-making has the mark of originality and inspiration all the more noteworthy for his youth. Mr. Dylan is vague about his antecedents and birthplace, but it matters less where he has been than where he is going, and that would seem to be straight up.

Woody Guthrie Visited by Bob Dylan: Brooklyn State Hospital, New York, 1961

DAVID WOJAHN

As a young man Dylan emulated Woody Guthrie in every way—song repertoire, style of clothing and manner of speech—and set out to meet him immediately upon arriving in New York. Guthrie, afflicted with Huntington's disease, was bedridden, unable to sing or play the guitar and permitted to leave New Jersey's Greystone Hospital only on Sundays to visit friends in nearby East Orange. Dylan first called upon Guthrie in East Orange and later saw him in the hospital. David Wojahn has written a poem about the legendary encounter. The piece ably depicts Dylan's youth and determination to impress, as well as the visit's ceremonial overtones—the handing of the torch from mentor to apprentice.

"Woody Guthrie Visited by Bob Dylan" is taken from *Mystery Train*, a collection of poems on blues and rock and roll. Wojahn is also the author of *Icehouse Lights* and *Glassworks*.

He has lain here for a terrible, motionless
Decade, and talks through a system of winks
And facial twitches. The nurse pops a cigarette
Between his lips, wipes his forehead. She thinks
He wants to send the kid away, but decides
To let him in—he's waited hours.
Guitar case, jean jacket. A corduroy cap slides

Down his forehead. Doesn't talk. He can't be more
Than twenty. He straps on the harmonica holder,
Tunes up, and begins his "Song to Woody,"
Trying to sound three times his age, sandpaper
Dustbowl growl, the song interminable, inept. Should he
Sing another? The eyes roll their half-hearted yes.
The nurse grits her teeth, stubs out the cigarette.

Flat Tire

PAUL NELSON AND JON PANKAKE

The *Freewheelin' Bob Dylan*, his second album with Columbia and the first to be primarily devoted to original material, elicited wide praise—Pete Seeger, *Sing Out!* and others believed it to be a major work—and some of its songs were popularized by ensembles like Peter, Paul and Mary. But a vocal, and unexpected, condemnation of the record came from *Little Sandy Review*, a newsletter for the Minneapolis folk community.

The journal's editors, Paul Nelson and Jon Pankake, met Dylan when he was at the University of Minnesota; in a favorable review of *Bob Dylan*, Nelson and Pankake warned: "we sincerely hope that Dylan will steer clear of the protesty people, continue to write songs near the traditional manner and continue to develop his mastery of his difficult, delicate, highly personal style." Their review of *Freewheelin'* is excessively negative at times and they brought unrealistic expectations to bear on the career of a twenty-two-year-old. Yet their criticism was in many ways prescient: Nelson and Pankake were the first to identify a tension and potential incompatibility between traditional and topical material, and spot Dylan's early attempts at pop melody. They also compare the songs on *Freewheelin'* with the standards from which they were derived, suggesting that Dylan had lost touch with his predecessors. If the editors err in mislabeling a masterpiece, their review correctly foreshadows the end of Dylan's topical songwriting and his move away from folk music.

"WITH MY THUMB OUT, my eyes asleep, my hat turned up an' my head turned on, I's driftin' and learnin' new lessons," Bob Dylan was quoted as saying in *Time*, May 31, 1963. Unfortunately, about half of his eagerly awaited second album suggests that both his eyes and his head were asleep.

Frankly, *The Freewheelin' Bob Dylan* is a great disappointment. That such a creative energy and driving force as Dylan would ever be satisfied with some of the material issued here is a great mystery. The virtues of the first album were an electrifying and mercurial inventiveness (both as a songwriter and as an interpreter) and a natural gift for genuine directness and simplicity in the finest folk-derived sense; those virtues barely exist here. As a songwriter, he has become melodramatic and maudlin, lacking all Guthriesque economy; his melodies bear more relation now to popular music than folk music. As a performer, he is at times affected and pretentious, although his harmonica technique has greatly improved. The main trouble now seems to be that he has no foundation or base for his songs; they seem to float vaguely above the ground in amorphous hazes; the talent is still apparent, but all the parts and working mechanisms seem to have broken down or gone out of control. Like Chaplin's feeding machine in *Modern Times*, the functions have gotten all mixed up, and the result is a mess.

"Blowin' in the Wind," Dylan's "This Land Is Your Land," gets the album off to a fine start; Bob sings and plays it well, and the song should be with us at least as long as the folk revival (and probably a lot longer). "Girl from the North Country" and "Bob Dylan's Dream" are examples of what the liner notes (by Nat Hentoff) describes as Dylan's "particular kind of lyricism." The latter is so mawkish and slushy that one wonders if he meant it as a joke, while the former, despite a pretty melody, is marred by a strangely foppish manner of singing. "Masters of War," Dylan's epic Protest song, is dull and monotonous both in text and performance; its total effect suggests a manufactured rather than a real anger. "A Hard Rain's A-Gonna Fall," being proclaimed by some as Dylan's masterpiece, seems far more a poem than a song (although Dylan says in the notes: "Anything I can sing I call a song"). Some of the images are striking and apt ("ten thousand talkers whose tongues were all broken"); others merely akin to bad beatnik poetry. The cut is, however, one of the most interesting on the record. "Oxford Town," about James Meredith, is a pleasant surprise: a protest song that ironically implies its "grimness" through common sense and good humor rather than baldly stating it.

Dylan wrote "Down the Highway" when his girl went to Italy for a few months. In it, he attempts to utilize Charlie Pickett's beautiful guitar run on an unrelated song of the same title that appears in *The Rural Blues*; the result is practically pure folknik, and Dylan has missed Pickett's point altogether. "Don't Think Twice, It's All Right," according to reports, is the next Dylan song that will be given the pop treatment by groups like the Chad Mitchell Trio and the Limeliters; it has a certain bittersweet charm to it. "Corrina, Corrina" makes feeble and cautious use of piano, bass, and drums in a pallid attempt at rhythm-and-blues. "Honey, Just Allow Me One More Chance" (from *Henry Thomas Sings the Texas Blues!* Origin Jazz Library) gets the same treatment from Dylan as did Jesse Fuller's "You're No Good" on the first album; perhaps it was a leftover cut from then, since its style is far more frantic and pell-mell than anything else on this record.

Undoubtedly the strangest, loosest, funniest, and least worked out pieces on the album are the three long nonsense and talking songs: "Bob Dylan's Blues," "Talking World War III," and "I Shall Be Free." All are by turns engaging and futile, and all eventually fail because there is no logical continuity or point to them. Dylan is brilliantly funny or touching one moment, then floundering hopelessly in arid and embarrassing improvisation the next. His imagery falls far short of Guthrie's magic, and his wacky verses don't quite have that flash of humanitarian genius that marked Woody's as the work of a true folk poet. Instead, they stumble and stagger along, going nowhere, and not always with much style. There is, however, a great jugband harmonica on "Talking World War III." "I Shall Be Free" uses roughly the same tune and form that Woody and Leadbelly used on their recordings of "We Shall Be Free" for Folkways, although Dylan's verses are completely different.

A fine local singer recently made a most perceptive remark about the urban folk scene in general, not particularly about Dylan. He said, "Some singers are 98 percent personality and only 2 percent folk music, but that 2 percent is a whole lot better than most of the people in folk music today." It seems a good summation of *The Freewheelin' Bob Dylan*, an album that, like Arthur Miller's salesman, is "way out there in the blue, riding on a smile and a shoeshine," and nothing else. Dylan bases everything here almost 100 percent on his own personality; there is hardly any traditional material, and most of the original material is not particularly folk-derived.

It is pure Bob Dylan (Bob Dylan's dream, as it were), with its foundations in nothing that isn't constantly shifting, searching, and changing. What Dylan needs to do is to square the percentages between traditional and original back to 50–50 (as in his first album) to give some anchor of solidarity to his work; his absurd concoctions and blendings miss their mark here (whereas before they landed dead center), and the album floats away into never-never land, a failure, but a most interesting one. Don't make the mistake of crossing off Bob Dylan yet, however; he still remains one of our most promising songwriters and performers. As it stands, he'll merely have a first and a third album.

Letter to *Broadside*

JOHNNY CASH

Urging everyone to "shut up and let him sing," Johnny Cash published this letter in the March 10, 1964, issue of *Broadside*, a short-lived but influential paper devoted to publishing folk songs. Dylan later wrote, "This was before I had ever met him, and the letter meant the world to me. I've kept the magazine to this day."* Although it is often tied to the ardent criticism directed toward Dylan later that year—particularly Irwin Silber's "Open Letter" in the November *Sing Out!*—Cash's short, sometimes playful lyric was actually a response to Dylan's own letter to *Broadside*, which had been published in January. In a six-page confession on the private difficulties and guilt that attended fame, Dylan asked, "Let me begin by not beginnin / let me start not by startin but by continuin"—lines that Cash echoes at the end of this piece.

Cash also penned the liner notes to Dylan's *Nashville Skyline*, which features their duet of "Girl from the North Country." His essential albums include *The Complete Original Sun Singles*, *At Folsom Prison*, *American Recordings* and *The Man Comes Around*. He died in 2003.

HI BROADSIDE: I got hung, but didn't choke . . . Bob Dylan slung his rope. I sat down and listened quick . . . Gravy from that brain is thick.

> He began by startin' alright . . . But the place he started . . .
> Was the way ahead, out of slight!
> In the night there's a light.

---

* Bob Dylan, "Remembering Johnny," *Rolling Stone*, October 16, 2003: 74.

A lamp is burning in all our dark . . . But . . . We must open our eyes to see it . . . As he listened for the wind . . . To hear it.

Near my shores of mental dying, Grasping straws and twigs, and drowning, Worthless I, But crying loudest, Came a Poet Troubadour, Singing fine familiar things.

Sang a hundred thousand lyrics, Right as Rain, Sweet as
   Sleep,
Words to thrill you . . . And to kill you.
Don't bad-mouth him, till you hear him,
Let him start by continuing, He's almost brand new,
SHUT UP! . . . AND LET HIM SING!

The Crackin', Shakin', Breakin' Sounds

NAT HENTOFF

In October 1964 *The New Yorker* published an engaging profile of Dylan by the journalist and jazz critic Nat Hentoff. Dylan was nearly a household name in the United States at this point—folk's enfant terrible and "the voice of a generation"—although as the profile makes clear, this was a time of great transition in his music.

In preparing the piece, Hentoff conducted extensive interviews. With a candor rarely displayed during the sixties, Dylan is forthright about the creative process and casting off the role of social activist in order to develop his own voice. Though at times he displays a youthful naïveté, his quotes betray a wariness of labels and pigeonholing, and an eagerness to explore more personal subjects in his writing.

Hentoff was also in Columbia's Studio A on the night of June 9, when *Another Side of Bob Dylan* was cut in a single six-hour session. Replete with dialogue and secondary characters, his prose gracefully depicts the casual atmosphere that became a trademark of Dylan's studio sessions. Hentoff assesses Dylan's performing style and recording technique, in turn both informal and exacting. The result is a perfectly rendered account of the songwriter at work.

These two maintained a close association throughout Dylan's early career. Hentoff wrote the liner notes to *Freewheelin'*, collaborated on the infamous *Playboy* interview of 1966 and later covered the Rolling Thunder Revue for *Rolling Stone*. A regular columnist at the *Village Voice*, he has published such books as *Boston Boy*, *The Jazz Life* and *The Nat Hentoff Reader*.

THE WORD "FOLK" in the term "folk music" used to connote a rural, homogeneous community that carried on a tradition of anonymously created music. No one person composed a piece; it evolved through generations of communal care. In recent years, however, folk music has increasingly become the quite personal—and copyrighted—product of specific creators. More and more of them, in fact, are neither rural nor representative of centuries-old family and regional traditions. They are so often city-bred converts to the folk style; and, after an apprenticeship during which they try to imitate rural models from the older approach to folk music, they write and perform their own songs out of their own concerns and preoccupations. The restless young, who have been the primary support of the rise of this kind of folk music over the past five years, regard two performers as their preeminent spokesmen. One is the twenty-three-year-old Joan Baez. She does not write her own material and she includes a considerable proportion of traditional, communally created songs in her programs. But Miss Baez does speak out explicitly against racial prejudice and militarism, and she does sing some of the best of the new topical songs. Moreover, her pure, penetrating voice and her open, honest manner symbolize for her admirers a cool island of integrity in a society that the folk-song writer Malvina Reynolds has characterized in one of her songs as consisting of "little boxes." The second—and more influential—demiurge of the folk-music microcosm is Bob Dylan, who is also twenty-three. Dylan's impact has been the greater because he *is* a writer of songs as well as a performer. Such compositions of his as "Blowin' in the Wind," "Masters of War," "Don't Think Twice, It's All Right," and "Only a Pawn in Their Game" have become part of the repertoire of many other performers, including Miss Baez, who has explained, "Bobby is expressing what I—and many other young people—feel, what we want to say. Most of the 'protest' songs about the bomb and race prejudice and conformity are stupid. They have no beauty. But Bobby's songs are powerful as poetry and powerful as music. And, oh, my God, how that boy can sing!" Another reason for Dylan's impact is the singular force of his personality. Wiry, tense, and boyish, Dylan looks and acts like a fusion of Huck Finn and a young Woody Guthrie. Both onstage and off, he appears to be just barely able to contain his prodigious energy. Pete Seeger, who, at forty-five, is one of the elders of American folk music, recently observed, "Dylan may well become the country's most creative troubadour—if he doesn't explode."

Dylan is always dressed informally—the possibility that he will ever be seen in a tie is as remote as the possibility that Miss Baez will perform in an evening gown—and his possessions are few, the weightiest of them being a motorcycle. A wanderer, Dylan is often on the road in search of more experience. "You can find out a lot about a small town by hanging around its poolroom," he says. Like Miss Baez, he prefers to keep most of his time to himself. He works only occasionally, and during the rest of year he travels or briefly stays in a house owned by his manager, Albert Grossman, in Bearsville, New York—a small town adjacent to Woodstock and about a hundred miles north of New York City. There Dylan writes songs, works on poetry, plays, and novels, rides his motorcycle, and talks with his friends. From time to time, he comes to New York to record for Columbia Records.

A few weeks ago, Dylan invited me to a recording session that was to begin at seven in the evening in a Columbia studio on Seventh Avenue near Fifty-second Street. Before he arrived, a tall, lean, relaxed man in his early thirties came in and introduced himself to me as Tom Wilson, Dylan's recording producer. He was joined by two engineers, and we all went into the control room. Wilson took up a post at a long, broad table, between the engineers, from which he looked out into a spacious studio with a tall thicket of microphones to the left and, directly in front, an enclave containing a music stand, two microphones, and an upright piano, and set off by a large screen, which would partly shield Dylan as he sang, for the purpose of improving the quality of the sound. "I have no idea what he's going to record tonight," Wilson told me. "It's all to be stuff he's written in the last couple of months."

I asked if Dylan presented any particular problems to a recording director.

"My main difficulty has been pounding mike technique into him," Wilson said. "He used to get excited and move around a lot and then lean in too far, so that the mike popped. Aside from that, my basic problem with him has been to create the kind of setting in which he's relaxed. For instance, if that screen should bother him, I'd take it away, even if we have to lose a little quality in the sound." Wilson looked toward the door. "I'm somewhat concerned about tonight. We're going to do a whole album in one session. Usually, we're not in such a rush, but this album has to be ready for Columbia's fall sales convention. Except for special occasions like this, Bob has no set schedule of recording dates. We think he's important enough to record whenever he wants to come to the studio."

Five minutes after seven, Dylan walked into the studio, carrying a battered guitar case. He had on dark glasses, and his hair, dark-blond and curly, had obviously not been cut for some weeks; he was dressed in blue jeans, a black jersey, and desert boots. With him were half a dozen friends, among them Jack Elliott, a folk singer in the Woody Guthrie tradition, who was also dressed in blue jeans and desert boots, plus a brown corduroy shirt and a jaunty cowboy hat. Elliott had been carrying two bottles of Beaujolais, which he now handed to Dylan, who carefully put them on a table near the screen. Dylan opened the guitar case, took out a looped-wire harmonica holder, hung it around his neck, and then walked over to the piano and began to play in a rolling, honky-tonk style.

"He's got a wider range of talents than he shows," Wilson told me. "He kind of hoards them. You go back to his three albums. Each time, there's a big leap from one to the next—in material, in performance, in everything."

Dylan came into the control room, smiling. Although he is fiercely accusatory toward society at large while he is performing, his most marked offstage characteristic is gentleness. He speaks swiftly but softly, and appears persistently anxious to make himself clear. "We're going to make a good one tonight," he said to Wilson. "I promise." He turned to me and continued, "There aren't any finger-pointing songs in here, either. Those records I've already made, I'll stand behind them, but some of that was jumping into the scene to be heard and a lot of it was because I didn't see anybody else doing that kind of thing. Now a lot of people are doing finger-pointing songs. You know—pointing to all the things that are wrong. Me, I don't want to write *for* people anymore. You know—be a spokesman. Like I once wrote about Emmett Till in the first person, pretending I was him. From now on, I want to write from inside me, and to do that I'm going to have to get back to writing like I used to when I was ten—having everything come out naturally. The way I like to write is for it to come out the way I walk or talk." Dylan frowned. "Not that I even walk or talk yet like I'd like to. I don't carry myself the way Woody, Big Joe Williams, and Lightnin' Hopkins have carried themselves. I hope to someday, but they're older. They got to where music was a tool for them, a way to live more, a way to make themselves feel better. Sometimes I can make myself feel better with music, but other times it's still hard to go to sleep at night."

A friend strolled in, and Dylan began to grumble about an interview that had been arranged for him later in the week. "I hate to say no, because, after all, these guys have a job to do," he said, shaking his head impatiently. "But it bugs me that the first question usually turns out to be 'Are you going down South to take part in any of the civil-rights projects?' They try to fit you into things. Now, I've been down there, but I'm not going down just to hold a picket sign so they can shoot a picture of me. I know a lot of the kids in SNCC—you know, the Student Nonviolent Coordinating Committee. That's the only organization I feel a part of spiritually. The NAACP is a bunch of old guys. I found that out by coming directly in contact with some of the people in it. They didn't understand me. They were looking to use me for something. Man, everybody's hung up. You sometimes don't know if somebody wants you to do something because he's hung up or because he really digs who you are. It's awful complicated, and the best thing you can do is admit it."

Returning to the studio, Dylan stood in front of the piano and pounded out an accompaniment as he sang from one of his own new songs:

> *Are you just for real, baby, or are you just on the shelf?*
> *I'm looking deep into your eyes, but all I can see is myself.*
> *If you're trying to throw me, I've already been tossed.*
> *If you're already trying to lose me, I've already been lost. . . .*

Another friend of Dylan's arrived, with three children, ranging in age from four to ten. The children raced around the studio until Wilson insisted that they be relatively confined to the control room. By ten minutes to eight, Wilson had checked out the sound balance to his satisfaction, Dylan's friends had found seats along the studio walls, and Dylan had expressed his readiness—in fact, eagerness—to begin. Wilson, in the control room, leaned forward, a stopwatch in his hand. Dylan took a deep breath, threw his head back, and plunged into a song in which he accompanied himself on guitar and harmonica. The first take was ragged; the second was both more relaxed and more vivid. At that point, Dylan, smiling, clearly appeared to be confident of his ability to do an entire album in one night. As he moved into succeeding numbers, he relied principally on the guitar for support, except for exclamatory punctuations on the harmonica.

Having glanced through a copy of Dylan's new lyrics that he had handed to Wilson, I observed to Wilson that there were indeed hardly any songs of social protest in the collection.

"Those early albums gave people the wrong idea," Wilson said. "Basically, he's in the tradition of all lasting folk music. I mean, he's not a singer of protest so much as he is a singer of *concern* about people. He doesn't have to be talking about Medgar Evers all the time to be effective. He can just tell a simple little story of a guy who ran off from a woman."

After three takes of one number, one of the engineers said to Wilson, "If you want to try another, we can get a better take."

"No." Wilson shook his head. "With Dylan, you have to take what you can get."

Out in the studio, Dylan, his slight form bent forward, was standing just outside the screen and listening to a playback through earphones. He began to take the earphones off during an instrumental passage, but then his voice came on, and he grinned and replaced them.

The engineer muttered again that he might get a better take if Dylan ran through the number once more.

"Forget it," Wilson said. "You don't think in terms of orthodox recording techniques when you're dealing with Dylan. You have to learn to be as free on this side of the glass as he is out there."

Dylan went on to record a song about a man leaving a girl because he was not prepared to be the kind of invincible hero and all-encompassing provider she wanted. "It ain't me you're looking for, babe," he sang, with finality.

During the playback, I joined Dylan in the studio. "The songs so far sound as if there were real people in them," I said.

Dylan seemed surprised that I had considered it necessary to make the comment. "There are. That's what makes them so scary. If I haven't been through what I write about, the songs aren't worth anything." He went on, via one of his songs, to offer a complicated account of a turbulent love affair in Spanish Harlem, and at the end asked a friend, "Did you understand it?" The friend nodded enthusiastically. "Well, I didn't," Dylan said, with a laugh, and then became somber. "It's hard being free in a song—getting it all in. Songs are so confining. Woody Guthrie told me once that songs don't have to rhyme—that they don't have to do anything like that. But it's not true. A song has to have some kind of form to fit into the music. You can bend the words and the meter, but it still has to fit somehow. I've been getting freer in the songs I write, but I still feel confined. That's why I write a lot of poetry—if that's the word. Poetry can make its own form."

As Wilson signaled for the start of the next number, Dylan put up his hand. "I just want to light a cigarette, so I can see it there while I'm singing," he said, and grinned. "I'm very neurotic. I need to be secure."

By ten-thirty, seven songs had been recorded.

"This is the fastest Dylan date yet," Wilson said. "He used to be all hung up with the microphones. Now he's a pro."

Several more friends of Dylan's had arrived during the recording of the seven songs, and at this point four of them were seated in the control room behind Wilson and the engineers. The others were scattered around the studio, using the table that held the bottles of Beaujolais as their base. They opened the bottles, and every once in a while poured out a drink in a paper cup. The three children were still irrepressibly present, and once the smallest burst suddenly into the studio, ruining a take. Dylan turned on the youngster in mock anger. "I'm gonna rub you out," he said. "I'll track you down and turn you to dust." The boy giggled and ran back into the control room.

As the evening went on, Dylan's voice became more acrid. The dynamics of his singing grew more pronounced, soft, intimate passages being abruptly followed by fierce surges in volume. The relentless, driving beat of his guitar was more often supplemented by the whooping thrusts of the harmonica.

"Intensity, that's what he's got," Wilson said, apparently to himself. "By now, this kid is outselling Thelonious Monk and Miles Davis," he went on, to me. "He's speaking to a whole new generation. And not only here. He's just been in England. He had standing room only in Royal Festival Hall."

Dylan had begun a song called "Chimes of Freedom." One of his four friends in the control room—a lean, bearded man—proclaimed, "Bobby's talking for every hung-up person in the whole wide universe." His three companions nodded gravely.

The next composition, "Motorpsycho Nitemare," was a mordantly satirical version of the vintage tale of the farmer, his daughter, and the traveling salesman. There were several false starts, apparently because Dylan was having trouble reading the lyrics.

"Man, dim the lights," the bearded friend counseled Wilson. "He'll get more relaxed."

"Atmosphere is not what we need," Wilson answered, without turning around. "Legibility is what we need."

During the playback, Dylan listened intently, his lips moving, and a cigarette cocked in his right hand. A short break followed, during which Dylan shouted, "Hey, we're gonna need some more wine!" Two of his friends in the studio nodded and left.

After the recording session resumed, Dylan continued to work hard and conscientiously. When he was preparing for a take or listening to a playback, he seemed able to cut himself off completely from the eddies of conversation and humorous byplay stirred up by his friends in the studio. Occasionally, when a line particularly pleased him, he burst into laughter, but he swiftly got back to business.

Dylan started a talking blues—a wry narrative in a sardonic recitative style, which had been developed by Woody Guthrie. "Now I'm liberal, but to a degree," Dylan was drawling halfway through the song. "I want everybody to be free. But if you think I'll let Barry Goldwater move in next door and marry my daughter, you must think I'm crazy. I wouldn't let him do it for all the farms in Cuba." He was smiling broadly, and Wilson and the engineers were laughing. It was a long song, and toward the end Dylan faltered. He tried it twice more, and each time he stumbled before the close.

"Let me do another song," he said to Wilson. "I'll come back to this."

"No," Wilson said. "Finish up this one. You'll hang us up on the order, and if I'm not here to edit, the other cat will get mixed up. Just do an insert of the last part."

"Let him start from the beginning, man," said one of the four friends sitting behind Wilson.

Wilson turned around, looking annoyed. "Why, man?"

"You don't start telling a story with Chapter Eight, man," the friend said.

"Oh, man," said Wilson. "What kind of philosophy is that? We're recording, not writing a biography."

As an obbligato of protest continued behind Wilson, Dylan, accepting Wilson's advice, sang the insert. His bearded friend rose silently and drew a square in the air behind Wilson's head.

Other songs, mostly of love lost or misunderstood, followed. Dylan was now tired, but he retained his good humor. "This last one is called 'My Back Pages,'" he announced to Wilson. It appeared to express his current desire to get away from "finger-pointing" and write more acutely personal material. "Oh, but I was so much older then," he sang as a refrain, "I'm younger than that now."

By one-thirty, the session was over. Dylan had recorded fourteen new songs. He agreed to meet me again in a week or so and fill me in on his background. "My background's not all that important, though," he said as we left the studio. "It's what I am now that counts."

DYLAN WAS BORN in Duluth, on May 24, 1941, and grew up in Hibbing, Minnesota, a mining town near the Canadian border. He does not discuss his parents, preferring to let his songs tell whatever he wants to say about his personal history. "You can stand at one end of Hibbing on the main drag an' see clear past the city limits on the other end," Dylan once noted in a poem, "My Life in a Stolen Moment," printed in the program of a 1963 Town Hall concert he gave. Like Dylan's parents, it appears, the town was neither rich nor poor, but it was, Dylan has said, "a dyin' town." He ran away from home seven times—at ten, twelve, at thirteen, at fifteen, at fifteen and a half, at seventeen, and at eighteen. His travels included South Dakota, New Mexico, Kansas, and California. In between flights, he taught himself the guitar, which he had begun playing at the age of ten. At fifteen, he was also playing the harmonica and the autoharp, and, in addition, had written his first song, a ballad dedicated to Brigitte Bardot. In the spring of

1960, Dylan entered the University of Minnesota, in Minneapolis, which he attended for something under six months. In "My Life in a Stolen Moment," Dylan has summarized his college career dourly: "I sat in science class an' flunked out for refusin' to watch a rabbit die. I got expelled from English class for using four-letter words in a paper describing the English teacher. I also failed out of communication class for callin' up every day and sayin' I couldn't come. . . . I was kept around for kicks at a fraternity house. They let me live there, an' I did until they wanted me to join." Paul Nelson and Jon Pankake, who edit the *Little Sandy Review*, a quarterly magazine, published in Minneapolis, that is devoted to critical articles on folk music and performers, remember meeting Dylan at the University of Minnesota in the summer of 1960, while he was part of a group of singers who performed at The Scholar, a coffeehouse near the university. The editors, who were students at the university then, have since noted in their publication: "We recall Bob as a soft-spoken, rather unprepossessing youngster . . . well-groomed and neat in the standard campus costume of slacks, sweater, white oxford sneakers, poplin raincoat, and dark glasses."

Before Dylan arrived at the university, his singing had been strongly influenced by such Negro folk interpreters as Leadbelly and Big Joe Williams. He had met Williams in Evanston, Illinois, during his break from home at the age of twelve. Dylan had also been attracted to several urban-style rhythm-and-blues performers, notably Bo Diddley and Chuck Berry. Other shaping forces were white country-music figures—particularly Hank Williams, Hank Snow, and Jimmie Rodgers. During his brief stay at the university, Dylan became especially absorbed in the recordings of Woody Guthrie, the Oklahoma-born traveler who had created the most distinctive body of American topical folk material to come to light in this century. Since 1954, Guthrie, ill with Huntington's chorea, a progressive disease of the nervous system, had not been able to perform, but he was allowed to receive visitors. In the autumn of 1960, Dylan quit the University of Minnesota and decided to visit Guthrie at Greystone Hospital, in New Jersey. Dylan returned briefly to Minnesota the following May, to sing at a university hootenanny, and Nelson and Pankake saw him again on that occasion. "In a mere half year," they have recalled in the *Little Sandy Review*, "he had learned to churn up exciting, bluesy, hard-driving harmonica-and-guitar music, and had absorbed during his visits with Guthrie not only the great Okie musician's unpredictable syntax but his very vocal color, diction, and inflection. Dylan's performance that spring evening of a selection of Guthrie . . . songs was hectic and shaky, but it contained all the elements of the now-perfected performing style that has made him the most original newcomer to folk music."

The winter Dylan visited Guthrie was otherwise bleak. He spent most of it in New York, where he found it difficult to get steady work singing. In "Talking New York," a caustic song describing his first months in the city, Dylan tells of having been turned away by a coffeehouse owner, who told him scornfully, "You sound like a hillbilly. We want folk singers here." There were nights when he slept in the subway, but eventually he found friends and a place to stay on the Lower East Side, and after he had returned from the spring hootenanny, he began getting more frequent engagements in New York. John Hammond, Director of Talent Acquisition at Columbia Records, who had discovered a sizable number of important jazz and folk performers during the past thirty years, heard Dylan that summer while attending a rehearsal of another folk singer, whom Hammond was about to record for Columbia Records. Impressed by the young man's raw force and by the vivid lyrics of his songs, Hammond auditioned him and immediately signed him to a recording contract. Then, in September 1961, while Dylan was appearing at Gerde's Folk City, a casual refuge for "citybillies" (as the young city singers and musicians are now called in the trade), on West Fourth Street, in Greenwich Village, he was heard by Robert Shelton, the folk-music critic for the *Times*, who wrote of him enthusiastically.

Dylan began to prosper. He enlarged his following by appearing at the Newport and Monterey Folk Festivals and giving concerts throughout the country. There have been a few snags, as when he walked off the Ed Sullivan television show in the spring of 1963 because the Columbia Broadcasting System would not permit him to sing a tart appraisal of the John Birch Society, but on the whole he has experienced accelerating success. His first three Columbia albums—*Bob Dylan, The Freewheelin' Bob Dylan,* and *The Times They Are A-Changin'*—have by now reached a cumulative sales figure of nearly four hundred thousand. In addition, he has received large royalties as a composer of songs that have become hits through recordings by Peter, Paul and Mary, the Kingston Trio, and other performers. At present, Dylan's fees for a concert appearance range from two thousand to three thousand dollars a night. He has sometimes agreed to sing at a nominal fee for new, nonprofit folk societies, however, and he has often performed without charge at civil-rights rallies.

MUSICALLY, Dylan has transcended most of his early influences and developed an incisively personal style. His vocal sound is most often characterized by flaying harshness. Mitch Jayne, a member of the Dillards, a folk group from Missouri, has described Dylan's sound as "very much like a dog with his leg caught in barbed wire." Yet Dylan's admirers come to accept and even delight in his harshness, because of the vitality and wit at its core. And they point out that in intimate ballads he is capable of a fragile lyricism that does not slip into bathos. It is Dylan's work as a composer, however, that has won him a wider audience than his singing alone might have. Whether concerned with cosmic specters or personal conundrums, Dylan's lyrics are pungently idiomatic. He has a superb ear for speech rhythms, a generally astute sense of selective detail, and a natural storyteller's command of narrative pacing. His songs sound as if they were being created out of oral street history rather than carefully written in tranquillity. On a stage, Dylan performs his songs as if he had an urgent story to tell. In his work there is little of the polished grace of such carefully trained contemporary minstrels as Richard Dyer-Bennet. Nor, on the other hand, do Dylan's performances reflect the calculated showmanship of a Harry Belafonte or of Peter, Paul and Mary. Dylan off the stage is very much the same as Dylan the performer—restless, insatiably hungry for experience, idealistic, but skeptical of neatly defined causes.

In the past year, as his renown has increased, Dylan has become more elusive. He felt so strongly threatened by his initial fame that he welcomed the chance to use the Bearsville home of his manager as a refuge between concerts, and he still spends most of his time there when he's not traveling. A week after the recording session, he telephoned me from Bearsville, and we agreed to meet the next evening at the Keneret, a restaurant on lower Seventh Avenue, in the Village. It specializes in Middle Eastern food, which is one of Dylan's preferences, but it does not have a liquor license. Upon keeping our rendezvous, therefore, we went next door for a few bottles of

Beaujolais and then returned to the Keneret. Dylan was as restless as usual, and as he talked, his hands moved constantly and his voice sounded as if he were never quite able to catch his breath.

I asked him what he had meant, exactly, when he spoke at the recording session of abandoning "finger-pointing" songs, and he took a sip of wine, leaned forward, and said, "I looked around and saw all these people pointing fingers at the bomb. But the bomb is getting boring, because what's wrong goes much deeper than the bomb. What's wrong is how few people are free. Most people walking around are tied down to something that doesn't let them really *speak*, so they just add their confusion to the mess. I mean, they have some kind of vested interest in the way things are now. Me, I'm cool." He smiled. "You know, Joanie—Joanie Baez—worries about me. She worries about whether people will get control over me and exploit me. But I'm cool. I'm in control, because I don't care about money, and all that. And I'm cool in myself, because I've gone through enough changes so that I know what's real to me and what isn't. Like this fame. It's done something to me. It's okay in the Village here. People don't pay attention to me. But in other towns it's funny knowing that people you don't know figure they know *you*. I mean, they think they know everything about you. One thing is groovy, though. I got birthday cards this year from people I'd never heard of. It's weird, isn't it? There are people I've really touched whom I'll never know." He lit a cigarette. "But in other ways being noticed can be a weight. So I disappear a lot. I go to places where I'm not going to be noticed. And I *can*." He laughed. "I have no work to do. I have no job. I'm not committed to anything except making a few records and playing a few concerts. I'm weird that way. Most people, when they get up in the morning, have to do what they *have* to do. I could pretend there were all kinds of things I *had* to do every day. But why? So I do whatever I feel like. I might make movies of my friends around Woodstock one day. I write a lot. I get involved in scenes with people. A lot of scenes are going on with me all the time—here in the Village, in Paris during my trips to Europe, in lots of places."

I asked Dylan how far ahead he planned.

"I don't look past right now," he said. "Now there's this fame business. I know it's going to go away. It has to. This so-called mass fame comes from people who get caught up in a thing for a while and buy the records. Then they stop. And when they stop, I won't be famous anymore."

We became aware that a young waitress was standing by diffidently. Dylan turned to her, and she asked him for his autograph. He signed his name with gusto, and signed again when she asked if he would give her an autograph for a friend. "I'm sorry to have interrupted your dinner," she said, smiling. "But I'm really not."

"I get letters from people—young people—all the time," Dylan continued when she had left us. "I wonder if they write letters like those to other people they don't know. They just want to tell me things, and sometimes they go into their personal hang-ups. Some send poetry. I like getting them—read them all and answer some. But I don't mean I give any of the people who write to me any *answers* to their problems." He leaned forward and talked more rapidly. "It's like when somebody wants to tell me what the 'moral' thing is to do, I want them to *show* me. If they have anything to say about morals, I want to know what it is they *do*. Same with me. All I can do is show the people who ask me questions how I live. All I can do is be me. I can't tell them how to change things, because there's only one way to change things, and that's to cut yourself off from all the chains. That's hard for most people to do."

I had Dylan's *The Times They Are-A-Changin'* album with me, and I pointed out to him a section of his notes on the cover in which he spoke of how he had always been running when he was a boy—running away from Hibbing and from his parents.

Dylan took a sip of wine. "I kept running because I wasn't free," he said. "I was constantly on guard. Somehow, way back then, I already knew that parents do what they do because they're up tight. They're concerned with their kids in relation to *themselves*. I mean, they want their kids to please them, not to embarrass them—so they can be proud of them. They want you to be what *they* want you to be. So I started running when I was ten. But always I'd get picked up and sent home. When I was thirteen, I was traveling with a carnival through upper Minnesota and North and South Dakota, and I got picked up again. I tried again and again, and when I was eighteen, I cut out for good. I was still running when I came to New York. Just because you're free to move doesn't mean you're free. Finally, I got so far out I was cut off from everybody and everything. It was then I decided there was no sense in running so far and so fast when there was no longer anybody there. It was fake. It was running for the sake of running. So I stopped. I've got no place to run from. I don't have to be anyplace I don't want to be. But I am by no means an example for any kid wanting to strike out. I mean, I wouldn't want a young kid to leave home because I did it, and then have to go through a lot of the things I went through. Everybody has to find his *own* way to be free. There isn't anybody who can help you in that sense. Nobody was able to help me. Like seeing Woody Guthrie was one of the main reasons I came East. He was an idol to me. A couple of years ago, after I'd gotten to know him, I was going through some very bad changes, and I went to see Woody, like I'd go to somebody to confess to. But I couldn't confess to him. It was silly. I did go and talk with him—as much as he could talk—and the talking helped. But basically he wasn't able to help me at all. I finally realized that. So Woody was my last idol."

There was a pause.

"I've learned a lot in these past few years," Dylan said softly. "Like about beauty."

I reminded him of what he had said about his changing criteria of beauty in some notes he did for a Joan Baez album. There he had written that when he first heard her voice, before he knew her, his reaction had been:

> *"I hate that kind a sound," said I*
> *"The only beauty's ugly, man*
> *The crackin', shakin', breakin' sounds're*
> *The only beauty I understand."*

Dylan laughed. "Yeah," he said. "I was wrong. My hang-up was that I used to try to *define* beauty. Now I take it as it is, however it is. That's why I like Hemingway. I don't read much. Usually I read what people put in my hands. But I do read Hemingway. He didn't have to use adjectives. He didn't really have to define what he was saying. He just said it. I can't do that yet, but that's what I want to be able to do."

A young actor from Julian Beck's and Judith Malina's Living Theatre troupe stopped by the table, and Dylan shook hands with him enthusiastically. "We're leaving for Europe soon," the actor said. "But when we come back, we're going out on the street. We're going to put on plays right on the street, for anyone who wants to watch."

"Hey!" said Dylan, bouncing in his seat. "Tell Julian and Judith that I want to be in on that."

The actor said he would, and took Dylan's telephone number. Then he said, "Bob, are you doing only your own songs now—none of the old folk songs at all?"

"Have to," Dylan answered. "When I'm up tight and it's raining outside and nobody's around and somebody I want is a long way from me—and with someone else besides—I can't sing 'Ain't Got No Use for Your Red Apple Juice.' I don't care how great an old song it is or what its tradition is. I have to make a new song out of what *I* know and out of what *I'm* feeling."

The conversation turned to civil rights, and the actor used the term "the Movement" to signify the work of the civil-rights activists. Dylan looked at him quizzically. "I agree with everything that's happening," he said, "but I'm not part of no Movement. If I was, I wouldn't be able to do anything else but be in 'the Movement.' I just can't have people sit around and make rules for me. I do a lot of things no Movement would allow." He took a long drink of Beaujolais. "It's like politics," he went on. "I just can't make it with *any* organization. I fell into a trap once—last December—when I agreed to accept the Tom Paine Award from the Emergency Civil Liberties Committee. At the Americana Hotel! In the Grand Ballroom! As soon as I got there, I felt up tight. First of all, the people with me couldn't get in. They looked even funkier than I did, I guess. They weren't dressed right, or something. Inside the ballroom, I really got up tight. I began to drink. I looked down from the platform and saw a bunch of people who had nothing to do with my kind of politics. I looked down and I got scared. They were supposed to be on my side, but I didn't feel any connection with them. Here were these people who had been all involved with the left in the thirties, and now they were supporting civil-rights drives. That's groovy, but they also had minks and jewels, and it was like they were giving the money out of guilt. I got up to leave, and they followed me and caught me. They told me I had to accept the award. When I got up to make my speech, I couldn't say anything by that time but what was passing through my mind. They'd been talking about Kennedy being killed, and Bill Moore and Medgar Evers and the Buddhist monks in Vietnam being killed. I had to say something about Lee Oswald. I told them I'd read a lot of his feelings in the papers, and I knew he was up tight. Said I'd been up tight, too, so I'd got a lot of his feelings. I saw a lot of myself in Oswald, I said, and I saw in him a lot of the times we're all living in. And, you know, they started booing. They looked at me like I was an animal. They actually thought I was saying it was a good thing Kennedy had been killed. That's how far out they are. I was talking about Oswald. And then I started talking about friends of mine in Harlem—some of them junkies, all of them poor. And I said they need freedom as much as anybody else, and what's anybody doing for *them*? The chairman was kicking my leg under the table, and I told him, 'Get out of here.' Now, what I was supposed to be was a nice cat. I was supposed to say, 'I appreciate your award and I'm a great singer and I'm a great believer in liberals, and you buy my records and I'll support your cause.' But I didn't, and so I wasn't accepted that night. That's the cause of a lot of those chains I was talking about—people wanting to be accepted, people not wanting to be alone. But, after all, what is it to be alone? I've been alone sometimes in front of three thousand people. I was alone that night."

The actor nodded sympathetically.

Dylan snapped his fingers. "I almost forgot," he said. "You know, they were talking about Freedom Fighters that night. I've been in Mississippi, man. I know those people on another level besides civil-rights campaigns. I know them as friends. Like Jim Forman, one of the heads of SNCC. I'll stand on his side any time. But those people that night were actually getting me to look at colored people as colored people. I tell you, I'm never going to have anything to do with any political organization again in my life. Oh, I might help a friend if he was campaigning for office. But I'm not going to be part of any organization. Those people at that dinner were the same as everybody else. They're doing their time. They're chained to what they're doing. The only thing is, they're trying to put morals and great deeds on their chains, but basically they don't want to jeopardize their positions. They got their jobs to keep. There's nothing there for me, and there's nothing there for the kind of people I hang around with. The only thing I'm sorry about is that I guess I hurt the collection at the dinner. I didn't know they were going to try to collect money after my speech. I guess I lost them a lot of money. Well, I offered to pay them whatever it was they figured they'd lost because of the way I talked. I told them I didn't care how much it was. I hate debts, especially moral debts. They're worse than money debts."

Exhausted by his monologue, Dylan sank back and poured more Beaujolais. "People talk about trying to change society," he said. "All I know is that so long as people stay so concerned about protecting their status and protecting what they have, ain't nothing going to be done. Oh, there may be some change of levels inside the circle, but nobody's going to learn anything."

The actor left, and it was time for Dylan to head back upstate. "Come up and visit next week," he said to me, "and I'll give you a ride on my motorcycle." He hunched his shoulders and walked off quickly.

NEWPORT 1965

Three accounts of the 1965 Newport Folk Festival, where Dylan played a short electric set accompanied by Al Kooper, Barry Goldberg and members of the Paul Butterfield Blues Band—a supposed jilt of the folk community as well as Dylan's musical roots and idealism. Fred Goodman, in *The Mansion on the Hill*, presents a concise overview of the Newport legend, concentrating on the traditionalists' point of view. At the center of Goodman's description is Dylan's role in rock's becoming (at the expense of folk) the music that appealed most to the country's disaffected youth, thus creating a turning point in the record industry.

From a revisionist perspective, David Hajdu notes how implausible it was that Dylan's electric set at Newport took anybody by surprise, and points out that the audience was reacting, above all, to miserable sound quality. This passage is taken from Hajdu's *Positively 4th Street: The Lives and Times of Joan Baez, Bob Dylan, Mimi Baez Fariña and Richard Fariña*. While researching that book, Hajdu interviewed several musicians and organizers present at the festival. These talks prompted insights unavailable elsewhere, resulting in a novel and carefully considered evaluation of what likely occurred that evening.

Paul Nelson, after editing the *Little Sandy Review*, joined *Sing Out!* as a managing editor. Once a major figure in the folk revival, Nelson had begun to reject the movement's politics; in this highly personal report for *Sing Out!*'s "What's Happening" column, he sets forth a lengthy blast at Pete Seeger. More important, Nelson's account is a passionate and eloquent defense of the electric songs, marked by an urgent tone that shows how seriously the music press regarded Dylan as a visionary.

Before writing *The Mansion on the Hill*, Goodman worked for several years as a reporter and editor at *Rolling Stone*. Hajdu writes about music for

The New York Review of Books and *The New Republic*, among other publications, and is the author of an acclaimed biography of Billy Strayhorn, *Lush Life*. After the appearance of this "What's Happening" column, Nelson left *Sing Out!*; he later joined the staff of *Rolling Stone* and continued to write widely on folk and rock music.

excerpt from *The Mansion on the Hill*

FRED GOODMAN

THE ULTIMATE BASTION of folk purity, the festival was structured as a nonprofit foundation, and its board of directors included musicologist Alan Lomax and performers Pete Seeger, Theodore Bikel, and Peter Yarrow. "The board was interested in the great and good of the folk movement," says Joe Boyd, who became the festival's production manager. "Everybody played for scale: fifty dollars a day. Bob Dylan did it for the same money as the prisoners from a Texas chain gang."

In 1963, the festival received a huge boost from the twenty-two-year-old Dylan. He appeared with Peter, Paul and Mary, sang with Joan Baez, took part in Pete Seeger's workshop on topical songs and new songwriters, and performed a feature set that was greeted with near reverence. The Newport Folk Festival—which had struggled from its inception in 1959—was finally a hit, the folk movement was reinvigorated, and Bob Dylan was the shining star of both.

Just two years later, however, cracks were beginning to appear in the movement's foundation. In June of 1965, two months before the festival, Dylan had released an electric single, "Like a Rolling Stone." The notion that the artistic and social intentions of folk could be expressed through a blatantly commercial medium like rock and roll horrified folk's old guard.

"There were lots of battles at that time about what a folk song was," recalls Peter Yarrow. "Whether urban singers like Peter, Paul and Mary were emasculating music. Whether we were too homogenized; who had the right to call themselves a folk singer. The battles about definition were fast and furious. In the midst of this there was a division between amplified instruments and acoustic. And that was a real line." The scene was set for a showdown. "This was the last outpost," says organist Barry Goldberg, who came from Chicago to perform with Butterfield at the '65 festival, "and the feeling was that the barbarians were at the gate." Introducing Butterfield's band, festival director Alan Lomax offered up a long-winded and snide rant to the effect that in his day *real* bluesmen didn't need a bunch of fancy electric hardware. Rising to the bait, Albert Grossman, who managed Dylan, Peter, Paul and Mary, and Butterfield, accosted Lomax as he came offstage. In an instant, the two were rolling around in the dust, trading wild punches.

Butterfield's performance was just the excuse for a fight that had been waiting to happen. "There was a clear generational and cultural gap widening as the weekend went on," says Boyd. "The year before, Dylan had been the pied piper in blue jeans. This year he was in a puffed polka-dotted dueling shirt and there were rumors that they were smoking dope. The old guard—Seeger, Lomax, Bikel—were very upset. They had gotten to the point of having all their dreams come true two years before . . . having this gigantic mass movement of politically active kids. And suddenly they could see it all slipping away in a haze of marijuana smoke and self-indulgence. As far as they were concerned, Grossman was the money changer at the gates of the temple."

The fisticuffs would prove just the undercard for the festival's main bout. The next evening an obviously nervous Dylan took the stage with an electric guitar and band. Pummeled by the opening chords of "Maggie's Farm," the audience was struck dumb. "There was almost no sound," remembers Yarrow. "Then after the interminable two or three seconds, there were boos and whistles. Overwhelmingly, people were in shock."

Onstage, Barry Goldberg could hear both cheers and boos. Backstage, the world was coming to an end. "Goddamnit, it's terrible!" shouted Pete Seeger. "You can't understand the words! If I had an ax I'd cut the cable right now!"

Seeger, Lomax, and Bikel grabbed Boyd. "You've got to get the sound down!" they yelled. "It's far too loud!" Dashing to the mixing board where Yarrow and Paul Rothchild were stationed, Boyd relayed the message. No one budged.

After three songs, Dylan walked off to continuing boos. "People were just horrified," says Yarrow, who, despite refusing to interfere with Dylan's music, sympathized with the crowd. "It was as if it was a capitulation to the enemy—as if all of a sudden you saw Martin Luther King Jr. doing a cigarette ad. It was unimaginable that of all people this poet would abandon the touchy-feely intimacy of the music."

Dylan was badly shaken, but Yarrow and festival promoter George Wein convinced him to mollify the crowd by going back onstage with an acoustic guitar and playing two songs. But there was no turning back, and it was soon obvious that the inability of folk's old guard to accept the validity of the electric music would cost them. The following week Butterfield received an unheard-of $100 a night to play Club 47—an amount that forced club manager Jim Rooney to clear the coffeehouse after each set like a standard nightclub rather than allow people to loiter all night over a fifty-cent mug of coffee. The Cambridge folk scene was dead.

excerpt from *Positively 4th Street*

DAVID HAJDU

SOME 15,000 PEOPLE saw Dylan's set, and everyone who touched a different part of that elephant came away with his or her own mental picture of the beast. The facts are the following. Bob Dylan took the stage at nine fifteen. In place of his old work clothes, he was wearing motorcycle boots and a black leather blazer over a pressed white dress shirt with a gold tab pinning the collar tight. His hair and sideburns were long, and he had a sunburst Fender Stratocaster electric guitar, the model Buddy Holly played, strapped over his shoulder. A band of other musicians followed him—Mike Bloomfield of Butterfield's group on electric guitar, Al Kooper on organ, Barry Goldberg on piano, and the Butterfield rhythm section, Jerome Arnold on bass and Sam Lay on drums. They played three songs, "Maggie's Farm," "Like a Rolling Stone," and an early version of "It Takes a Lot to Laugh, It Takes a Train to Cry," and left the stage. A few minutes later Dylan returned alone with an acoustic guitar, and he sang two more songs, "It's All Over Now, Baby Blue" and "Mr. Tambourine Man."

From that sprang one of the most enduring myths of postwar popular culture: having affronted his fans by "going electric," Dylan was booed off the Newport stage, thrown from the temple for propagating a new faith in rock and roll too radical for his old followers to accept; humbled, teary-eyed, Dylan returned to sing in his folk style, an act of contrition. As a poetic allegory, the story dramatizes the emergence of a new music through the union of folk and rock with themes close to young people—generational conflict, style, and rage. But the mythic tale of Dylan's 1965 Newport performance has never borne scrutiny well.

The Newport audience was mostly young, predominantly college students and others their age. By July 25 they were thoroughly steeped in Bob Dylan's new music. *Bringing It All Back Home* and the single of "Subterranean Homesick Blues" had been in release for more than a third of the year. Dylan's current single, moreover, was "Like a Rolling Stone"—his venomous rock-and-roll masterpiece, written on his way back from London ("as a long piece of vomit," he said). It was a Top 40 hit; you could hardly drive to Newport with the radio on and not hear it, repeatedly. ("Like a Rolling Stone" would peak at number two on the pop music charts on August 14, 1965.) While some folk traditionalists in the Newport audience may have been startled to hear "Maggie's Farm," far more had been listening to it for months. "It was a huge festival, not a recital for a musicological society," John Cooke said. "My own view, and I was sitting there, was that most people in that audience had heard 'Like a Rolling Stone,' and they probably bought tickets purposely to see Bob Dylan and hear it, not in some weird hope that Dylan would go back in time and do stuff he hadn't done on his last two albums." Nor could the sound of a group playing rock and roll on electrified instruments have come as much of a shock that evening. The Paul Butterfield Blues Band had done a whole set of hard-driving R&B on Sunday afternoon, the Chambers Brothers had played the same day, and both groups had gotten wildly enthusiastic receptions.

What about that booing, then? There was consternation during Dylan's first song, although accounts differ on its nature and intent. Historian and musician Sam Charters, who has studied Vanguard's archival recordings, the documentary film soundtrack, and private tapes of Dylan's set, insists that the audience was not booing but hollering complaints about the sound quality. "There were no boos," he said, "and the complaints weren't about the music—my God, Dylan was the hottest thing going. The sound system at Newport was not set up properly for electric instruments, so people were yelling out because all they could hear was noise." As Jack Elliott put it, "The music was good. It sounded like horseshit." Among those who did hear booing, Geoff Muldaur assumed it was a reaction to the execution, not the style, of Dylan's music. "I don't believe people were booing because the music was revolutionary," Muldaur said. "It was just that Dylan wasn't very good at it. He had no idea how to play the electric guitar, and he had very second-rate musicians with him, and they hadn't rehearsed enough. It just didn't work. The musicians didn't play good. There's no doubt in my mind, people were booing because it stank."

Dylan was among those convinced that the audience was booing him, and he attributed it to a faction of musical reactionaries. "It was in Newport—well, I did this very crazy thing," Dylan said. "I mean, I didn't really know what was going to happen, but they certainly booed, I'll tell you that. You could hear it all over the place. I don't know who they were, though, and I'm certain whoever it was did it twice as loud as they normally would. . . .

"I was kind of stunned," he recalled. "But I can't put anybody down for coming and booing. After all, they paid to get in. They could have been maybe a little quieter and not so persistent, though. There were a lot of old people there, too. Lots of whole families had driven down from Vermont, lots of nurses and their patients, and, well, like they just came to hear some relaxing hoedowns, you know, maybe an Indian polka or two. And just when everything's going all right, here I come on, and the whole place turns into a beer factory. . . .

"I think there's always a little 'boo' in all of us. I don't even understand it. . . . They can't hurt me with a boo. . . . There were a lot of people there who were very pleased that I got booed. I saw them afterward. I do resent somewhat, though, that everybody that booed said they did it because they were old fans."

Backstage, the traditional folk power brokers watched Dylan in exasperation. Folklorist Alan Lomax and Pete Seeger sputtered and fumed about this violation of everything Dylan represented, at least to them. Seeger at one point spouted something widely repeated as a threat to chop the power cord with an ax if Dylan were not pulled off immediately. (Years later Seeger would say he had indeed been furious, but only because the volume on the instruments was obscuring the socialist message of "Maggie's Farm.") When Dylan left the stage after only three songs—not in retreat, but because the band had only rehearsed those three—he walked into the wall of Lomax, Seeger, George Wein, Theodore Bikel, and Peter Yarrow (the latter two of whom had been arguing in Dylan's favor). "I told him, 'Bob—people are very upset,'" Wein recalled. "I didn't know how upset the audience was. Maybe they were thrilled. I was trying to keep things under control, and I knew people backstage were very upset. I said, 'Bob, you've gotta go back and sing something and calm things down.' He said to me, 'I only have my electric guitar.' I said, 'Does anybody here have a guitar for Bob Dylan?' Twenty people raised their hands with guitars. He picked one out of the air, and he did go out there."

Dylan would insist he was not upset by either the booing he thought he heard or the reaction he found backstage. "I wasn't shattered by it," he said. "I didn't cry." The strap on the guitar he borrowed was too short and pulled the instrument high up on his chest; he looked uneasy, and his singing was soft and vulnerable. He seemed wrought with emotion. There is a picture of this moment by photographer Rick Sullo, who was on the side of the stage and used a telephoto lens to catch Dylan close up, in profile. Bob is glaring ahead at the audience as he sings, and a tear trails from his left eye down his cheek.

What's Happening

PAUL NELSON

FOR ALL ITS EMPHASIS on tradition and its quiet high points, Newport is still a place for the Big Moment, the Great Wham, that minuscule second of High Drama that freezes the blood and sparks the brain into the kind of excitement that stays forever in one's memory. Nothing approaching such a moment happened at Newport in 1964 (it was a dull circus), but Bob Dylan provided it on Sunday night this year: the most dramatic scene I've ever witnessed in folk music.

Here are two accounts of it, the first sketched quickly in my notebook at the time:

"Dylan, doing his new R&R, R&B, R&? stuff knocked me out. . . . I think his new stuff is as exciting as anything I've heard lately in any field. The Newport crowd actually booed the electric guitar numbers he did, and there followed the most dramatic thing I've seen: Dylan walking off the stage, the audience booing and yelling 'Get rid of that electric guitar,' Peter Yarrow trying to talk the audience into clapping and trying to talk Dylan into coming back, Yarrow announcing that Dylan was coming back, George Wein asking Yarrow in disbelief, '*Is* he coming back?,' Dylan coming back with tears in his eyes and singing 'It's All Over Now, Baby Blue,' a song that I took to be his farewell to Newport, an incredible sadness over Dylan and the audience, the audience finally clapping now because the electric guitar was gone, etc." (Dylan did only his first three numbers with electric guitar and band.)

The second account is from a long report on Newport by Jim Rooney of Cambridge, Massachusetts:

"Nothing else in the festival caused such controversy. His [Dylan's] was the only appearance that was genuinely disturbing. It was disturbing to the Old Guard, I think, for several reasons. Bob is no longer a neo–Woody Guthrie, with whom they could identify. He has thrown away his dungarees and shaggy jacket. He has stopped singing talking blues and songs about 'causes'—peace or civil rights. The highway he travels now is unfamiliar to those who bummed around in the thirties during the Depression. He travels by plane. He wears high-heel shoes and high-style clothes from Europe. The mountains and valleys he knows are those of the mind—a mind extremely aware of the violence of the inner and outer world. 'The people' so loved by Pete Seeger are 'the mob' so hated by Dylan. In the face of violence, he has chosen to preserve himself alone. No one else. And he defies everyone else to have the courage to be as alone, as unconnected . . . as he. He screams through organ and drums and electric guitar, 'How does it feel to be on your own?' And there is no mistaking the hostility, the defiance, the contempt for all those thousands sitting before him who aren't on their own. Who can't make it. And they seemed to understand that night for the first time what Dylan has been trying to say for over a year—that he is not theirs or anyone else's—and they didn't like what they heard and booed. They wanted to throw him out. He had fooled them before when they thought he was theirs. . . . Pete [Seeger had] begun the night with the sound of a newborn baby crying, and asked that everyone sing to that baby and tell it what kind of a world it would be growing up into. But Pete already knew what he wanted others to sing. They were going to sing that it was a world of pollution, bombs, hunger, and injustice, but that PEOPLE would OVERCOME. . . . [But] can there be no songs as violent as the age? Must a folk song be of mountains, valleys, and love between my brother and my sister all over the land? Do we allow for despair only in the blues? . . . [That's all] very comfortable and safe. But is that what we should be saying to that baby? Maybe, maybe not. But we should ask the question. And the only one in the entire festival who questioned our position was Bob Dylan. Maybe he didn't put it in the best way. Maybe he was rude. But he shook us. And that is why we have poets and artists."

Indeed that's why we have poets and artists. Newport 1965, interestingly enough, split apart forever the two biggest names in folk music: Pete Seeger, who saw in Sunday night a chance to project his vision of the world and sought to have all others convey his impression (thereby restricting their performances), and Bob Dylan, like some fierce young Spanish outlaw in dress leather jacket, a man who could no longer accept the older singer's vague humanistic generalities, a man who, like Nathanael West, had his own angry vision to project in such driving electric songs as "Like a Rolling Stone" and "Maggie's Farm."

And, like it or not, the audience had to choose. Whether, on the one hand, to take the word of a dignified and great humanitarian whose personal sincerity is beyond question but whose public career more and more seems to be sliding like that other old radical Max Eastman's toward a *Reader's Digest*–Norman Rockwell version of how things are (Pete's idea of singing peace songs to a newborn baby makes even the most middle-brow *Digest* ideas seem as far out as anything William Burroughs ever did!); or whether to accept as truth the Donleavy-Westian-Brechtian world of Bob Dylan, where things aren't often pretty, where there isn't often hope, where man isn't always noble, but where, most importantly, there exists a reality that coincides with that of this planet. Was it to be marshmallows and cotton candy or meat and potatoes? Rose-colored glasses or a magnifying glass? A nice guy who has subjugated and weakened his art through his constant insistence on a world that never was and never can be, or an angry, passionate poet who demands his art to be all, who demands not to be owned, not to be restricted or predicted, but only, like Picasso, to be left alone from petty criticisms to do his business, wherever that may take him?

Make no mistake, the audience had to make a clear-cut choice and they made it: Pete Seeger. They chose to boo Dylan off the stage for something as superficially silly as an electric guitar or something as stagnatingly sickening as their idea of owning an artist. They chose the safety of wishful thinking rather than the painful, always difficult stab of art. They might have believed they were choosing humanity over a reckless me-for-me attitude, but they weren't. They were choosing suffocation over invention and adventure, backwards over forwards, a dead hand instead of a live one. They were afraid, as was Pete Seeger (who was profoundly disturbed by Dylan's performance), to make a leap, to admit, to consider, to think. Instead, they took refuge in the Seeger vision as translated by the other less-pure-at-heart singers on the program, indeed, by all other than Seeger: the ghastly second half of Sunday night's program, where practically all forms of Social Significance ran completely out of control in a sickening display of egomania and a desperate grasping for publicity and fame. The second half of Sunday night (from all reports) was more ugly and hysterical than anything in a Dylan song; and, remember, the impetus for it was not Dylan at all, but Pete Seeger. (Ironically, although the audience chose the Seeger vision, it was a hollow victory for Pete, who felt he'd failed badly.)

It was a sad parting of the ways for many, myself included. I choose Dylan. I choose art. I will stand behind Dylan and his "new" songs, and I'll bet my critical reputation (such as it may be) that I'm right.

excerpt from KQED Press Conference, December 3, 1965

BOB DYLAN

Like the Beatles, whose wit and charisma were always on display before the camera, Dylan learned to have fun at the media's expense. The first of his press conferences to be televised in its entirety, this hourlong session at San Francisco's KQED studio is a masterly performance. Asked for his opinion on a variety of topics, political, musical and otherwise, he responds with a blend of sarcasm and deflection. Clearly ad-libbing in search of the most absurd answer to each query, Dylan spoke very slowly and in a deadpan voice. Often he was unable to conceal a wide, diffident smile. Wary of being the subject of so much attention, he gave several such conferences during this period of his career. At his most funny and eccentric, the transcript typifies Dylan's caustic, edgy attitude toward the press.

PRESS: *I'd like to know about the cover of your forthcoming album, the one with "Subterranean Homesick Blues" on it. I'd like to know about the meaning of the photograph with you in the Triumph T-shirt.*

DYLAN: What would you like to know about it?

Well, I'd like to know if that's an equivalent photograph. It means something. It's got a philosophy in it. I'd like to know visually what it represents to you, because you're a part of that.

I haven't really looked at it that much.

I've thought about it a great deal.

It was just taken one day when I was sitting on the steps, you know. I don't really remember too much about it.

Well, what about the motorcycle as an image in your songwriting? You seem to like that.

Oh, we all like motorcycles to some degree.

Do you think of yourself primarily as a singer or as a poet?

I think of myself more as a song-and-dance man, you know.

A what?

A song-and-dance man.

Why?

Oh, I don't think we have enough time to really go into that.

You were quoted in the Chicago Daily News *as saying that when you're really wasted you may enter into another field. How "wasted" is really wasted, and do you foresee it?*

No, I don't foresee it, but it's more or less like a ruthless type of feeling. Very ruthless and intoxicated to some degree.

The criticism that you've received for more or less leaving folk for folk-rock hasn't seemed to bother you very much. Do you think you'll stick with folk-rock or are you going on into more writing?

I don't play folk-rock.

What would you call your music?

I would call it, ah, I like to think of it more in terms of vision music. It's mathematical music.

Would you say that the words were more important than the music?

The words are just as important as the music. There would be no music without the words.

Which do you write first, ordinarily?

The words.

Do you think there will ever be a time when you will paint or sculpt?

Oh yes. Oh sure.

What poets do you dig?

Oh, Rimbaud, I guess. W. C. Fields. The family, you know, the trapeze family in the circus. Smokey Robinson, Allen Ginsberg, Charlie Rich—he's a good poet.

In a lot of your songs you are hard on a lot of people. In "Like a Rolling Stone" you're pretty hard on the girl and in "Positively 4th Street" you're pretty hard on a supposed friend. Are you hard on them because you want to torment them or because you want to change their lives, to make them notice?

I want to needle them.

Do you still sing your older songs?

No. I just saw a songbook last night. I don't really see too many of those things, but there's a lot of songs in those books I haven't even recorded, you know. I've just written down, you know, and put little tunes to them and they published them. A lot of the songs I just don't even know anymore, even the ones I did sing. There doesn't seem to be enough time, you know.

What do you think of people that analyze your songs? Do they usually end up with the same meaning that you wrote, or . . .

I welcome them with open arms.

The University of California mimeographed the lyrics to all the songs on the last album and had a symposium discussing them. Do you welcome that?

Oh sure. I'm just kind of sad I'm not around to be a part of it, but . . . it was nice.

It'd be pretty wild if you had been.

Yes.

Mr. Dylan, Josh Dunson, in his new book Freedom in the Air, *implies that you have sold out to commercial interests and the topical song movement. Do you have any comments, sir?*

Well, no comments, no arguments. No, I sincerely don't feel guilty.

If you were going to sell out to a commercial interest, which one would you choose?

Ladies' garments.

If you were draftable at present, do you have any feelings of what your actions might be?

No, I'd probably just do what had to be done.

What would that be?

Well, I don't know. I never really speak in terms of what if, you know, so I don't really know.

You're considered by many people to be symbolic of the protest movement in the country for young people. Are you going to participate in the Vietnam Day Committee demonstration in front of the Fairmont Hotel tonight?

No, I'll be busy tonight.

Are you planning any demonstrations?

Well, we thought of one. I don't know if it could be organized in time.

Would you describe it?

Well, it was a demonstration where I make up the cards, you know. They have a group of protestors here, perhaps carrying cards with pictures of jack of diamondses on them and the ace of spades on them. Pictures of mules, maybe words and, oh, maybe about twenty-five to thirty thousand of these things printed up and just picket—carry signs and picket in front of the post office.

What words?

Oh, words. Camera, microphone, loose. Just words, names of some famous people.

Do you consider yourself a politician?

Do I consider myself a politician? Oh, I guess so. I have my own party, though.

Does it have a name?

No. There's no presidents in the party. There's no presidents, or vice-presidents, or secretaries or anything like that, so it makes it kind of hard to get in.

Is there any right wing or left wing in that party?

No. It's more or less in the center, kind of on the uppity scale.

Do you think your party could end the war with China?

I don't know. I don't know if they have any people over there that would be in the same kind of party. You know? So it might be kind of hard to infiltrate. I don't think my party would ever be approved by the White House or anything like that.

Is there anyone else in your party?

No. Most of us don't even know each other, you know. It's hard to tell who's in it and who's not in it.

Would you recognize them if you see them?

Oh, you can recognize them if you see them.

Mr. Dylan, how would you define folk music?

As a constitutional replay of mass production.

Would you call your songs folk songs?

No.

Are protest songs "folk songs"?

I guess. If they're a constitutional replay of mass production.

Do you prefer songs with a subtle or obvious message?

With a what?

A subtle or obvious message.

I don't really prefer those kinds of songs at all. "Message," you mean like . . . what songs with a message?

Well, like "Eve of Destruction" and things like that.

Do I prefer that to what?

I don't know, but your songs are supposed to have a subtle message.

Subtle message?

Well, they're supposed to.

Where did you hear that?

In a movie magazine.

Oh my God! Well, we don't discuss those things here.

Are your songs ever about real people, like occasional poetry?

Sure they are. They're all about real people.

Particular ones?

Particular people? Sure, I'm sure you've seen all the people in my songs at one time or another.

Who's Mr. Jones?

Mr. Jones, I'm not going to tell you his first name. I'd get sued.

What does he do for a living?

He's a pin boy. He also wears suspenders.

Can you explain your attraction as a performer, your writing?

Attraction to what?

Your attraction, your popularity, your mass popularity.

No, I really have no idea. That's the truth. I always tell the truth. That is the truth.

What are your own personal hopes for the future, and what do you hope to change in the world?

Oh, my hopes for the future. To be honest, you know, I don't have any hopes for the future, and I just hope to have enough boots to be able to change them. That's all, really, it doesn't boil down to anything more than that. If it did, I would certainly tell you.

In Berkeley They Dig
Bob Dylan

RALPH J. GLEASON

Not long after Newport, Dylan left for a world tour that would feature four excellent musicians—Robbie Robertson on guitar, Rick Danko on bass, Richard Manuel on piano and Garth Hudson on organ (various drummers were used aside from Levon Helm, the group's original drummer, who plays on *The Basement Tapes*). Later known as the Band, they played more than seventy concerts with Dylan in 1965 and '66 and formed an integral part in his switch from solo performer to bandleader.

Ralph J. Gleason reviewed their December 3 and 4, 1965, concerts at Berkeley's Community Theater for the *San Francisco Chronicle*. Gleason devotes most of his commentary to the electric half of the performance, and the ways in which the Band enlivened Dylan's singing and stage presence. He also observes the unique responsiveness of the West Coast audience, who didn't find anything wrong with Dylan playing blues and rock and roll alongside his acoustic set. Though other audiences would not be as tolerant, this tour has long been considered among the high points of Dylan's performing career.

Gleason was a pop and jazz critic for the *Chronicle* for many years; he also cofounded *Rolling Stone* and collected a number of his essays in *Celebrating the Duke*.

THEY DIDN'T BOO BOB Dylan in Berkeley when he brought out his electric guitar and his rock-and-roll band. Instead they cheered and shouted, "bravo! bravo!" when he finished his hit, "Positively 4th Street."

On both the Friday and Saturday night shows, a curious rapport existed with the audience. Each show opened—as is apparently from his pattern these days—with Dylan on stage alone, singing seven or eight of his better known numbers accompanied only by his own guitar with occasional harmonica solos to offset it.

Both nights, Dylan, resplendent in a brown shetland suit with perpendicular, black, inch-wide houndstooth jagged checks, his hair, like thin brownish wires standing out from his head, stood at the microphone raising himself on tiptoe to mark the emphasis of a word or an accent singing the familiar songs, "Gates of Eden," "To Ramona," "Baby Blue," "Love Minus Zero" and "Tambourine Man." Except for "Baby Blue" and "Desolation Row" and a new song he sang on Saturday night, "Freeze Out," I got the impression both nights that he was less than wildly concerned at first.

Each night as he got further into the opening half, he dug into the numbers more until, on both nights, "Baby Blue" followed by "Desolation Row" brought down the house.

Both nights, too, the second half wiped everybody out. Dylan's rock-and-roll band, which caused such booing and horror-show reaction at the Newport Folk Festival and elsewhere, went over in Berkeley like the discovery of gold.

It made a great night. Here was one of America's greatest singers (who is also America's greatest poet) standing there like an I. Magnin mannikin clutching an electric guitar, backed by racks of amplifiers, loudspeakers, flanked by an electric organ, a piano, another guitarist, an electric bassist and a drummer and overhead, making a surrealistic stage set, four paintings by Bob Neuarth. In each painting, from the space man to the rock 'n' roll players, the figures were an abstraction of Dylan's own image, or so it seemed to me after two glasses of milk and a Hershey bar.

The band is great. Just great. The lead guitarist, Robbie Robertson, is eloquent and exciting and the bassist, Rick Danko, seems like he could swing Colt Tower.

Dylan has taken several of his older songs, "I Don't Believe You," "Baby Let Me Follow You Down" and "It Ain't Me Babe" and rearranged them for the band. "It Ain't Me Babe" is a literal demonstration of how the composer wants his music played, addressed to the recent pop hit by the Turtles, it strikes me.

Then the rest of the songs are from his latest albums, "Tombstone Blues," "Just Like Tom Thumb's Blues," "Ballad of a Thin Man," "Positively 4th Street" and "Like A Rolling Stone" plus a new one whose title was lost both nights in the hurricane of sound.*

It is a loud band, but an exciting and delightful band full of kicks and flashes of great moments. It is obvious Dylan blows his mind playing with them. He even broke a guitar string Saturday night and did a couple of numbers without the guitar, just wailing on the harmonica.

The climaxes and explosions that build like great waves of sound in "Rolling Stone" are an amazing emotional experience complimenting fully the lyrics of the songs. The dirge-like quality of "Mr. Jones" is enhanced by the band's treatment of it and Dylan's own singing, from the piano bench. And "Positively 4th Street" brought screams of joy both nights.

Dylan is obviously in transition. His program now represents the midpoint and it is clear that at any minute he will abandon the solo singing except for occasional numbers, and do the whole show with the band. The next step will be a portable lighting system to enhance the surrealistic effect the paintings and Dylan's costume already give the stage.

Phil Ochs, in his *Broadside* interview, called Dylan "LSD on stage." This may or may not be true. I wouldn't know. But I do know it is a powerful experience in more than musical terms to dig his concerts. The audience's relationship to the singer is possibly the most direct and powerful I have ever witnessed. He moves them in a deep and sometimes disturbing way and the occasional bad sound doesn't interfere; enough comes through emotionally.

Dylan returns Saturday to the Masonic Memorial (Sunday he's in San Jose). Friday night two major American poets (Allen Ginsberg and Lawrence Ferlinghetti), a major novelist (Ken Kesey) and two Hell's Angels were in the front row. Dozens of university professors were scattered in the audience, some looking rather shattered by the experience. On

---

* Most likely "Long Distance Operator," a song premiered in Berkeley though never recorded in the studio. —ED.

both nights, the audience lingered in the hall and on the steps outside the Community Theater. They simply didn't want to go home.

Something most certainly *is* happening here and perhaps we have been given through Dylan's muse an opportunity to see a glimpse of the future as it works. In any case it is a very special and highly emotional happening every time he comes alive on the stage.

excerpt from Rock Lyrics Are Poetry (Maybe)

ROBERT CHRISTGAU

Here, Robert Christgau offers a sensible corrective to the hyperbole common during the height of Dylan's popularity in the mid-1960s, when many declared him the greatest contemporary American poet. Christgau discusses how a song—"My Back Pages," in particular—can seem silly without accompaniment, while allowing that the need to rhyme and adapt lyrics to music relaxes one's literary standards. Dylan holds a similar opinion; he has always preferred not to be known as a poet, but as an entertainer or singer.

Christgau, a senior editor at the *Village Voice*, is one of the writers whose work in the sixties and seventies established a community of serious rock criticism. He has published several books, including *Any Old Way You Choose It: Rock and Other Pop Music, 1967–1973*.

THE SONGWRITER who seems to sound most like a poet is Bob Dylan. Dylan is such an idiosyncratic genius that it is perilous to imitate him—his faults, at worst annoying and at best invigorating, ruin lesser talents. But imitation is irresistible. Who can withstand Paul Nelson of *Little Sandy Review*, who calls Dylan "the man who in every sense revolutionized modern poetry, American folk music, popular music. And the whole of modern-day thought"? Or Jack Newfield of the *Village Voice*, wandering on about "symbolic alienation . . . new plateaus for poetic, content-conscious songwriters . . . put poetry back into song . . . reworks T. S. Eliot's classic line . . . bastard child of Chaplin, Céline, and Hart Crane," while serving up tidbits from Dylan's corpus, some of which don't look so tasty on a paper plate? However inoffensive "The ghost of electricity / Howls in the bones of her face" sounds on vinyl, it is silly without the music. Poems are read or said. Songs are sung.

Dylan gets away with it simply cause there is so much there. The refrain of "My Back Pages," his renunciation of political protest—"I was so much older then / I'm younger than that now"—may be the finest line he has ever written. Its opening—"Crimson flames tied to my ears"—may be the worst. The song bulges with metaphors and epithets, some apt, some tucked in to fill out the meter. The tired trick of using a noun for a verb to spice things up reaches an all-time low with the word (?) "foundationed." Dylan's obsession with rhyme (which he has lately begun to parody: "Hear the one with the mustache say, Jeeze / I can't find my knees") compels him to match "now" with "somehow" three times in six stanzas. Twice this is totally gratuitous. But the third time—"Good and bad, I define these terms, quite clear no doubt somehow"—"somehow" becomes the final qualification in a series of qualifications, and works perfectly: a typical hit among misses.

"My Back Pages" is a bad poem. But it is a good song, supported by a memorable refrain which couldn't possibly bear the weight of a whole poem. The music softens our demands, the importance of what is being said somehow overbalances the flaws in how, and Dylan's delivery—he sounds as if he's singing a hymn at a funeral—adds a portentous edge not present just in the words. Because it's a good song, "My Back Pages" can be done in other ways. The Byrds' version depends on intricate, up-tempo music that pushes the words into the background. However much they mean to David Crosby, the lyrics—except for that refrain—could be gibberish and the song would still succeed. Repeat: Dylan is a songwriter, not a poet. A few of his most perfect efforts—"Don't Think Twice," say, or "Just Like a Woman"—are tight enough to survive on the page. But they are exceptions.

John Wesley Harding

ROBERT CHRISTGAU

O n July 29, 1966, Dylan crashed his motorcycle on a back road near Woodstock; though the nature of the accident and the extent of injuries suffered by Dylan remain vague, the crash released him from an exhausting touring schedule and allowed him to withdraw from public scrutiny. Dylan reposed in upstate New York for the next year and a half, raising a family and making a series of informal recordings with the Band in the summer of 1967 that were later released as *The Basement Tapes*.

When he finally returned to the studio, in October 1967, it was to record an acoustic album built largely on biblical themes and characters entitled *John Wesley Harding*. Released the same year as the "summer of love," the album surprised many for its soft-spoken quality and stark instrumentation. Reviewing it for *Esquire*, Robert Christgau praises these reductive qualities, emphasizing the ways in which they contrast the excesses of contemporary rock as well as Dylan's earlier music. In so doing, he also provides a fresh analysis of the songwriter's youthful style.

BOB DYLAN'S long-awaited *John Wesley Harding* will doubtless stand as the funniest album of the year. Even if it failed as music (it doesn't), it would succeed as strategy, and that would be enough. Pop music does not exist in the future. Immediacy is its most salient virtue. And at the moment there couldn't be a more salutary record than *John Wesley Harding*.

Dylan had not been heard from since May 1966, when he presented his work at its most involuted, neurotic, and pop—and exhilarating—in *Blonde on Blonde*. Then he racked himself up in a motorcycle accident, went into hiding, and inspired a legend. But while he was away, the music in which he has been a prime mover continued to evolve—and mutate. Art and Social Commentary were absorbed, almost painlessly, by the world's schlockiest business, so that the trade journal *Record World* could review a new single as "a highly commercial rock allegory of perishing society." Apparently, society itself would perish before the record industry.

All this was made possible by the charismatic rebelliousness of the brightest pop stars. For them, terms like "highly commercial" were irrelevant; they were highly commercial, however they chose to manifest themselves, and the industry could just hangdog along. The luminaries had a double goal: to find their own thing and to make sure it was heavier than anyone else's. A Heavy Thing. Thus, the Beach Boys arrived at something unique and almost perfect, *Smiley Smile*, but because it was so slight, it was outshone by the Doors' muscular but misshapen *Strange Days*, and in eight months the Doors came from nowhere to reign as America's heaviest group.

Dylan, of course, does not operate on such a modest level of competition. His only rivals are the Beatles and the Stones. In his absence the Beatles redefined the contest as (a) conceptual and (b) musical. Everything had to be placed in an abstract framework—even cover art was the pop star's responsibility—and while good lyrics were important, new music was even more important. For lesser talents, these preconditions usually insured that "heavy" meant "overburdened." No one was sure how they'd affect Dylan.

It should be added that Dylan does not necessarily relish combat. His retreat emphasized what was already clear: He would rather do his thing in private. The spotlight puts him off. Only the odd happenstance that he is an entertainer, forced by the nature of his thing to compete for public acclaim, induces him to fight at all.

So he fought and won, by redefining the rules of war. His battle cry was the album's title, as kinky as "Greensleeves," and his standard the jacket, done in gray and featuring a Polaroid snapshot of the artist and some friends in the woods. Turn it over, and there are the song titles, six on a side, just like Lawrence Welk. There are notes by Dylan, not as willful as usual, but still the first written comment on a major album in several years. And then the credits—three musicians all told, drums and acoustic bass and (for two songs only) steel guitar, plus Dylan on acoustic guitar, harmonica, and (twice) piano. Psychedelic!

The title song opens the record, introduced by a few passes at the guitar that sound no different from what Dylan was doing at nineteen—a little more subdued, perhaps. Then bass and drums enter; they provide a beat, but they also remind us that the record was not resurrected from the 1963 reject can. Such a reminder is necessary, for on first hearing, *John Wesley Harding* sounds monotonous, old-fashioned, and very folky.

In fact it is all that and represents a starting artistic advance anyway. Instead of plunging forward, Dylan looked back. Instead of grafting, he pruned. Dylan's work has always been marked by derelictions of taste that have become almost an endearing trademark. He has never hesitated to fill the meter with a useless word or to wrench tone in the service of rhyme. Much of his best work is simply too long, like *Clarissa* or Satyajit Ray's *Apu Trilogy*. Despite all the talk about "poetry," Dylan has always been a word-crazy dramatist; his "images" are mostly situations full of incongruities and awkward in syntax and diction. Even his best stanzas seem ready to burst like waterlogged beanbags. But on the new album Dylan has learned the value of understatement.

Only one of the new songs, a ballad, runs more than five minutes, and nine of the remaining eleven are under the two-hundred-second mark so dear to radio programmers. They have only three stanzas. Diction is spare, traditional (almost all the songs function as parodies), and abstract. Everything is so careful that a well-placed detail or linguistic self-indulgence carries the weight that a whole stanza used to, so the familiar sense of unreality prevails, reinforced by the fact that many of the songs seem to end in the middle. The Dylan flavor is unquestionably there. But it has been achieved for the first time with no waste of materials.

This is also the most impersonal record Dylan has ever made. Persona has always been important in his work, but this time the "I," when it appears, is almost anonymous. And although the songs seem obscure, they are often quite straightforward: Whatever other levels are also present, "I Pity the Poor Immigrant" is still really about working-class protofascists, Tom Paine is really a character in "As I Went Out One Morning," and, in

"I'll Be Your Baby Tonight," that big old moon really does shine like a spoon. But the directness of attack is so uncharacteristic that it undercuts itself, becoming a source of mystery and surprise—imagine, a Dylan album that is most admirable for its straightforwardness.

When *John Wesley Harding* was in the stores for a week, it had already sold 250,000 copies—Dylan's fastest moving album on mystique alone. Let's hope everyone listens, too. Let's hope that songwriters, instead of deciding that folk (which this is not) is in again, will learn to concentrate on line before they attempt oratorios, and that the fans will finally be weaned from some of our more excessive poetasters.

Dylan seems finally to have found his own ground. Almost alone among the pop stars, he no longer comes on like a questing adolescent. Politically, he is neither the true believer nor the dropout. His country accent has never been less self-conscious or more effective. The piano and steel guitar work better than four sitars and a Moog synthesizer. Only the harmonica is occasionally intrusive, and I'm sure we'll all forgive him that—after all, he probably planned it that way.

This is not a better record than *Sgt. Pepper*, but it should have better effect. It is mature work that still shows room for rich development. If only it were so easy to say that of the Beatles.

excerpt from Owl Farm—
Winter of '68

HUNTER S. THOMPSON

Hunter S. Thompson, author of *Fear and Loathing in Las Vegas* and one of the first New Journalists, began his eulogy for the sixties by expressing a popular sentiment: Dylan's music reflected, and in some cases, fostered the era's unsettling social events.* (Accordingly, Dylan's withdrawal after his motorcycle accident is often seen as foreshadowing the counterculture's end.) Thompson notes the curious rise of Dylan's national prominence, and considers the ways in which his music appealed to a radical and rebellious generation. The idea of interpreting Dylan's life as allegory is a common one, and though he doesn't like to be known as a political or social icon, it has persisted throughout his career.

1967 WAS THE YEAR of the hippy. As this is the last meditation I intend to write on that subject, I decided, while composing it, to have the proper background. So, in the same small room with me and my typewriter, I have two huge speakers and a 100 watt music amplifier booming out Bob Dylan's "Mr. Tambourine Man." This, to me, is the Hippy National Anthem. It's an acid or LSD song—and like much of the hippy music, its lyrics don't make much sense to anyone not "cool" or "with it" or "into the

---

* Although Thompson and others label "Mr. Tambourine Man" as a drug song, Dylan later contradicted this—"drugs never played a part in that song. Drugs were never that big a thing with me. I could take 'm or leave 'm, never hung me up" (*Biograph* liner notes, 50).

drug scene." I was living in San Francisco's Haight-Ashbury district when the word "hippy" was coined by *San Francisco Chronicle* columnist Herb Caen—who also came up with "beatnik," in the late 1950s—so I figure I'm entitled to lean on personal experience in these things. To anyone who was part of that (post-beat) scene before the word "hippy" became a national publicity landmark (in 1966 and 1967), "Mr. Tambourine Man" is both an epitaph and a swan-song for the lifestyle and the instincts that led, eventually, to the hugely-advertised "hippy phenomenon."

Bob Dylan was the original hippy, and anyone curious about the style and tone of the "younger generation's" thinking in the early 1960s has only to play his albums in chronological order. They move from folk-whimsy to weird humor to harsh social protest during the time of the civil rights marches and the Mississippi summer protests of 1963 and '64. Then, in the months after the death of President Kennedy, Dylan switched from the hard commitments of social realism to the more abstract "realities" of neo-protest and disengagement. His style became one of eloquent despair and personal anarchism. His lyrics became increasingly drug-oriented, with double-entendres and dual meanings that were more and more obvious, until his "Rainy Day Women #12 and 35" was banned by radio stations from coast to coast . . . mainly because of the chorus line saying "Everybody must get stoned. . . ."

By this time he was a folk hero to the "under thirty generation" that seemed to be in total revolt against everything their elders were trying to believe in. By this time, too, Dylan was flying around the country—from one sold-out concert to another—in his private jet plane, worth about $500,000. His rare press conferences were jammed by reporters who treated them more like an audience with a Wizard than a question and answer session with an accidental public figure. At the same time, Dylan's appearance became more and more bizarre. When he began singing in Greenwich Village about 1960 his name was Bob Zimmerman and he looked like a teen-age hobo in the Huck Finn tradition . . . or like Nick Adams in the early Hemingway stories. But by 1965 he had changed his last name to Dylan & was wearing shoulder-length hair and rubber-tight, pin-stripe suits that reflected the colorful & sarcastically bisexual image that was, even then, becoming the universal style of a sub-culture called "hippies."

This focus on Dylan is no accident. Any culture—and especially any sub-culture—can be at least tentatively defined by its heroes ... and of all the hippy heroes, Bob Dylan was the first and foremost. He appeared at a time when Joan Baez was the Queen Bee of that world of the young and alienated ... but unlike Joanie, who wrote none of her own songs and preferred wistful ballads to contemporary drug anthems, Dylan moved on to become the voice of an anguished and half-desperate generation. Or at least that part of a generation that saw itself as doomed and useless in terms of the status-quo, business-as-usual kind of atmosphere that prevailed in this country as the war in Vietnam went from bad to worse and the United States, in the eyes of the whole world's "under thirty generation," seemed to be drifting toward a stance of vengeful, uncontrolled militarism.

PART TWO

BLOOD ON THE TRACKS
(1970–1978)

"Songwriting is a lot like fishing in a stream;
you put in your line and hope you catch something. And I don't think anyone downstream from
Bob Dylan ever caught anything."

—*Arlo Guthrie*

Self Portrait No. 25*

GREIL MARCUS

Few writers have chronicled Dylan's career with as much wit and perspicacity as Greil Marcus. A former editor at *Rolling Stone* and the author of books such as *Mystery Train: Images of America in Rock 'n' Roll Music*; *Lipstick Traces: A Secret History of the 20th Century;* and *The Dustbin of History*, Marcus is one of the most important critics and cultural historians to give serious study to rock and roll. In a mostly unfavorable review of Dylan's first album of the 1970s—beginning with what is probably the most famous lead in all of rock journalism—he addresses a number of issues: the pressures that Dylan's early success bring to bear on his fans and music, the increasing importance of bootlegs, "song-stealing" and the significance of the arts in America.

In the piece, Marcus takes issue with a lack of ambition that he believes is the ruin of *Self Portrait*. This lack of ambition relates to the Dylan myth, a catch-22 of sorts: the myth provides license for Dylan to release any kind of material, good or bad, that he likes, and it prevents fans from taking an honest approach to new works. At this point the critical dialogue on Dylan begins to change. Everyone looks back to the sixties to find the criteria for greatness, and as a consequence the tone of most reviews and commentary becomes dominated by impatience.

Depicting various concerns and impressions that follow the album in sequential order, "Self Portrait No. 25" is not entirely the blast that it comes

---

*When it appeared in the July 23, 1970, *Rolling Stone*, the article's byline read, "Written and arranged by Greil Marcus. Chorus: Charles Perry, Jenny Marcus, Jann Wenner, Erik Bernstein, Ed Ward, John Burks, Ralph Gleason, Langdon Winner, Bruce Miroff, Richard Vaughn and Mike Goodwin."

off as; some of its passages are among the most thoughtful and personal of tributes to Dylan. The end, in particular, is elegiac: "Dylan's songs can serve as metaphors, enriching our lives, giving us random insight into the myths we carry and the present we live, intensifying what we've known and leading us toward what we've never looked for. . . ." This essay, though an acerbic criticism of *Self Portrait* and what Marcus thinks it represents, is also a retrospective that seeks to place Dylan's efforts up to 1970 in their rightful context.

(1)

What is this shit?

(1) "All the Tired Horses" is a gorgeous piece of music, perhaps the most memorable song on this album. In an older form it was "All the Pretty Ponies in the Yard"; now it could serve as the theme song to any classic western. Can you hear the organ standing in between the beautiful strings and voices? Shane comes into view, and The Magnificent Seven: gunmen over the hill and out of time still got to ride. It sounds like Barbara Stanwyck in Forty Guns singing, as a matter of fact.

The beauty of this painted signpost promises what its words belie, and the song's question becomes the listener's: he can't ride when the horse is asleep in the meadow.

(2)

"I don't know if I should keep playing this," said the disc jockey, as the album made its debut on the radio. "Nobody's calling in and saying they want to hear it or anything . . . usually when something like this happens people say 'Hey, the new Dylan album,' but not tonight."

Later someone called and asked for a reprise of "Blue Moon." In the end it all came down to a telephone poll to determine whether radioland really cared. The DJ kept apologizing: "If there is anyone who needs . . . or deserves to have his whole album played through it's Bob Dylan."

(2) After a false beginning comes "Alberta #1," an old song now claimed by Dylan. One line stands out: "I'll give you more gold than your apron can hold." We're still at the frontier. The harmonica lets you into the album by its nostalgia, and it's the song's promise that matters, not the song itself, which fades.

(3)

"What was it?" said a friend, after we'd heard thirty minutes of *Self Portrait* for the first time. "Were we really that impressionable back in '65, '66? Was it that the stuff really wasn't that good, that this is just as good? Was it some sort of accident in time that made those other records so powerful, or what?

"My life was really turned around, it affected me—I don't know if it was the records or the words or the sound or the noise—maybe the interview: 'What is there to believe in?' I doubt if he'd say that now, though."

We put on "Like a Rolling Stone" from *Highway 61 Revisited* and sat through it. "I was listening to that song five, ten times a day for the last few months, hustling my ass, getting my act together to get into school . . . but it's such a drag to hear what he's done with it . . ."

(3) Something like a mood collapses with the first Nashville offering, "I Forgot More Than You'll Ever Know," a slick exercise in vocal control that fills a bit of time. After getting closer and closer to the Country Music Capitol of the World—and still keeping his distance with Nashville Skyline, *one of the loveliest rock-and-roll albums ever made—the visitor returns to pay his compliments by recording some of their songs. How does it sound? It sounds alright. He's sung himself into a corner. It sounds alright. Sign up the band.*

(4)

GM: "It's such an unambitious album."

JW: "Maybe what we need most of all right now is an unambitious album from Dylan."

GM: "What we need most of all is for Dylan to get ambitious."

JW: "It's such a . . ."

GM: ". . . though it is a really . . ."

GM & JW: ". . . *friendly* album . . ."

(4) "Days of '49" is a fine old ballad. Dylan's beginning is utterly convincing, as he slips past the years of the song (listen to the vaguely bitter way he sings "But what cares I for praise?"). He fumbles as the song moves on, and the cut collapses, despite the deep burr of the horns and the drama generated by the piano. It's a tentative performance, a warm-up, hardly more than a work tape. The depths of the history the song creates—out of the history of

pathos Johnny Cash gave "Hardin Wouldn't Run" (sounding like it was recorded in the shadows of an Arizona canyon) or "Sweet Betsy from Pike"— has been missed. The song is worth more effort than it was given.

(5)

"It's hard," he said. "It's hard for Dylan to do anything real, shut off the way he is, not interested in the world, maybe no reason why he should be. Maybe the weight of the days is too strong, maybe withdrawal is a choice we'd make if we could. . . ." One's reminded that art doesn't come— perhaps that it can't be heard—in times of crisis and destruction; art comes in the period of decadence that precedes a revolution, or after the deluge. It's prelude to revolution; it's not contemporary with it save in terms of memory.

But in the midst of it all artists sometimes move in to re-create history. That takes ambition.

(5) When you consider how imaginative the backing on other Dylan records has been, the extremely routine quality of most of the music on Self Portrait *can become irritating. It is so uninteresting. "Early Mornin' Rain" is one of the most lifeless performances of the entire album; a rather mawkish song, a stiff well-formed-vowel vocal, and a vapid instrumental track that has all the flair of canned laughter.*

(6)

THE FOUR QUESTIONS: The four sons gazed at the painting on the museum wall. "It's a painting," said the first son. "It's art," said the second son. "It's a frame," said the third son, and he said it rather coyly. The fourth son was usually considered somewhat stupid, but he at least figured out why they'd come all the way from home to look at the thing in the first place. "It's a signature," he said.

(6) "In Search of Little Sadie" is an old number called "Badman's Blun-der" (or sometimes "Badman's Ballad" and sometimes "Little Sadie") that Dylan now claims as his own composition. As with "Days of '49," the song is superb—it's these kinds of song that seem like the vague source of the music the Band makes—and what Dylan is doing with the tune, leading it on a switchback trail, has all sorts of possibilities. But again, the vocal hasn't been

given time to develop and the song loses whatever power it might have had to
offer, until the final chorus, when Bob takes off and does some real singing.

This bit about getting it all down in one or two takes only works if you get
it all down. Otherwise it's at best "charming" and at worst boring, alluding to
a song without really making music.

(7)

Imagine a kid in his teens responding to *Self Portrait*. His older brothers
and sisters have been living by Dylan for years. They come home with the
album and he simply cannot figure out what it's all about. To him, *Self Portrait* sounds more like the stuff his parents listen to than what he wants to
hear; in fact, his parents have just gone out and bought *Self Portrait* and
given it to him for his birthday. He considers giving it back for Father's Day.

To this kid Dylan is a figure of myth; nothing less, but nothing more.
Dylan is not real and the album carries no reality. He's never seen Bob
Dylan; he doesn't expect to; he can't figure out why he wants to.

(7) The Everly Brothers version of "Let It Be Me" is enough to make you
cry, and Bob Dylan's version is just about enough to make you listen. For all of
the emotion usually found in his singing, there is virtually none here. It is a
very formal performance.

(8)

"Bob should go whole-hog and revive the Bing Crosby Look, with its
emphasis on five-button, soft shoulder, wide-collar, plaid country-club
lounge jackets (Pendleton probably still makes them). And, like Der Bin-
gle, it might do well for Dylan to work a long-stemmed briar pipe into his
act, stopping every so often to light up, puff at it, raise some smoke, and
gaze, momentarily, toward the horizon, before launching into [this is John
Burks in *Rags*, June 1970] the next phrase of 'Peggy Day.' Then, for his
finale—the big 'Blue Moon' production number with the girls and the
spotlights on the Mountains—he does a quick costume change into one of
those high-collar 1920s formal shirts with the diamond-shaped bow tie,
plus, of course, full length tails and the trousers with the satin stripe down
the side, carnation in the buttonhole, like Dick Powell in *Gold Diggers of
1933*. Here comes Dylan in his tails, his briar in one hand, his megaphone

in the other, strolling down the runway, smiling that toothpaste smile. 'Like a *roll*-ing stone . . .'"

(8) "Little Sadie" is an alternate take of "In Search of . . ." I bet we're going to hear a lot of alternate takes in the coming year, especially from bands short on material who want to maintain their commercial presence without working too hard. Ordinarily, when there are no striking musical questions at stake in the clash of various attempts—alternate takes have been used as a graveyard rip-off to squeeze more bread out of the art of dead men or simply to fill up a side. "Little Sadie" fills up the side nicely.

(9)

"It's a high school yearbook. Color pictures this year, because there was a surplus left over from last year, more pages than usual too, a sentimental journey, 'what we did,' it's not all that interesting, it's a memento of something, there's a place for autographs, lots of white space, nobody's name was left out . . . It is June, after all."

(9) "Woogie Boogie" is fun. The band sounds like it's falling all over itself (or maybe slipping on its overdubs) but they hold on to the beat. There is as much of Dylan's feel for music here as on anything else on Self Portrait. *If you were a producer combing through a bunch of* Self Portrait *tapes for something to release, you might choose "Woogie Boogie" as a single—backing "All the Tired Horses," of course.*

(10)

Self Portrait most closely resembles the Dylan album that preceded it: *Great White Wonder.* The album is a two-record set masterfully assembled from an odd collection of mostly indifferent recordings made over the course of the last year, complete with alternate takes, chopped endings, loose beginnings, side comments, and all sorts of mistakes. Straight from the can to you, as it were. A bit from Nashville, a taste of the Isle of Wight since you missed it, some sessions from New York that mostly don't make it, but dig, it's Dylan, and if you wanted *Great White Wonder* and *Stealin'* and *John Birch* and *Isle of Wight* and *A Thousand Miles Behind, Self Portrait* will surely fill the need.

I don't think it will. It's true that all of the bootlegs (and the *Masked Marauders,* which was a fantasy bootleg) came out in the absence of new music from Dylan, but I think their release was related not to the absence of his recordings but to the absence of the man himself. We are dealing with myth, after all, and the more Dylan stays away the greater the weight attached to anything he's done. When King Midas reached out his hand everything he touched not only turned to gold, it became valuable to everyone else, and Dylan still has the Midas touch even though he'd rather not reach out. It is only in the last two years that the collecting of old tapes by Dylan has really become a general phenomena, and there are many times more tapes in circulation than are represented on the bootlegs. There is a session with the Band from December of 1965, live albums, ancient recordings, tapes of Dylan at the Guthrie Memorial, with the Band last summer in Missouri, radio shows from the early sixties, the live "Like a Rolling Stone." It sometimes seems as if every public act Dylan ever made was recorded, and it is all coming together. Eventually, the bootleggers will get their hands on it. Legally, there is virtually nothing he can do to stop it.

He can head off the theft and sale of his first drafts, his secrets, and his memories only with his music. And it is the vitality of the music that is being bootlegged that is the basis of its appeal. The noise of it. *Self Portrait*, though it's a good imitation bootleg, isn't nearly the music that *Great White Wonder* is. "Copper Kettle" is a masterpiece but "Killing Me Alive" will blow it down. *Nashville Skyline* and *John Wesley Harding* are classic albums; but no matter how good they are they lack the power of the music Dylan made in the middle sixties. Unless he returns to the marketplace, with a sense of vocation and the ambition to keep up with his own gifts, the music of those years will continue to dominate his records, whether he releases them or not. If the music Dylan makes doesn't have the power to enter the lives of his audience—and *Self Portrait* does not have that power—his audience will take over his past.

(10) Did Dylan write "Belle Isle?" Maybe he did. This is the first time I've ever felt cynical listening to a new Dylan record.

(11)

In the record industry music is referred to as "product." "We got Beatle product." When the whirlwind courtship of Johnny Winter and Columbia was finally consummated everyone wanted to know when they would get product. They got product fast but it took them a while longer to get music. Such is show biz, viz. *Self Portrait*, which is already a triple gold record, the way "O Captain! My Captain" is more famous than "When Lilacs Last in the Dooryard Bloom'd," is the closest to pure product in Dylan's career, even more so than *Greatest Hits*, because that had no pretensions. The purpose of *Self Portrait* is mainly product and the need it fills is for product—for "a Dylan album"—and make no mistake about it, the need for product is felt as deeply by those who buy it, myself included, of course, as by those who sell it, and perhaps more so.

As a throw-together album it resembles *Flowers*; but it's totally unlike *Flowers* in that the album promises to be more than it is, rather than less. By its title alone *Self Portrait* makes claims for itself as the definitive Dylan album—which it may be, in a sad way—but it is still something like an attempt to delude the public into thinking they are getting more than they are, or that *Self Portrait* is more than it is.

(11) "Living the Blues" is a marvelous recording. All sorts of flashes of all sorts of enthusiasms spin around it: The Dovells cheering for the Bristol Stomp, Dylan shadow-boxing with Cassius Clay, Elvis smiling and sneering in Jailhouse Rock *("Baby you're so square, I don't care!"). The singing is great—listen to the way Bob fades off "deep down insyyy-hide," stepping back and slipping in that last syllable. For the first time on this album, Dylan sounds excited about the music he's making. The rhythm section, led by the guitar and the piano that's rolling over the most delightful rock-and-roll changes, is wonderful. The girls go through their routine and they sound— cute. Dylan shines. Give it 100.*

(12)

"... various times he thought of completing his baccalaureate so that he could teach in the college and oddly enough [this is from *A Rimbaud Chronology*, New Directions Press] of learning to play the piano. At last he went to Holland, where, in order to reach the Orient, he enlisted in the Dutch Army and sailed for Java in June of 1876. Three weeks after his arrival in Batavia [Charles Perry: "We know Dylan was the Rimbaud of his generation; it seems he's found his Abyssinia."] he deserted, wandered among the natives of the jungle and soon signed on a British ship for Liverpool. After a winter at home he went to Hamburg, joined in a circus as interpreter-manager to tour the northern countries, but the cold was too much for him and he was repatriated from Sweden, only to leave home again, this time for Alexandria. Again, illness interrupted his travels and he was put off the ship in Italy and spent a year recovering on the farm in Roche. In 1878 he was in Hamburg again, trying to reach Genoa to take a ship for the East. Once more he tried to cross the Alps on foot [Charles Perry: "We know that Dylan was the Rimbaud of his generation; it seems he's found his Abyssinia."] but in a snowstorm he almost perished. Saved by monks in a Hospice, he managed to reach Genoa and sail to Alexandria where he worked as a farm laborer for a while. In Suez, where he was stopped on his way to Cyprus, he was employed as a ship-breaker to plunder a ship wrecked on the dangerous coast at Guardafui. Most of the first half of 1879 he worked as foreman in a desert quarry on Cyprus, and went home in June to recuperate from typhoid fever."

(12) "Like A Rolling Stone"—Dylan's greatest song. He knows it, and so do we. Not only that, but the greatest song of our era, on that single, on High-way 61 Revisited, *on the tape of a British performance with the Hawks in 1966. If one version is better than the other it's like Robin Hood splitting his father's arrow.*

1965: "Alright. We've done it. Dig it. If you can. If you can take it. Like a complete *unknown, can you feel that?"*

We could, and Bob Dylan took over. All that's come since goes back to the bid for power that was "Like a Rolling Stone."

"Can you keep up with this train?" The train no longer runs; I suppose it depends on where your feet are planted.

Dylan from the Isle of Wight is in your living room and Dylan is blowing his lines, singing country flat, up and down, getting through the song somehow, almost losing the whole mess at the end of the second verse. You don't know whether he dropped the third verse because he didn't want to sing it or because he forgot it. It's enough to make your speakers wilt.

Self Portrait *enforces or suggests a quiet sound. "Like a Rolling Stone" isn't "Blue Moon" but since most of* Self Portrait *is more like "Blue Moon" than "Like a Rolling Stone," and since it is a playable album that blends together, you set the volume low. But if you play this song loud—really loud, until it distorts and rumbles, you'll find The Band is still playing as hard as they can, for real. The strength cut in half by the man who recorded it, but volume will bring it back up.*

Some of "Like a Rolling Stone" is still there. A splendid beginning, announcing a conquest; Levon Helm beating his drums over the Band's Motown March (ba-bump barrummmp, ba-bump barrrummmp), smashing his cymbals like the glass-breaking finale of a car crash; and best of all, Garth Hudson finding the spirit of the song and holding it firm on every chorus. Near the end when the pallid vocalizing is done with Dylan moves back to the song and he and the Band begin to stir up a frenzy that ends with a crash of metal and Bob's shout: "JUST LIKE A ROLLING STONE!" There is something left.

1965: "BAM! Once upon a time . . ." The song assaults you with a deluge of experience and the song opens up the abyss. "And just how far would you like to go in?" "Not too far but just far enough so's we can say we've been there." That wasn't good enough. "When you gaze into the abyss, the abyss looks back at you." It peered out through "Wheel's on Fire" and "All Along the Watchtower," but it seems Dylan has stepped back from its edge.

The abyss is hidden away now, like the lost mine of a dead prospector. "Like a Rolling Stone," as we hear it now, is like a fragment of a faded map leading back to that lost mine.

(13)

I once said I'd buy an album of Dylan breathing heavily. I still would. But not an album of Dylan breathing softly.

(13) Why does "Copper Kettle" shine (it even sounds like a hit record) when so many other cuts hide in their own dullness? Why does this performance evoke all kinds of experience when most of Self Portrait is so one-dimensional and restrictive? Why does "Copper Kettle" grow on you while the other songs disappear?

Like "All the Tired Horses," it's gorgeous. There are those tiny high notes punctuating the song in the mood of an old Buddy Holly ballad or "The Three Bells" by the Browns, and that slipstream organ, so faint you can barely hear it—you don't hear it, really, but you are aware of it in the subtlest way. There is the power and the real depth of the song itself, that erases our Tennessee truck-stop postcard image of moonshining and moves in with a vision of nature, an ideal of repose, and a sense of rebellion that goes back to the founding of the country. "We ain't paid no whiskey tax since 1792," Bob sings, and that goes all the way back—they passed the whiskey tax in 1791. It's a song about revolt as a vocation, not revolution, merely refusal! Old men hid-ing out in mountain valleys, keeping their own peace.

[The old moonshiners are sitting around a stove in Thunder Road, *trying to come up with an answer to the mobsters that are muscling in on the valley they've held since the Revolution. "Blat sprat muglmmph ruurrrp fffft," says one. The audience stirs, realizing they can't understand his Appalachian dialect. "If you'd take that tobacco plug out of your mouth, Jed," says another whiskey man, "maybe we could understand what you said."]*

What matters most is Bob's singing. He's been the most amazing singer of the last ten years, creating his language of stress, fitting five words into a line of ten and ten into a line of five, shoving the words around and opening up spaces for noise and silence that through assault or seduction or the gift of good timing made room for expression and emotion. Every vocal was a sur-prise. You couldn't predict what it would sound like. The song itself, the struc-ture of the song, was barely a clue. The limits were there to be evaded. On "Copper Kettle" that all happens, and it is noticeable because this is the only time on Self Portrait *that it happens.*

"Not all great poets—like Wallace Stevens—are great singers," Dylan said a year ago. "But a great singer—Billie Holiday—is always a great poet." That sort of poetry—and it's that sort of poetry that made Dylan seem like a "poet"—is all there on "Copper Kettle," in the way Bob changes into the lines "... or the ROTTEN wood ..." fading into "(they'll get you) by the smo-oke ..." The fact that the rest of the album lacks the grace of "Copper Kettle" isn't a matter of the album being "different" or "new." It is a matter of the music having power, or not having it.

(14, 15, 16)

". . . very highly successful in terms of money. Dylan's concerts in the past have been booked by his own firm, Ashes and Sand, rather than by [this is from *Rolling Stone*, December 7, 1968] private promoters. Promot-ers are now talking about a ten city tour with the possibility of adding more dates, according to *Variety*.

"Greta Garbo may also come out of retirement to do a series of per-sonal appearances. The Swedish film star who wanted only 'to be alone' after continued press invasions of her life is rumored to be considering a series of lavish stage shows, possibly with Dylan . . ."

And we'd just sit there and *stare.*

(14) "Gotta Travel On." Dylan sings "Gotta Travel On."

(15) We take "Blue Moon" as a joke, a stylized apotheosis of corn, or as further musical evidence of Dylan's retreat from the pop scene. But back on Elvis's first album, there is another version of "Blue Moon," a deep and moving performance that opens up the possibilities of the song and reveals the failure of Dylan's recording.

Hoofbeats, vaguely aided by a string bass and guitar, form the background to a vocal that blows a cemetery wind across the lines of the song. Elvis moves back and forth with a high phantom wail, singing that part that Doug Kershaw plays on Dylan's version, finally answering himself with a dark murmur that fades into silence. "It's a revelation," said a friend. "I can't believe it."

There is nothing banal about "Blue Moon." In formal musical terms, Dylan's performance is virtually a cover of Elvis's recording, but while one man sings toward the song, the other sings from behind it, from the other side.

(16) "The Boxer": remember "How I Was Robert McNamara'd into Submission," or whatever it was called, with that friendly line, "I forgot my harmonica, Albert?" Or Eric Andersen's "The Hustler?" Maybe this number means "no hard feelings." Jesus, it is awful.

(17)

Before going into the studio to set up the Weathermen, he wrote the Yippies' first position paper, although it took Abbie Hoffman a few years to find it and Jerry Rubin had trouble reading it. A quote:

"I'm going to grow my hair down to my feet so strange till I look like a walking mountain range then I'm gonna ride into Omaha on a horse out to the country club and the golf course carrying a *New York Times* shoot a few holes blow their minds."

"Dylan's coming," said Lang.

"Ah, you're full of shit," [said Abbie Hoffman in *Woodstock Nation*], he's gonna be in England tonight, don't pull that shit on me."

"Nah I ain't kiddin, Abby-baby, he called up and said he might come..."

"You think he'd dig running for president?"

"Nah, that ain't his trip he's into something else."

"You met him, Mike? What's he into?"

"I don't know for sure but it ain't exactly politics. You ever met him?"

"Yeah, once about seven years ago in Gerde's Folk City down in the West Village. I was trying to get him to do a benefit for civil rights or something . . . hey Mike will you introduce us? I sure would like to meet Dylan . . . I only know about meetin' him through Happy Traum . . ."

"There's an easier way . . . Abbs . . . I'll introduce you. In fact he wants to meet you . . ."

Would *Self Portrait* make you want to meet Dylan? No? Perhaps it's there to keep you away?

(17) "The Mighty Quinn" sounds as if it were a gas to watch. It's pretty much of a mess on record, and the sound isn't all that much better than the bootleg. The Isle of Wight concert was originally planned as an album, and it's obvious why it wasn't released as such—on tape, it sounded bad. The performances were mostly clumsy or languid and all together would have made a lousy record. Two of the songs had something special about them, on the evidence of the bootleg, though neither of them made it to Self Portrait. *One was "Highway 61 Revisited," where Bob and the Band screamed like Mexican tour guides hustling customers for a run down the road: "OUT ON HIGHWAY SIXTY-ONE!" The other was "It Ain't Me Babe." Dylan sang solo, playing guitar like a lyric poet, transforming the song with a new identity, sweeping in and out of the phrases and the traces of memory. He sounded something like Billie Holiday.*

(18)

It's certainly a rather odd "self portrait": other people's songs and the songs of a few years ago. If the title is serious, Dylan no longer cares much about making music and would just as soon define himself on someone else's terms. There is a curious move toward self-effacement; Dylan's removing himself from a position from which he is asked to exercise power in the arena. It's rather like the Duke of Windsor abdicating the throne. After it's over he merely goes away, and occasionally there'll be a picture of him getting on a plane somewhere.

(18) "Take Me as I Am or Let Me Go." The Nashville recordings of Self Portrait, *taken together, may not be all that staggering but they are pleasant—a sentimental little country melodrama. If the album had been cut to "Tired Horses" at the start and "Wigwam" at the end, with the Nashville*

tracks sleeping in between, we'd have a good record about which no one would have gotten very excited one way or the other, a kind of musical disappearing act. But the Artist must make a Statement, be he Bob Dylan, the Beach Boys, or Tommy James and the Shondells. He must enter the studio and come out with that masterpiece. If he doesn't or hasn't bothered, there'll be at least an attempt to make it look as if he had. If Dylan was releasing more music than he's been—a single three times a year, an album every six months or so—then the weight that fixes itself on whatever he does release would be lessened. But the pattern is set now, for the biggest stars—one a year, if that. It's rather degrading for an artist to put out more than one album a year, as if he has to keep trying, you know? Well, three cheers for John Fogerty.

(19)

Because of what happened in the middle sixties, our fate is bound up with Dylan's whether he or we like it or not. Because *Highway 61 Revisited* changed the world, the albums that follow it must—but not in the same way, of course.

(19) "Take a Message to Mary": the backing band didn't seem to care much about the song, but Dylan did. My ten-year-old nephew thought "It Hurts Me Too" sounded fake but he was sure this was for real.

(20)

Ralph Gleason: "There was this cat Max Kaminsky talks about in his autobiography who stole records. He stole one from Max. He *had* to have them, you know? Just had to have them. Once he got busted because he heard this record on a jukebox and shoved his fist through the glass of the box trying to get the record out.

"We all have records we'd steal for, that we need that bad. But would you steal this record? You wouldn't steal this record."

You wouldn't steal *Self Portrait*? It wouldn't steal you either. Perhaps that's the real tragedy, because Dylan's last two albums were art breaking and entering into the house of the mind.

(20) Songwriting can hardly be much older than song-stealing. It's part of the tradition. It may even be more honorable than outright imitation; at least it's not as dull.

Early in his career, Bob Dylan, like every other musician on the street with

*a chance to get off it, copped one or two old blues or folk songs, changed a
word or two, and copyrighted them (weirdest of all was claiming "That's
Alright Mama," which was Elvis's first record and written—or at least written down—by Arthur Crudup). As he developed his own genius, Dylan also
used older ballads for the skeletons of his own songs: "Bob Dylan's Dream" is
a recasting of "Lord Franklin's Dream"; "I Dreamed I Saw St. Augustine"
finds its way back to "I Dreamed I Saw Joe Hill." "Pledging My Time" has the
structure, the spirit, and a line from Robert Johnson's "Come On in My
Kitchen"; "Don't the moon look lonesome, shining through the trees," is a
quote from an old Jimmy Rushing blues. "Subterranean Homesick Blues"
comes off of Chuck Berry's "Too Much Monkey Business." This is a lovely way
to write, and to invite, history, and it is part of the beauty and the inevitabil-
ity of American music. But while Dylan may have added a few words to "It
Hurts Me Too," from where he sits, it's simply wrong to claim this old blues,
recorded by Elmore James among others, as his own. That* Self Portrait *is
characterized by borrowing, lifting, and plagiarism simply means Bob will
get a little more bread and thousands of kids will get a phony view of their
own history.*

(21, 22)

That splendid frenzy, the strength of new values in the midst of some
sort of musical behemoth of destruction, the noise, the power—the *totality* of it! So you said well, alright, there it is . . .

The mythical immediacy of everything Dylan does and the relevance
of that force to the way we live our lives is rooted in the three albums and
the two incredible singles he released in 1965 and 1966: *Bringing It All
Back Home, Highway 61 Revisited, Blonde on Blonde,* "Like A Rolling
Stone," and "Subterranean Homesick Blues." Those records defined and
structured a crucial year—no one has ever caught up with them and most
likely no one ever will. What happened then is what we always look for.
The power of those recordings and of the music Dylan was making on
stage, together with his retreat at the height of his career, made Dylan into
a legend and virtually changed his name into a noun. Out of that Dylan
gained the freedom to step back and get away with anything he chose to
do, commercially and artistically. The fact that more than a year now separates one album from another heightens their impact, regardless of how

much less they have to offer than the albums which established this matrix of power in the first place. In a real way, Dylan is trading on the treasure of myth, fame, and awe he gathered in '65 and '66. In mythical terms, he doesn't have to do good, because he has done good. One wonders, in mythical terms of course, how long he can get away with it.

(21) "Minstrel Boy" is the best of the Isle of Wight cuts; it rides easy.

(22) The Band plays pretty on "She Belongs to Me" and Dylan runs through the vocal the way he used to hurry through the first half of a concert, getting the crowd-pleasers out of the way so he could play the music that mattered. Garth Hudson has the best moment of the song.

(23)

VOCATION AS A VOCATION: Dylan is, if he wants to be, an American with a vocation. It might almost be a calling—the old Puritan idea of a gift one should live up to—but it's not, and vocation is strong enough.

There is no theme richer for the American artist than the spirit and the themes of the country and the country's history. We have never figured out what this place is about or what it is for, and the only way to even begin to answer those questions is to watch our movies, read our poets, our novelists, and listen to our music. Robert Johnson and Melville, Hank Williams and Hawthorne, Bob Dylan and Mark Twain, Jimmie Rodgers and John Wayne. America is the life's work of the American artist because he is doomed to be an American. Dylan has a feel for it; his impulses seem to take him back into the forgotten parts of our history, and even on *Self Portrait*, there is a sense of this vocation; Bob is almost on the verge of writing a western. But it's an ambitious vocation and there is not enough of that, only an impulse without the determination to follow it up.

Dylan has a vocation if he wants it; his audience may refuse to accept *his* refusal unless he simply goes away. In the midst of that vocation there might be something like a Hamlet asking questions, old questions, with a bit of magic to them; but hardly a prophet, merely a man with good vision.

(23) "Wigwam" slowly leads the album to its end. Campfire music, or "3 AM, After the Bullfight." It's a great job of arranging, and the B-side of the album's second natural single, backing "Living the Blues." "Wigwam" puts you to bed, and by that I don't mean it puts you to sleep.

(24)

SELF PORTRAIT, THE AUTEUR, AND HOME MOVIES: "*Auteur*" means, literally, "author," and in America the word has come to signify a formula about films: movies (like books) are made by "authors," i.e., directors. This has led to a dictum which tends to affirm the following: movies are about the personality of the director. We should judge a movie in terms of how well the "*auteur*" has "developed his personality" in relation to previous films. His best film is that which most fully presents the flower of his personality. Needless to say such an approach requires a devotion to mannerism, quirk, and self-indulgence. It also turns out that the greatest *auteurs* are those with the most consistent, obvious, and recognizable mannerisms, quirks, and self-indulgences. By this approach *Stolen Kisses* is a better film than *Jules and Jim* because in *Stolen Kisses* we had nothing to look for but Truffaut while in *Jules and Jim* there was this story and those actors who kept getting in the way. The spirit of the *auteur* approach can be transferred to other arts; and by its dictum, *Self Portrait* is a better album than *Highway 61 Revisited* because *Self Portrait* is *about* the *auteur*, that is, Dylan, and *Highway 61 Revisited* takes on the world, which tends to get in the way. (*Highway 61 Revisited* might well be about Dylan too, but it's more *obvious* on *Self Portrait*, and therefore more relevant to Art, and . . . please don't ask about the music, really . . .)

Now Dylan has been approached this way for years, whether or not the word was used, and while in the end it may be the least interesting way to listen to his music it's occasionally a lot of fun and a game that many of us have played (for example, on "Days of '49" Dylan sings the line "just like a roving sign" and I just can't help almost hearing him say "just like a rolling stone" and wondering if he avoided that on purpose). One writer, named Alan Weberman, has devoted his life to unraveling Dylan's songs in order to examine the man himself; just as every artist once had his patron now every *auteur* has his critic, it seems.

[CONTINUED]

(24) Self Portrait *is a concept album from the cutting room floor. It has been constructed so artfully, but as a cover-up, not a revelation. Thus "Alberta #2" is the end, after a false ending, just as "Alberta #1" was the beginning, after a false beginning. The song moves quickly, and ends abruptly. These*

alternate takes don't just fill up a side, they set up the whole album, and it works, in a way, because I think it's mainly the four songs fitted in at the edges that make the album a playable record. With a circle you tend to see the line that defines it, rather than the hole in the middle.

SELF PORTRAIT, THE AUTEUR, AND HOME MOVIES, CONT.: We all play the *auteur* game: We went out and bought *Self Portrait* not because we knew it was great music—it might have been but that's not the first question we'd ask—but because it was a Dylan album. What we *want*, though, is a different matter—and that's what separates most people from auteurists—we *want* great music, and because of those three albums back in '65 and '66, we expect it, or hope for it.

I wouldn't be dwelling on this but for my suspicion that it is exactly a perception of this approach that is the justification for the release of *Self Portrait*, to the degree that it is justified artistically (the commercial justification is something else—self-justification). The *auteur* approach allows the great artist to limit his ambition, perhaps even abandon it, and turn inward. To be crude, it begins to seem as if it is his habits that matter, rather than his vision. If *we* approach art in this fashion, we degrade it. Take that second song on *John Wesley Harding*, "As I Went Out One Morning," and two ways of hearing it.

Weberman has determined a fixed meaning for the song: It relates to a dinner given years ago by the Emergency Civil Liberties Committee at which they awarded Bob Dylan their Thomas Paine prize. Dylan showed up, said a few words about how it was possible to understand how Lee Harvey Oswald felt, and got booed. "As I Went Out One Morning," according to Weberman, is Dylan's way of saying he didn't dig getting booed.

I sometimes hear the song as a brief journey into American history; the singer out for a walk in the park, finding himself next to a statue of Tom Paine, and stumbling across an allegory: Tom Paine, symbol of freedom and revolt, co-opted into the role of Patriot by textbooks and statue committees, and now playing, as befits his role as Patriot, enforcer to a girl who runs for freedom—in chains, to the *South*, the source of vitality in America, in America's music—*away* from Tom Paine. We have turned our history on its head; we have perverted our own myths.

Now it would be astonishing if what I've just described was on Dylan's mind when he wrote the song. That's not the point. The point is that

Dylan's songs can serve as metaphors, enriching our lives, giving us random insight into the myths we carry and the present we live, intensifying what we've known and leading us toward what we never looked for, while at the same time enforcing an emotional strength upon those perceptions by the power of the music that moves with his words. Weberman's way of hearing, or rather seeing, is more logical, more linear, and perhaps even "correct," but it's sterile. Mine is not an answer but a possibility, and I think Dylan's music is about possibilities, rather than facts, like a statue that is not an expenditure of city funds but a gateway to a vision.

If we are to be satisfied with *Self Portrait* we may have to see it in the sterile terms of the *auteur*, which in our language would be translated as "Hey, far out, Dylan singing Simon and Garfunkel, Rodgers and Hart, and Gordon Lightfoot . . ." Well, it is far out, in a sad sort of way, but it also vapid, and if our own untaught perception of the *auteur* allows us to be satisfied with it, we degrade our own sensibilities and Dylan's capabilities as an American artist as well. Dylan did not become a force whose every movement carries the force of myth by presenting desultory images of his own career as if that was the only movie that mattered—he did it by taking on the world, by assault, and by seduction.

In an attack on the *auteur* approach, as it relates to film, Kevin Brownlow quotes an old dictionary, and the words he cites reveal the problem: "The novel (the film) (the song) is a subjective epic composition in which the author begs leave to treat the world according to his own point of view. It is only a question, therefore, whether he has a point of view. The rest will take care of itself."

Two Poems

A friend of Dylan's, and occasional collaborator, was beat poet Allen Ginsberg, the author of *Kaddish*, *Reality Sandwiches*, 1956's epic *Howl* and other books. The two met in Greenwich Village in 1963; each acknowledged an influence from the other's work— Dylan had been reading the beats since his late teens—and Ginsberg accompanied the Rolling Thunder Revue in 1975. (See "Rolling Thunder Stones" in Ginsberg's *Collected Poems* [New York: Harper and Row, 1988].)

Before then, in the fall of 1971, Ginsberg and Dylan made a series of informal, spontaneous recordings together. After watching him improvise on a harmonium at a reading in New York, Dylan began jamming with Ginsberg and encouraged him to write his own songs. When Ginsberg collected these lyrics in his book *First Blues*, he dedicated it "To Minstrel Guruji Bob Dylan" and included two poems addressed to the songwriter, reprinted below.

Postcard to D----

Chuggling along in an old open bus
    past the green sugarfields
        down a dusty dirt road
            overlooking the ocean in Fiji,
thinking of your big Macdougal street house
    & the old orange peels
        in your mail-garbage load,
            smoggy windows you clean with a squeejee

                    3 March 1972

On Reading Dylan's Writings

Now that it's dust and ashes
now that it's human skin
Here's to you Bob Dylan
a poem for the laurels you win

Sincerest form of flattery
is imitation they say
I've broke my long line down
to write a song your way

Those 'chains of flashing images'
that came to you at night
were highest farm boys' day dreams
that glimpse the Angels' light

And tho the dross of wisdom's come
and left you lone on earth
remember when the Angels call
your soul for a new birth

It wasn't dope that gave you truth
no money that you stole
—was God himself that entered in
shining your heavenly soul.

27 July 1973, London

Dylan

HENDRIK HERTZBERG AND GEORGE TROW

In 1974 Hendrik Hertzberg and George Trow crafted this piece for "The Talk of the Town" column in *The New Yorker*. In discussing Dylan's evening show at Madison Square Garden that January 31, Hertzberg and Trow humorously capture the skepticism and confusion that can divide Dylan's fans, with a consensus regarding his post-sixties music rarely found. While some of the article's claims reflect on that particular era, other ideas—the typical fan's frustration at not being able to recognize a melody when played live, for instance—have followed Dylan for decades.

WE HAD BREAKFAST Thursday morning with two friends (one blond, the other dark-haired, both recently turned thirty) who had been to the Bob Dylan concert at Madison Square Garden the night before. "I'll tell you some people who were there," our blond friend said. "Yoko Ono was there. Her seat was two rows in front of Dick Cavett's. Pete Hamill and Shirley MacLaine were there and had seats four rows ahead of Yoko Ono's. That's six ahead of Dick Cavett. James Taylor and Carly Simon were in the vicinity, and I want to tell you that this is only the *back* part of the front section of the orchestra I'm talking about. I couldn't see the *front* part of the front section, where one assumes the real heavies, Yeats and so forth, were sitting. I'll tell you some people who weren't there. There were no blacks there, and no transvestites, and there were very few people in embroidered jeans. Instead, there were extraordinary numbers of people who seemed to have come directly from registration at the New School. A very earnest group. One of my problems with old Dylan has to do with humor, you see. I don't think he has any. Which is why the blacks and the transvestites stay away. I personally don't *trust* any rock-and-roll concert without a single transvestite, but never mind. The point is that Dylan has irony—I mean, he knows how to milk a juxtaposition—but no humor. He reminds me of a guy I went to school with who was very bright and very ambitious and who just missed starring in *Zabriskie Point*. My schoolmate sang songs about Franco in the offices of our school newspaper in 1957, but luckily he was completely tone-deaf and had to go into the social sciences."

"What's *that* all about?" our dark-haired friend said. "We're talking about a *Bob Dylan concert*. Look at it from the Dylan-can-do-no-wrong angle, which is how I look at it. All through his career, Dylan has been a highly elusive figure. He always manages to free himself from the expectations of his audience. When they were expecting folk songs about the struggles of the thirties, he gave them folk songs about the struggles of the sixties. When they were expecting a revolutionary anthem with all the answers, he gave them a revolutionary anthem that was all questions. 'The answer is blowin' in the wind'—was there ever a better summing up of the intuitive, improvisatory, unreflective approach of what we used to call 'the Movement'? When people expected acoustic, he gave them electric. When they expected funk, he gave them mysticism. When they expected psychedelia, he gave them simple country love tunes. When they finally learned not to expect anything in particular except genius, he gave them mediocrity. So. The first half of the concert felt strange—a little disappointing, a little disorienting. Dylan sang too fast, in a sort of strong, high chant, and he virtually obliterated the melodies—to no purpose. Or so I thought at intermission time. But in light of what happened in the second half of the concert, I look upon the whole first half as a necessary softening-up process for both Dylan and the audience. The room was full of complicated yearnings, after all. He was singing his old songs, and he had to avoid the dangers of a 'Dylan's Greatest Hits' atmosphere, so he recast them in such a way that you had a hard time recognizing them and a rather hard time enjoying them. He was nervous but not hostile. He had to establish the right mixture of friendliness and distance. He had to make it plain that he goes his way and others, including the audience, go theirs."

"And the second half of the concert?" we asked.

"Ah," our dark-haired friend went on. "Dylan came out all alone, small and brave, with just his harmonica and his acoustic guitar. I was too far away to see the details of his face, but I could see his hair, curly and mousy, and that tense, crabbed stance. He sang 'The Times They Are A-Changin'' and 'Don't Think Twice, It's All Right' and 'Gates of Eden'—still too fast, still in that almost strangled high chant. Then, halfway through 'Just Like a Woman,' it started to get magical, and when he sang 'It's Alright Ma (I'm Only Bleeding)' it all fell into place. He was still fooling with the melody, but with a purpose. I felt I was hearing that song for the first time instead of the thousandth. When he sang the line about 'But even the President of the United States sometimes must have to stand naked,' everyone cheered, of course, but they cheered even louder for the line 'And it's all right, Ma, I can make it.' After the Band came back on again, he sang a couple of very pretty new songs, and then 'Like a Rolling Stone.' People began streaming down the aisles, and everyone stood up—there was no particular cue; we just all stood up at once. Dylan's accompaniment for the chorus was the whole audience—twenty thousand people singing 'HOW DOES IT FEEL?' at the top of their lungs. The houselights were turned on, so we could all see each other, and four huge klieg lights went on behind Dylan, making everything—Dylan, us, the music—seem half again as big. He did two encores: a reprise of 'Most Likely You Go Your Way (and I'll Go Mine),' much more melodic and accessible this time, and 'Blowin' in the Wind.' I'd never heard him sing it quite that way before. He never does anything the same way twice. His voice was clear, strong, and true. He pulled it off—he kept the myth intact."

"Personally," our blond friend said, "when it comes to mythic figures I prefer the ones like Elvis Presley, who stay mythic in spite of themselves. Dylan was never really a successful archetype, if you know what I mean. He was only someone who seemed to be somewhere we thought we ought to be. That's why people worried so much about his changes of style. People worried about where Dylan was and what he was doing because they wanted to know where *they* should be and what *they* should be doing. The style changes prophesied—falsely, perhaps—some kind of movement, and that mercurial quality of his appealed to our generation's love of novelty. But now, you see, he has run out of ways to seem some distance *ahead*, and has fallen back on devices that will allow him to seem (at all but a few carefully chosen moments) some distance *away*. It's a little sad to fight so hard for Mythic Distance."

"But that's precisely what I like about him," said our dark-haired friend. "He lives by his wits."

Bringing Some of It All Back Home

CLIVE JAMES

After the release of such poorly received albums as *Self Portrait*, *New Morning* and *Planet Waves*, Dylan's so-called slump was perceived to be not a slump at all, but a genuine and permanent abating of his songwriting ability. In *Creem* magazine (the essay was later reprinted in *New Musical Express*), Clive James summed up this attitude, while arguing that the rock culture was ill equipped to understand Dylan's most recent, disappointing efforts. In this way, he provides a thoughtful evaluation and critique of the era's leading modes of rock criticism.

James also does an able job of identifying the raw and "unstudied" element of Dylan's songwriting. Analyzing song structure as a whole and a stanza of "Gates of Eden," he finds that the songs contain a fascinating, and frustrating, unevenness. The spontaneity of the lyrics seem to work against the need for aesthetic or poetic uniformity. Even though he had not "dried up," as James originally thought, the idea of Dylan as an instinctive writer remains accurate, and this is a persuasive vantage point from which to understand his creative process.

James writes for the *Times Literary Supplement, The New Yorker, The New York Review of Books* and other publications; he has authored more than twenty books of nonfiction, poetry and fiction—most recently the collection of essays *As of This Writing*.

IF SUCH A THING as the rock culture can be said to exist, then a thoroughgoing anti-intellectualism was probably a fundamental requirement for its coming into being.

Artistry can't afford to be inhibited by criticism—not, at any rate, until it has passed the point of mere self-assertion and reached a stage of self-assurance. In the last long interview he gave before his suicide, John Berryman pointed out that in his early days he simply couldn't allow himself to think about how his poems stood up against the poems of Yeats: he would have had to stop writing.

From all the other arts, and from all the other artistic epochs, hundreds more such individual cases could be adduced. It's a kind of willed deafness—a way of not letting any outside voices interfere with the attention you are struggling to pay to an interior voice which is not yet speaking clearly.

And what has always been true for individuals was also true, I think, for the rock culture as a whole. It was establishing itself in spite of massive contradictions, and the only way to deprive them of their disintegratory force was to find a way of not listening to them: anti-intellectualism had to be institutionalized.

Pretending to be in revolt against capitalism, the rock culture could scarcely afford to listen to anybody who pointed out that the rock culture was entirely and exclusively a capitalist product and depended for its continuance on capitalism continuing, too. Favoring a "new" music over an older music, the rock culture could equally ill afford to consider that this very act of comparison was in itself a critical act, implying further critical acts to infinity.

Total discrimination against the past, and totally indiscriminate enthusiasm for the music of a continuous present: the only way to handle such a frightful contradiction was to switch off the collective mind and drain the vocabulary of many terms other than the purely—and inertly—descriptive.

At bottom this was a protective tactic, and I don't need to point out that a defensive stance was fully justified: the bitter counteroffensive mounted by the established culture was in nearly all cases utterly irrational, as those of us who tried to ward it off in the pages of established publications are well aware.

But a consequence of this protective tactic was a widespread tendency to elevate the key creators in the rock field to a plane of historic destiny—in a word, determinism. And the charismatic intellectual mode of determinism is not investigation by criticism, but justification by description: an intellectual mode which might just as well be called anti-intellectual, since no matter how much information it aspires to deal with it can never arrive at a judgment.

The rock culture grew up in a mental vacuum: and the fact that it grew at all—and grew so fast—was in itself sufficient proof of the aesthetic truism that creativity is a primal urge, antecedent to rational mentality. Making and understanding might appear to be unified, but the consequences of insisting on this unity are disastrous when the unity breaks down.

The established culture, noticing that the rock culture was devoid of understanding, assumed that no making could possibly be taking place. The rock culture, assuming that making was understanding, declared a separate system of understanding to be not only unnecessary but actively noxious.

Logic belonged to neither side, and in fact can only belong to the less immediately employable (but finally the only possible) philosophical truth—which is that making and understanding are separate, and have to be separate in order to be connected.

Recognition of this truth was long delayed, the necessity for it obscured by the clamor as the rock culture built up on its dangerously shallow beachhead. But eventually, the recognition did come, and came thorough the inadvertent instigation of Bob Dylan.

AS A RULE OF THUMB, it can be said that every change in Dylan's musical course—except the last change—was accepted uncritically, and that this uncritical acceptance was, on the whole, correct.

By saying this, one is trying to give the receptivity of the rock culture its due. Dylan's change from acoustic to electric music, for example, was in the end a fruitful change, and the reaction against that change was correctly identified as a prejudice, not a valid criticism.

To take an earlier, instance, in Richard Mabey's neglected book of 1969, *The Pop Process*, Mabey quotes *in extenso* from an intelligent article by

David Horowitz, responding unfavorably in late 1964 to Dylan's fourth album, *Another Side*. Horowitz was fully capable of appreciating Dylan's command of language, but he was too quick to decide that the confusions on that album were retrogressive: as we now know, they were the birth pangs of a whole new elaboration. Horowitz's article was a clear case of artificially stabilizing a process. But he didn't arrive at this through being critical. He arrived at it through not being critical enough.

When we look at this retrospective analysis of the previous albums, we find his procedures damagingly titled toward the descriptive: he hasn't done much to discriminate between the disciplined and the undisciplined in Dylan's writing, so what he's asking for is that Dylan should stabilize himself on an unpredictable course by refining the qualities he already possesses.

A good deal of the intelligent criticism leveled at Dylan had this bias, leaving us with the paradox that unintelligent receptivity was better adapted to events as they subsequently occurred. At its best, the criticism was simply an articulation of the silent, mass receptivity, which never got further than liking some Dylan songs more than others. The basic critical problem—whether the good songs were really as good as they could be—was left untouched.

I've said already why this problem remained undealt with: it was in the rock culture's best interests not to deal with it. But one could easily conjecture that it wasn't even seen to be a problem, and that the question of dealing with it consequently didn't need to be ignored, since it didn't even arise.

An argument about the real quality of Dylan's achievement would have to center itself in Dylan's handling of language, and for a whole generation Dylan *was* language—discrimination would have meant not just soul-searching but a painful dissection of one's own vocal mechanisms, performed without anesthetic.

From within or from without Dylan's cultural context, his leading gift went largely unexamined, even during the most violent changes of emphasis: the question of his symbolism's validity, for instance, never focused on the language he was creating the symbols with. Briefly, Dylan's verbal talent was held to be a monolith: the idea that there might be conflicts inside the talent itself simply never gained ground.

Not, that is, until his talent began going into abeyance.

FROM *NASHVILLE SKYLINE* onward, the creative pressure was felt to be slackening. In the same way that Altamont was a political crisis for the rock culture, Dylan's retreat into the unremarkable was an aesthetic crisis—a far greater one, in my view, than the breakup of the Beatles.

The Beatles' split dramatized a political problem for the rock culture, but glossed over the aesthetic one.

As the Beatles transferred from a cozy collective to bristling individuality, the rock culture was left to make what it could of the occurrence—which mainly meant sticking with the all-purpose opinion that collectivism and individuality were somehow the same thing. The aesthetic problem was taken care of, as usual, by sheer description: if the music of the separate Beatles was less interesting than the music of the *ur*-group, it must be because of the split.

As a matter of fact, however, the music of the Beatles was already wandering toward vaporous sophistication before the split happened. The Beatles had hit the point where they were required to take on new mental materials by conscious effort: the point every artist is bound to reach once his initial stock is used up.

What the Beatles then assimilated was mainly destructive of the accurate simplicities they had previously achieved: instead of moving on to accurate complexity, they moved on to inaccurate complexity.

But the crisis in their creativity was almost wholly obliterated by the brouhaha kicked up when they split, so the aesthetic problem was never clearly dramatized. With Dylan it was a different case.

Inspiration had clearly dried up, and political or sociological reasons for its disappearance were not all that easy to point to. For the first time, the rock culture was faced with a Cinerama-sized example of creativity running out of road. A full-scale intellectual crisis rapidly developed—a devil of a thing to happen in an intellectual vacuum.

AT THE MOMENT the response to Dylan's artistic evaporation seems to have shaped itself up into two main kinds of argument: the sociopolitical argument, and the argument by manifest destiny.

The sociopolitical argument tends to discover reasons in Dylan's life for his loss of creative drive, and has been given great weight by Anthony Scaduto's biography.

Scaduto's book is an able effort praiseworthy on the storytelling level and reasonable in its minor judgments. But the art and the life of its hero are drawn together in a simplistic pattern of correspondence which sweeps the question of cause and effect under the carpet.

It emerges—all too readily emerges—that Dylan was a calculating little handful when his work was still challenging, but eventually transmogrified himself into a home-making citizen whose comfortable music now gently celebrates his oneness with existence.

On Scaduto's terms, it would be very difficult to introduce the notion that Dylan's later phase might have something to do with his running out of creative potential. At best, the reader of this "intimate biography" might concede that Dylan had run out of will.

The argument by manifest destiny has nothing so impressive as Scaduto's book to support itself with, but stays potent simply through the flywheel effect of the last fifteen years, in which scarcely any other kind of argument has been allowed about anybody.

On this view, *Self Portrait* was an expansion of Dylan's range of musical apprehension, the signal for a fresh, comprehensive identification with modern America. It followed as the night the day that the suppression of Dylan's biting individuality was a deliberate sacrifice, and any song that failed was *meant* to fail.

Like the appreciators of the latter-day Godard, adherents of this argument take positive courage from the fragmentary and the inadequate—disintegration being the final proof of the hero's integrity in pursuit of his historical role.

A THIRD LINE of argument, more realistic than either of these two, has been gradually coming to the surface.

It would have surfaced faster if it could have been confident of its terms, but of necessity these terms had to be critical terms, a commodity in short supply.

When a properly critical view of Dylan is at last formulated, I think it will look to be lacking in self-confidence compared with the two lines of argument I've sketched above. To begin with, it won't be anything like so generous in making biographical references, or cheerful about supposing Dylan capable of perceiving his own historical role.

What it *will* do is make Dylan look more like other artists who have done good things for a while and then dried up. And by that I don't mean Arthur Rimbaud (who is so often mentioned in the same breath with Dylan, but who really was a full-blown genius, and no arguments): I mean all the young rock artists who have worked out their vein of material and found themselves ill equipped to go further.

Early collapse isn't a law of rock, but it is a characteristic: not of the musical form itself but of the mental patterns which have so far given rise to it. Like other artists, Dylan went to the limit of the instinctive, unstudied spontaneity—went to the limit of all those terms which the rock culture fondly imagines are automatic guarantees of quality.

Since Dylan's stock of instinctive, unstudied spontaneity was almost incomparably more abundant than anybody else's, his limits lay a long way down the pike. But eventually he got to them, confirming the principle that at some point an artist must either find a way of ensuring inspiration's arrival or else wave it farewell.

The element of uncaringness in Dylan was always a portent.

His expansiveness was always the undisciplined enemy of his intensity: his inclusiveness was always at war with his grasp of detail, and when he finally discovered that he could suggest the totality of experience without going to the trouble of concentrating on any part of it, the temptation to rest on his oars became irresistible.

Such an estimate—which is made with a full realization of the lasting importance of his achievement—is, in my view, easily deduced from his handling of language throughout his career.

The freedom of his linguistic invention, even at its most marvelous, has always had something to do with a fatal detachment from the discipline of concrete perception: Dylan makes a virtue of not knowing exactly what he means. He can't distinguish, in his own work, between the idea that is resonant and the idea that postures toward significance, the image that is highly charged and the image that is merely portentous.

The long receptivity which uncritically appreciated everything Dylan did was admiring the cancer as part of the body, which didn't matter so long as they both expanded together, but which mattered a great deal when the body started to shrink as a result of the cancer's growth.

THE DIFFERENCE between Dylan and Rimbaud, if it still needs pointing out, is that Rimbaud's unbelievably rapid ascent was an ascent to purity of utterance—it wasn't just an expensive giganticism. You look at a poem like "Bateau Ivre" and see instantly that such writing can't go much further.

But even in the best of Dylan songs—"Like a Rolling Stone"—your critical faculties can't be silenced for more than a single stanza: they're at war all the time with your acceptance of what's on offer, wincing at the song's slipshod organization, missed opportunities, easy rhymes, unfocused images.

Unless of course, those same critical faculties have been anesthetized by the means of descriptive justification, which refers every awkwardness back to the traditions from which Dylan drew his influence.

On that view, there isn't a limp or stumble which hasn't got its validation in Big Joe Williams, Woody Guthrie or elsewhere: once again, awkwardness and incompleteness are certificates of authenticity.

But the elementary counter to that view is that Dylan sets standards in one part which automatically criticize his performance in another part— his unevenness is self-demonstrating.

To take a glaring example, isn't the stanza about the Mystery Tramp in "Like a Rolling Stone" the first stanza of that song that anybody learns to quote entire, and the stanza beside which all the others are felt to be disjointed or blurred? And the *order* of the stanzas is not established as inevitable with the consequence that a whole dimension—the dimension of emotional progress—is heard to be missing.

Nobody contends that what is superb in the song isn't superb.

One only contends that the superbness shows up the barely adequate in a cruel light, proving Dylan's sense of strategy to be fragmentary even at its peak.

The maturity of lyricism occurs when the poet sees that the forces operating to unite his best image must be followed until they unite the entire lyric—at which point the lyrics can be said to be complete. This is the maturity Dylan hasn't reached: instead, he has developed his precocity.

DYLAN'S UNSTABLE sense of organization is most readily noticeable in the long songs that don't justify their length.

"Sad-Eyed Lady of the Lowlands" is too obvious a case to bear examination—it would be a dunce indeed who imagined that in purchasing *Blonde on Blonde* he had got hold of much more than one and a half LPs.

Less obvious cases are "Desolation Row" and "Gates of Eden." In "Desolation Row" the boredom attendant on Dylan's compulsively additive writing has been widely felt, but is usually accepted as contributory, as if the cleverest thing a song about desolation can do is to make the listener feel desolate with ennui.

In refutation, all we need to do is point out that the song would have a greater point if it were more concentrated—while remembering to insist that concentration means more than just lopping a few stanzas off.

"Gates of Eden," however, is a more rewarding case, since here, in order to articulate our sense of the song's inadequacy, we're obliged to get down to the level of the language.

Using those extended stanzas which are his biggest single contribution to rock writing, Dylan is exploiting a colossal buildup of argument which—when the trick is worked successfully—explodes into the tag line with a whopping release of tension. The effect can't fail so long as the stanza's argument remains intelligible.

Yet intelligibility is precisely what he throws away. Taking a representative stanza, we find the argument developing like this:

> *The motorcycle black Madonna*
> *Two-wheeled gypsy queen*
> *And her silver-studded Phantom*
> *Cause the gray flanneled dwarf to scream*

A detailed criticism could be made of this, but it wouldn't alter the fact that some kind of story is going forward in a way the listener can just follow, so long as he takes the essentially private nature of the imagery for granted and forgives the makeshift syntax. (If the Madonna's on a motor-cycle, by the way, we already know how many wheels she's got and don't need to be told again—but let it pass.)

The crippling blow comes in the next two lines, when Dylan shifts the field of attention, snaps the continuity and turns his big effect into a fizzler.

> *As he weeps two wicked birds of prey*
> *Who pick upon his breadcrumb sins*
> *And there are no sins inside the Gates of Eden.*

The blurred imagery wouldn't matter so much if it were grouped around a solid narrative spine: but with the narrative so spongy—so obviously willing to go anywhere—the stanza is robbed of its drive. It's not just that "breadcrumb sins" is a weak notion—it's that the ideas in the stanza are diminishing all the time, each one being introduced under less logical pressure than the last, with the sole object of passing the stanza out toward its big finish.

And the Q.E.D. clinching line callously demonstrates the hollowness of what has led up to it. Dylan's ability to invent such a flexibly argumentative stanza, coupled with his inability to see that he must argue in it and not just flannel: the two things amount to a crashing contradiction.

DYLAN'S TALENT for discovering capacious stanzaic forms comes from the precise side of his gift—he has an enviable intuitive grasp of how a lyrical stanza should be shaped in order to be best inhabited by music.

This intuitive grasp can be enjoyed by the listener even when the subsidiary forms occupying the stanza are inadequate: indeed half the thrill of Dylan lies in following his clear architectural outline and emotionally solidifying it with an imaginative content it hasn't really got.

Unfortunately the patchiness of the imaginative content it *has* got can't usually be overlooked for long enough to keep the thrill going.

The imprecise side of his gift is just too confoundedly fertile. His handling of language is self-forgiving at a fundamental level, the level of craft: never has so much arbitrary stressing met so much melodic angularity in so many awkward marriages.

By the time we get to the level of imagination, the reluctance to blot a line is an open invitation for almost any old notion to amble in and set up shop. Yet when all is sung and done, it can't be denied that the total effect is on a huge scale: he dreams great buildings, even if the walls remain untimbered and the roofs are open to the sky.

AS A CRITICAL estimate of Dylan comes within reach, it will always be necessary to remember that we seek it out of gratitude.

If we place limitations on his achievement, we place them out of our desire to see exactly how much has been done—which is the only way we will be able to see what needs to be done next. A purely descriptive survey of his work can only give us an account of subject matter, leading us into the fallacy by which it is assumed that certain subjects ("Protest," for example) have been exhausted.

What Dylan has exhausted is not any kind of subject matter, but a specific kind of approach to the song: the approach that relies on the indiscriminate imagination.

If rock is ever again to produce anything to equal what he has done, it will have to be something considered, disciplined and integrated. No resonance without clear statement: no radiance without clean edges.

That's the rule which, by breaking it, the most talented songwriter in rock proved to be binding.

Blood on the Tracks

RICK MOODY

In January 1975 Dylan released *Blood on the Tracks*, which many consider to be his single greatest album—"the truest, most honest account of a love affair from tip to stern ever put down on magnetic tape," according to Rick Moody. This speech, published here for the first time, was given at a celebration of Dylan's sixtieth birthday on May 19, 2001, at Town Hall in New York City. With rich and kinetic prose, Moody cites the qualities that make *Blood on the Tracks* a memorable album: the honesty of the lyrics, their universal ambivalence, the pointed contrast in instrumentation from song to song and the thematic range that Dylan creates out of a single subject. Moody's appreciation is unique insofar that he doesn't see it only as an album of love songs—though it is obviously that—but as a narrative of its own, depicting a single love affair whose breach results in a pathos of considerable authority.

Moody is the author of three novels, including *The Ice Storm* and *Purple America*; two collections of short stories; and *The Black Veil: A Memoir with Digressions*.

BLOOD ON THE TRACKS of thee I sing, best album ever made, or that's my hypothesis, best rock-and-roll record ever, more heroic than *The Sun Sessions*, more consistent than *Exile on Main Street*, more serious than *Never Mind the Bollocks*, better than *Revolver* because there's no "Good Day Sunshine" on it, more discerning in its rage than *Nevermind*, more accepting than *What's Going On*, less desperate than *Pet Sounds*, and more adult than *Blonde on Blonde* and *Highway 61 Revisited*; leagues beyond even the nearest runners-up, *Blue, Who's Next, Pink Moon, Horses, Let It Be* by the Replacements, *Sister Lovers* by Big Star, *Loaded* by the Velvet Underground—no filler, no topicalities, no gimmicks, unless you count the open D tuning that allegedly confounded the backing musicians when the author tried to instruct them in the tunes. Every now and then the heavens get it straight, see, *like a simple twist of fate*, and the inexplicable difficulties of the heart, the kinds of things that you spend your life trying to get down if you're working this variety of job, are rendered in all their infinite complexity in lines as blunt as Picasso's, *I can't help it if I'm lucky; I can change I swear; when something's not right, it's wrong; friends will arrive, friends will disappear;* of thee I sing, album of love found and lost, document of how desire comes on you and the decades seem to align, as you are *nearly swept off your feet,* and your circumstances, the stuff that has to be moved to accommodate this madness, just gets shoved aside; the practicalities vanish and your life is like the life of an outlaw, or like the lives of players on the stage, even the birds sing for you *at their own expense;* certain inevitable futures fall out of your hands, and it's this way even if the lawyers come with their subpoenas and impossible demands; *then* just as you're settling in to the luxury of this madness, as though desire is a great lyric that can be improvised and unrevised, you start to see the ominous intimations on the horizon, stories get planted in the press, *beware of lightning that might strike, the priest wears black, smoke pours out of a boxcar door,* and the very thing you loved, the very object, *the very person,* the very alignment, the very feeling that so buoyed you, it starts to spook and feint, even the elements seem fell and dumb, the wind, the air, the earth; if I sing of love on *Blood on the Tracks,* isn't love a variety of rage, isn't love a song of *rage and glory,* so that the good part, the blessedness of love is just the doorway into that much more complicated disdain and contempt and that implicates you the lover, the disdain that blows the neglected dust down off the shelf; now the very interpretation that made you a great believer in love makes you a better disbeliever, everywhere are plots and stratagems, *gravity, destiny,* the obverses of the *fatedness* that brought you together in the first place, back when you stupidly believed that you could see a lover across a room; now the people around you don't know you, even the sound of leaves rustling is fierce, and you realize you have let a lot of things go, things that were lovely and promising, you have blundered, you have erred, and thus the resignation and remembrance of the promise of things lost; it all gets quiet; all the drums and organs and bile of *Blood on the Tracks* give way to tracks of just acoustic guitar and bass, *situations have ended sad, relationships have all been bad,* nothing artful about it, it's just the experience of one troubadour, events are not exemplary, they are like the lazy, improvised insights of the blues, *they say the darkest hour is right before dawn, look at that sun sinking like a ship,* and *fatedness* is a dream you had, like in dreams where gambling stands as an emblem for divine order, the outcome of a hand of cards being the text for a divination, just as the lover is preoccupied with the details and effects and narratives of the vanished beloved, *Has your luck run out, she laughed at him, well, I guess you must have known it would some day;* don't pay any mind to the hanging judge, the colt revolver, the bank safe, the woman on the gallows, *it's all about gamblers and their systems, it's all about signs and portents, it's all about that error which surmises that winners are favored by God;* of thee I sing, album of love only briefly found and then voluminously, expertly, incisively lost, album that proves that all love has something *lost* in it, that *love lost* is the idiom known to all men; these are the mistakes *people make,* it's all in the lines, *we had a falling out, as lovers often will,* or *the bitter taste still lingers on from the night I tried to make her stay,* or *either I'm too sensitive or else I'm getting soft;* insights into love, you see, are a danger to their narrator, don't believe the narrator of a love song, who welters in his own spilt blood, so that his insights are likely hallucinatory ravings; of him I sing, of the untrustworthy narrator of the best love songs, who at his darkest, most forsaken moment launches into the iterations and reiterations of *shelter from the storm;* has ever the destitute lover articulated such riches? And with such perspicacity? In which the mere daily habits of want and sustenance are made universal? *Try imagining a place where it's always safe and warm,* you know what it is to be loved, and you *may never get it,* after which, of course, those *buckets of rain, all you can do is you do what you must;* of thee I sing, of an acoustic guitar flat-picked with bass and little other accompaniment, and the truest, most honest account of a love affair from tip to stern ever put down on magnetic tape, the kind of thing that counsels patience, steers a true course, keeps the wretched off of bridges, leads the estranged back into the arms of those they forsook, of thee I sing, of *blood,* that Old English syllable, *Blood, he speaks terribly,* and of Middle English *tracks, Myght I fynde the track of his hors I shold not fayle to fynde the knyghte.* When you close in on it, when you close in on the significance of these most ancient things, *blood* speckling the album *tracks,* well, it's like *the light coming through a beat-up shade;* of thee I sing, you masterpiece.

Shelter from the Storm

BOB DYLAN

Dylan has devoted energy to all sorts of musical styles. Yet his lyrics concentrate on a consistent set of themes; love and spirituality are his most common subjects. Often, in his best songs, the two become one and the same. Lost love is allied to a sense of spiritual extinction, or to put it another way, grace cannot be sought or achieved alone. "Shelter from the Storm," the next-to-last cut on *Blood on the Tracks*, is a good example of this idea, featuring a classic Dylan character—bloodied and wandering—as well as his keenest observation on the bond between love and holiness: "if I could only turn back the clock to when God and her were born." Like most songs on that album, the lyrics are supported by a hypnotic use of repetition. A single bar of music, built on the three major chords in the key of E, is played over and over beneath the melody, with bass as the only other form of accompaniment.

Blood on the Tracks was a breakthrough in Dylan's writing. He attributed much of the album's strength to his continued interest in painting, and the teachings of New York artist Norman Raeben in particular. The ability to depict so many events on a single plane, the brevity of line—these were qualities Dylan had never displayed so consistently before, and were ones he associated with the visual arts. "I wanted to defy time, so that the story took place in the present and the past at the same time. When you look at a painting, you can see any part of it, or see all of it together."* For this reason, perhaps, musical or literary terms often seem imprecise in describing

---

* Quoted in Clinton Heylin, *Behind the Shades Revisited* (New York: William Morrow, 2001), 370.

the album. "Shelter from the Storm" and other songs resist this sort of clas-
sification—their intense introspection exhausts and ultimately breaks free
of the traditional ballad form.

'Twas in another lifetime, one of toil and blood
When blackness was a virtue and the road was full of mud
I came in from the wilderness, a creature void of form.
"Come in," she said,
"I'll give you shelter from the storm."

And if I pass this way again, you can rest assured
I'll always do my best for her, on that I give my word
In a world of steel-eyed death, and men who are fighting to be
        warm.
"Come in," she said,
"I'll give you shelter from the storm."

Not a word was spoke between us, there was little risk involved
Everything up to that point had been left unresolved.
Try imagining a place where it's always safe and warm.
"Come in," she said,
"I'll give you shelter from the storm."

I was burned out from exhaustion, buried in the hail,
Poisoned in the bushes an' blown out on the trail,
Hunted like a crocodile, ravaged in the corn.
"Come in," she said,
"I'll give you shelter from the storm."

Suddenly I turned around and she was standin' there
With silver bracelets on her wrists and flowers in her hair.
She walked up to me so gracefully and took my crown of thorns.
"Come in," she said,
"I'll give you shelter from the storm."

Now there's a wall between us, somethin' there's been lost
I took too much for granted, got my signals crossed.
Just to think that it all began on a long-forgotten morn.
"Come in," she said,
"I'll give you shelter from the storm."

Well, the deputy walks on hard nails and the preacher rides a
        mount
But nothing really matters much, it's doom alone that counts
And the one-eyed undertaker, he blows a futile horn.
"Come in," she said,
"I'll give you shelter from the storm."

I've heard newborn babies wailin' like a mournin' dove
And old men with broken teeth stranded without love.
Do I understand your question, man, is it hopeless and forlorn?
"Come in," she said,
"I'll give you shelter from the storm."

In a little hilltop village, they gambled for my clothes
I bargained for salvation an' they gave me a lethal dose.
I offered up my innocence and got repaid with scorn.
"Come in," she said,
"I'll give you shelter from the storm."

Well, I'm livin' in a foreign country but I'm bound to cross the line
Beauty walks a razor's edge, someday I'll make it mine.
If I could only turn back the clock to when God and her were
        born.
"Come in," she said,
"I'll give you shelter from the storm."

excerpt from *The Old, Weird America**

GREIL MARCUS

In 1975 a selection of the basement tapes—the informal recordings Dylan made with the Band in the summer and fall of 1967—was finally released, after repeated demands for their release and the appearance of several bootlegs featuring basement songs. The album was quickly recognized as among the most sophisticated and inspired music of Dylan's career. Greil Marcus, in *The Old, Weird America*, finds the basements ripe with inheritance, and sets forth a remarkable examination of their thematic and musical origins.

In particular, he ties the basement experiment to Harry Smith's *Anthology of American Folk Music*—a collection of eighty-four songs recorded between 1927 and 1932 that, upon its release in 1952, became a potent force in the folk revival as well as American songwriting as a whole. By pointing back to the *Anthology*, the characters that populate its songs and the culture behind the folk music of Appalachia, Dock Boggs, Frank Hutchison and so forth, Marcus believes that *The Basement Tapes* represent a salient cultural phenomenon. The tapes constitute, he writes, a map of an invisible world, a country of their own—"where, for a few months, certain bedrock strains of American cultural language were retrieved and reinvented."

This "invisible republic" can be divided into two towns: Smithville, the world of Harry Smith's *Anthology*, its characters and social mores; and Kill

---

* When it was first published in 1997, the book carried the title of *Invisible Republic*; it has since been renamed.

Devil Hills (named after a small town in eastern North Carolina), the territory that Dylan and the Band created in 1967. Here, Marcus muses on differences and similarities between the two, the timelessness of the recordings made during a volatile year in American history and the disappearance of folk's old guard. He returns, at the end, to the book's central thesis. Just as Marcus thinks that the basements conjure a "perfectly metaphorical America," he also proves, in the course of this unique study, that there can be perfectly metaphorical readings of Dylan's music.

THERE IS LESS at stake in Kill Devil Hills than in Smithville. The town is far more playful. There is loss and there is guilt, but little if anything is final—as opposed to Smithville, where whatever doesn't seem completed seems preordained.

That is how the music feels—and all that begins to change with a series of songs set down in August and September of the basement summer. They're taken slowly, with crying voices. Dylan's voice is high and constantly bending, carried forward not by rhythm or even melody but by the discovery of the true terrain of the songs as they're sung. Richard Manuel's and Rick Danko's voices are higher still, more exposed, though for everyone in the basement, with these songs—"Goin' to Acapulco," "Too Much of Nothing," "This Wheel's on Fire," "I Shall Be Released"—the only mask between nakedness and the invisible public of the secret songs is one of knowledge, craft, and skill.

In two of the basement songs that are part of this series—that emerge from the shifting ground laid by all the other songs—the stakes may be higher than they ever are in Smithville. In "Tears of Rage" and "I'm Not There," you can sense the presence of something that can't be found in Smithville, unless it's the keen wishfulness and utter abandonment of Ken Maynard's "Lone Star Trail," and that is tragedy. This is the sung and played embodiment of crimes that float in terms of argument and evidence but are immovable as verdicts, in their weight: sins committed, perhaps even without intent, that will throw the world out of joint, crimes that will reverberate across space and time in ways that no one can stop. What language do you speak when you speak of things like this?

You speak the language, as Bob Dylan would say in the fall of the year, recording *John Wesley Harding* in Nashville with Nashville musicians, of not speaking falsely. How do you do that? You go as far into your song as you can. When Bob Dylan asked himself how far you could go with a song—with words and melody that on paper or in your head said next to nothing and in the air made a world suspended within it—Dock Boggs always had an answer: this far, and maybe no farther.

"where i live now," Dylan wrote in the mid-1960s, for a book that would be published in 1971 as *Tarantula*, in a voice one does not have to push very hard to hear as Dylan's idea of something Boggs might have written, or wanted to, "the only thing that keeps the area going is tradition—as you can figure out—it doesnt count very much—everything around me rots . . . i dont know how long it has been this way, but if it keeps up, soon i will be an old man—& i am only 15—the only job around here is mining—but jesus, who wants to be a miner . . . i refuse to be part of such a shallow death."

Bob Dylan knew better than most that the death in Boggs's music was no shallower than the hole the singer puts Pretty Polly in. "I dug on your grave two thirds of last night," Boggs's Willie tells her, brazenly, drunkenly, proudly, as he leads her to the sacred spot, hallowed by the countless pilgrimages lovers before them have made to this shaded grove. Speaking his life to Mike Seeger, Boggs called up a context, a setting, but the tension in his story is all in his will not to be reduced to his setting, not to be taken for anybody else.

The death Boggs made wasn't shallow but faked, and it was faked because it was art, not life. As a folk-lyric song, "Country Blues" was a mild, ritualized version of the everyday life Boggs described over the years, a celebration of certain choices, a dramatized refusal to take them back. As a ballad older than any family legend, "Pretty Polly" was a mythic version of the desires Boggs felt welling up within himself, the wish for vengeance that all his life diffused into nothing here focused on a single anagogic object. In the culture of which Boggs was a part, that was what songs like these were for, if you could rise to them, or past them. Boggs could, and probably no one ever sang these songs as he did, or took them as far. As a primitive modernist, he accepted their invitation to transform commonplaces into unique emotive events, where the performer draws out what he or she has—what he is, or what she is afraid she could become—and measures it against the artifact of the occasion: the song and all the past lives that it contains. What results is not a reflection of real life for the singer any more than it is for the listener, but a vision, a *lo!* and *behold!* of possible life—lives the singer and the listener may have ahead of them, to realize or lose, lives that may already be behind them, deprived of oblivion only because of what the singer does with the song.

This is the territory of "Country Blues" and "Pretty Polly," and it's the territory of "Tears of Rage" and "I'm Not There." The difference is that the words and sounds in Dylan's new songs only seem commonplace, borrowed, transformed, resting in an aura of somehow having always been present, not made up one summer when the country was burning and five people in a Catskills basement were looking for a good way to pass the time.

"That's the sound he's got now," Bruce Springsteen said of Dylan in 1995, when he heard Dock Boggs for the first time. Springsteen was speaking of Dylan's early 1990s embrace of old music, of *Good as I Been to You* and *World Gone Wrong*. Was Springsteen hearing sound or aura? For sound—for pitch and intonation, for the unstable flatness, for the yowl—there is more of Boggs in "Like a Rolling Stone" as Dylan recorded it in 1965 than there is in "Little Maggie" as he recorded it in 1992 or "Delia" as he recorded it in 1993. In the aura, though, was the peculiar intensity of the absence, and here the intensity of a vanished culture making itself felt, like a Rayograph turning up on a roll of Kodachrome you bought last week, the old America rustling in the drawers of any mall's Fotomat. "That world!" as Denis Johnson shouts in his novel *Jesus' Son*. "These days it's all been erased and they've rolled it up like a scroll and put it away somewhere. Yes, I can touch it with my fingers. But where is it?"

In 1993, two years before Bruce Springsteen heard Bob Dylan in Dock Boggs, Dylan played shows that included the new/old material of *Good as I Been to You* and *World Gone Wrong*: the Appalachian standard "Jack-a-Roe," the blues "Ragged and Dirty," the Memphis street song "Blood in My Eye." Here critic Dave Marsh heard Bruce Springsteen in Bob Dylan, and after one show he asked Dylan about that: about the question of Springsteen's then-stalled career, caught between an established audience that could produce huge sales for a greatest-hits package and an unknown audience that might have as little to say to Springsteen as they thought he had to say to them.

People like Springsteen had missed something, Dylan said, with Springsteen only eight years younger and still born too late: "They weren't there to see the end of the traditional people. But I was." What was he saying? He might have been saying that as in 1963 he watched Boggs, Mississippi John Hurt, Skip James, Clarence Ashley, Buell Kazee, Sara and Maybelle Carter— "the traditional people," standing on the Newport stage, for Dylan's cryptically perfect phrase, both as themselves and as a particularly American strain of fairy folk—he had learned something about persistence and renewal. Or he might have been saying something simpler, and harder: I saw a vanishing. He was present to witness an extinction, to see the last members of a species disappear. Thus it was left to him to say what went out of the world when the traditional people left the stage.

Where the past is in the basement tapes—what the past is—has more to do with this sort of question than with the question of any direct transmission of style or manner from one performer to another. In the basement tapes, an uncompleted world was haphazardly constructed out of the past, out of Smith's *Anthology* and its like, out of the responses people like Bob Dylan, Mike Seeger, and so many more brought to that music, its stories, and to the world—another country—implicit within it. The uncompleted world of the basement tapes was a fantasy beginning in artifacts refashioned by real people, dimly apprehended figures who out of the kettle of the folk revival appeared in the flesh to send an unexpected message. The vanished world they incarnated—as history, a set of facts and an indistinct romance; as a set of artifacts, as a work of art, complete and finished—was going to die, and you were going to be the last witness. Through your own performance, whenever it might take place, in 1963, 1965, or 1966, in 1967, 1992, or 1993, through its success or failure, you were to sign your name to the death certificate. You were to certify that a certain race of people had vanished from the earth, which was also a way of testifying that they once had been at large upon it—and as a result of your witnessing, what traces these people might have left behind were to be lodged in you.

It's a possibility that instantly raises its own question. What will go out of the world with *you*? This is the sense of loss and finality that is a bridge to the sense of tragedy in "Tears of Rage" and "I'm Not There." The past that drives these songs is this past.

The playfulness, the lowered stakes of Kill Devil Hills when measured against Smithville, is the only right backdrop for tragedy here: an arena where tragedy can be discovered and yet not claim the whole of life. It will throw the rest of life into relief: only tragedy can justify a place with a name like this, can give its pleasures memory, its drunks true sleep.

Smithville is definitively settled, and in Smithville there is no tragedy because there is no guilt. Fatalism overshadows everything else. Kill Devil Hills is not only unfinished, it is transitory. At times it can feel less like a town than a depot, a stopping-off point, like so many earlier American towns—not the utopian seventeenth-century Puritan communities, with so many masked against their inability to live up to their word to follow god's, or the scattered, multiplying perfectionist settlements of the late eighteenth and early nineteenth centuries, but the frontier towns, with the guilt and doubt of utopians and perfectionists no less present in their air than the free rapaciousness of traders, con artists, and killers, all walking streets where a mask was just part of the wardrobe. Here fatalism is nothing to the daredevil. Everything seems open, any turn can be made at any time—at least until a certain dead end is reached, and then no mask, no secret identity, no change of name or face will protect you, and for a moment all masks come off.

Night of the Hurricane

SAM SHEPARD

D ylan played a series of shows in small venues throughout the northeast United States, as well as Toronto, Montreal and Quebec City, in the fall of 1975. Known as the Rolling Thunder Revue, the tour was an ensemble act featuring some of Dylan's closest friends and accomplished peers, including Joan Baez, Joni Mitchell, Ramblin' Jack Elliott and Allen Ginsberg. Playwright Sam Shepard was hired to write the screenplay for a movie that was to be based on the Revue; although this became a loose, improvised affair with no script, Shepard stayed on the road and eventually published a memoir entitled *Rolling Thunder Logbook*.

Shepard's book captured one of the most historic nights in Dylan's live career—a benefit for Rubin "Hurricane" Carter at Madison Square Garden. A boxer who was falsely tried and convicted of murder, Carter was the basis for "Hurricane," the opening track on *Desire* and one of Dylan's better-known songs. Held on December 8, 1975, "The Night of the Hurricane" featured another popular figure who actively supported Carter: Muhammad Ali. Shepard recalls the evening's unusual excitement and gives a lively play-by-play of the band's performance. In addition to portraying the energy of the Revue, he also describes the tour's backstage activities, affording the reader a look rarely had by outsiders. (Perhaps overcome by the moment, Dylan was convinced by the end of the concert that Carter had been set free. This was not to be: although Carter was granted a second trial in March 1976, he was found guilty again and would not be acquitted until 1985.)

In the course of this excerpt, Shepard alludes to several other Rolling Thunder personnel: guitarists Bobby Neuwirth, Mick Ronson and T-Bone

Burnett, multi-instrumentalist David Mansfield, the actress and singer Ronee Blakley, bassist Rob Stoner and drummer Howard Wyeth.

Shepard's works, some of the most important in contemporary American theater, include the plays *Buried Child, Curse of the Starving Class* and *True West,* as well as the story collections *Cruising Paradise* and *Great Dreams of Heaven.* His "A Short Life of Trouble," a one-act play, appears on page 182.

DECEMBER 8—MADISON SQUARE GARDEN. The Garden is sold out for the concert within five hours after the box office opens. The question is, why the Garden after all that talk of keeping the show on a small-town level? Why wrap it up with a giant fandango in New York City? It seems a combination of helping to heal the costs of money lost on the New England circuit plus a genuine interest in aiding Rubin Carter. It is billed as a benefit, and it's for sure that the "public interest" generated by the presence of Muhammad Ali and Dylan in the same space is going to leak down to that New Jersey jailhouse and work its own kind of leverage on the law. Already the papers are talking about reprieves and retrials, and there's no doubt that this event will add some muscle to the whole cause.

In the afternoon the Garden is totally empty except for a few janitors and the Neuwirth band doing a sound check. The levels are generally too high, which seems to be coming from the impulse to put the music across in this gigantic tomb after playing to so many tiny halls for weeks on end. Mansfield has a superkeen ear and it doesn't take long before the vocals match up with the bottom end. I climb my way up to the very top of the volcanolike auditorium until the band looks like a miniaturized Punch and Judy show. Nobody's face is recognizable. Only certain random gestures give any clues as to who they are. It's very strange to know these people and then see them from the audience's point of view. The Garden is a stupefying piece of suspended architecture. Not beautiful or even aesthetic, but you can't help but wonder how they came up with a design for this gargantuan ceiling that seems to be just hanging in midair. No pillars or columns anywhere. Just cables all coming into a central hub and somehow holding the whole thing up. Seeing it with only a few people in it really adds to the immensity of it. I keep moving around to different places in the auditorium and sitting for a few minutes just to see what it's like. I begin to notice certain sections filling up with people. In one section all the people are wearing blue. In another section, white. Then a whole section of brown people. I start descending the mountain to take a closer look at this phenomenon. It turns out that the blue people are cops. All of them sitting within a definite perimeter, sucking on coffee cops, jackets open, feet up on the backs of chairs, and talking to each other. The brown people are ushers, doing more or less the same thing as the cops and carrying flashlights. The white people are technicians. Each section totally cut off from the other section like little territories on a topographical map. There's something very warming to me about all this, but I can't figure out what it is.

I make my way backstage, imaging all the different atmospheres this place has contained and how amazing it is that it still remains without a physical identity of its own. It's just a building and then a whole world enters into it and takes it over and then goes away again. Dog shows, rodeos, circuses, prizefights, hockey games, basketball, horse shows, ballets, musical events. The smell of hot roasted chestnuts and sauerkraut brings me out of my stupor. Barry Imhoff has done it again. He's hired a hot-dog man and a pretzel man from off the street, and they're both handing out their steaming stuff to anyone who wants it. It's been a while since I've had a real New York hot dog with mustard and sauerkraut and onions, so I stop. As I'm standing there waiting for the little fat man to pile all these layers onto two white buns resting in a piece of cellophane, I notice what seems to be a small army of black men in pinstripe suits, grim-set faces, eyes darting in all directions, all swarming around an even bigger, taller black man dressed completely in black and looking a lot like the "heavyweight champeen of the whole entire world." My two hands go paralyzed, one reaching in my pocket for change and the other one reaching for the hot dog as my eyes try to shake loose from this vision. Ali is cool and graceful while all around him these other guys never stop rotating their heads and twitching their pockets. If there aren't any assassins around, it looks like they'd just as soon dream one up right there on the spot just to let somebody know they're not fooling around. They move off down the hallway like a colony of worker ants surrounding the queen. The little fat hot-dog man is making "fed up" noises in a New York accent. I pay up and stagger off toward the dressing rooms. This must be the American way all right. Nothing's important or has any value until it's blown up into "bigger than life" proportions. "Get the biggest damn fucking hall in the whole entire planet! Get the heavyweight champ of the whole entire world! Get the greatest folk singer since Edith Piaf! The most incredible poet-musician phenomenon the world has ever seen and throw 'em all together in front of the biggest goddamn flesh-and-blood toe-tappin' audience this side of the Rio Grande! And we'll have ourselves a show, folks!" I'm game.

I veer into a dressing room marked Guam and come to rest on a metal bench. The table in the middle of the room looks like it couldn't support any more flowers and nuts and fruit. Barrels full of cans of beer, soft drinks resting on ice in every corner. Telegrams from all over pinned to the walls. Ginsberg comes bouncing in wearing a suit and tie plus his youthful tennis shoes. It's a good feeling seeing him in this atmosphere. Like a little breeze of sanity blowing through the door. "My father's out there. He's eighty years old and he's never seen a rock concert." I ask Allen if he's not afraid his father might have a heart attack at that age. "Naw, my father's a poet." He laughs and goes off bopping into the men's room. He shouts out of the bathroom to me. "He is! A real poet! We gave a reading together the other day at a college up north!" Neuwirth joins us, spinning on both heels, nervous as a cat. Already he's worked himself up into a lather. He growls something unintelligible, cranes his neck as though looking for someone, and then pivots back out the door. Most everyone is catching this drift of emotional frenzy. I can't remember the feeling of tension being like this at any other time on the tour except for maybe the very first concert at Plymouth. But that was mostly just butterflies, hoping the show would get off the ground on an up note. But this is more verging on anxiety. To add to it, Roberta Flack has been called in at the last minute because Aretha Franklin was tied up with dates in Los Angeles. Roberta makes no bones about being picked as second string to the great Aretha. She comes on like full-tilt Hollywood, storming around backstage in a flashy bandanna, decked out in jewelry and shouting orders to her entourage. There's a definite taste of black-white tension going on backstage, which is another new ingredient that was lacking on the New England schedule. Nothing weird or violent, just these two totally different streams of musical culture swimming by each other without mixing. Almost as though there were two different concerts to be given on the same bill, having nothing in common. I keep coming back to the idea that it's a black man that the concert's being given for. A benefit for a black convict initiated by a white singer with black support. It's too sticky to figure out. Ali's been trying to trump up support for Carter for quite a while. Before Dylan even. But it took Dylan to get this whole thing together.

THE WHOLE ATMOSPHERE has changed now with the coming of the crowds. Even the air is different. New York really is the testing ground for any experiment. It's plain as day. If you want the world to know about it, bring it to New York. Better yet, bring it to the Garden!

The band kicks off into "Good Love Is Hard to Find" and the volcano erupts. Rolling Thunder meets itself head-on in the voice of over thirty-five hundred screaming beings from earth. Dylan may be just a kid from Minnesota but this here is his hometown. No matter how many politico-music critics find disappointment in his recent lyrics and his lifestyle, the people here tonight are saying *yes* in full strength. Bring on the punk who changed the entire face of American youth consciousness in one fell swoop! Generally the musicians seem to be pushing themselves to the point where the music seems strained and speeded up compared to the more informal concerts up north. Ronson, on the other hand, really gets off on this monster crowd. His initial style is broad and theatrical anyway, coming from English "rave-up" and David Bowie. He begins to uncork all the flash he's been holding back throughout the tour. Giant, spread-eagle leaps into thin air. Triple vertical spins, wrapping the guitar cord around him like a boa constrictor, slashing at the guitar with full-arm uppercuts. Platinum-blond hair spraying in all directions. Then stalking around the stage, stiff legged, Frankenstein macho strutting, shaking the neck of the guitar with his vicious chord hand as though throttling his weaker brother. All the time, never losing a lick. Through every motion playing genius, inspirational lead lines, then melting into the background again to support the other musicians. Neuwirth seems on the verge of exploding through his skin from sheer tension. His voice is splitting down the middle through every song. The band holds it together though. Right down the line it's the music that's making this whole thing happen. The solid experience behind every member of the band. Joni Mitchell blows the top off the place again, just by walking on. She looks incredibly small from where I'm sitting. Like a vulnerable little girl trying to sing a song she's written for a huge living room full of adults. One of Neuwirth's standard introduction lines at every concert has been, "Welcome to your living room," and tonight's the first night I've really seen what he means. The set rolls on and then Muhammad Ali is introduced. This is becoming like a study in emotional trauma. It's hard to believe how the space can contain any more hysteria than it's already had, but Ali is like nitroglycerin wherever he appears and tonight is no exception. He cools the audience down and starts in with one of his casual lines that make you feel like he's talking to you personally and not thousands. "You know, when they asked me to come here tonight, I was wondering who this guy Bob Dylan was. Then I show up and see that all these people come to pay money and I think this Bob Dylan must be something. I thought I was the only one who could pack this joint out. Did all you girls really come here tonight to see Bob Dylan?" Huge cheer explodes from the house. "All right, all right. He ain't as purty as me though, you'll have to admit. Now I just want to say that it's a pleasure to see such a turnout here tonight, especially when it's for the cause of helping a black man in jail. 'Cause everyone knows that you got the complexion and the connections to get the protection." Now here comes the real theatrics. One of Ali's aides walks out onto the stage carrying a telephone. Someone interrupts him at the microphone and whispers in his ear. The whole thing's been planned long in advance but it's being put across like it's just now happening. Ali pulls back from the man and grabs the microphone. "I've just been told that we have a special phone call right here that's been put through all the way from New Jersey by special order from the governor. We've got Mr. Rubin 'Hurricane' Carter on the phone and you're going to be able to hear his voice as he's speaking to me." Ali picks up the phone and Carter's voice can be heard as though it's coming through thousands of miles of submerged cable. It sounds much farther away than New Jersey but comes across totally clearheaded and eloquent. In fact, Hurricane Carter sounds more present just through his voice than most of the flesh-and-blood people here. The whole reality of his imprisonment and our freedom comes through loud and clear. "I'm sitting here in jail and I'm thinking that this is truly a revolutionary act when so many people in the outside world can come together for someone in jail." Ali is still aware of the audience and tries to lighten it. "Listen, Rubin, just promise me one thing. If you get out, just don't come and challenge me for the title, all right?" Rubin keeps on, not having to pay dues to an audience he's not even in front of. "On a more serious note, I'm speaking from deep down in the bowels of a New Jersey penitentiary." The dialogue keeps on and the audience is surprisingly intent on listening to Carter even with the anticipation of Dylan still in the cards. The solitary voice keeps sailing into every corner of the place like a phantom. The imagination is working double time conjuring up images of this man, locked up and speaking over a phone somewhere to an audience he can't even see. The phone call ends and Ali spins into his next piece of histrionics. "Now, ladies and gentlemen, I'd like to introduce to you tonight the next President of the United States." What's going on now? Nobody's prepared for this one. Dylan's backstage ready to go on for the second half of the show and Ali's up there pulling off a sleeper on everyone. "Now, you know that I'm known for making predictions. And if it hadn't been for this man getting me his own private plane at the very last minute, I couldn't have been here with you tonight." Ali leaves to the sound of massive booing as his white "candidate" appears from out of nowhere, looking like a cross between Howard Hughes and ex-mayor Lindsay. The booing keeps up and rises in volume and intensity as the man tries to speak a few words on his own behalf. It's a pathetic demonstration of bad timing and totally out in left field in terms of what the whole concert and tour has been about. The "next President of the United States" gets about three words in underneath the mounting din of disapproval, then slinks sheepishly off stage. By this time everybody's champing at the bit for Dylan. As usual he just appears. Nobody announces him, he simply sidles out there with his head slightly down, plumes shaking, white-face thicker than usual, and starts singing. He's always got the jump on the audience that way. He knows he's out there way before they do, and it gives him the edge every time. Now the place is storming again. He's rocking back on both heels, doing a duet with Neuwirth on "My Masterpiece." Wyeth's jackhammer drums are splitting the four-four time into smithereens. He has a right hand that's not to be believed. It comes down on the accent and then plays half a dozen little cluster strokes in between striking two or three cymbals for added color. A drummer like this usually goes totally unnoticed, since he lacks the obvious flash of the more athletic types who leap around the set using twice as many muscles as they need to. Howie sits there like he's driving a '58 Impala, cruising down the highway while his arms and legs follow the patterns with the minimum of effort.

Halfway through the set Baez has worked out a "groupie" routine where she dashes on stage in blue hot pants, blond wig, and high heels. The security guards go along with the gag and drag her off stage kicking and howling. Later, she pulls off a real showstopper by coming on dressed completely as Dylan. For a second you think you're seeing double for sure until she tries to sing like him. Then the whole thing dissolves. It's like an apparition up there. Both of them the same height, dark eyes peering out through white-moon makeup. The same straight-brimmed hat, black vests. There's so many mixtures of imagery coming out, like French clowns, like medicine show, like minstrels, like voodoo, that your eyes stay completely hooked and you almost forget the music is going on all this time. Down by the side of the stage, one of the cops is asking me which one is Dylan. I point to him up on stage. "You mean that guy with the funny hat? I was just talking to him!" He jabs one of his sidekick cops with his elbow. "Hey, I was just talking to Bob Dylan! I didn't even know it was him." His sidekick tells him to pipe down and listen to the music. Even the cops are tapping their blackjacks to the band now. The whole joint is like one huge humming organism. I thought I left this whole thing behind up in the far north of Maine, but here I am. No way to walk out on this one. No way for anyone to deny the power of this event.

Back in the dressing room Dylan rushes in ripping the harmonica brace off his neck, makeup dripping in long streams, red eyes popping out. "Rubin's been acquitted! He'll be out by Christmas!" I'm the only one there and I don't know what to say. We just stare at each other. I wish I had something to say back to him but I can't find a thing. Nothing comes out. He turns and darts back out the door.

excerpt from Shaman Hisses You Slide Back into the Night

ANNE WALDMAN

Poetry, according to Anne Waldman, "arises out of an oral yearning and attraction. I hear words before I 'see' them." Waldman was one of the Revue's "poets-in-residence"; as she writes in its preface, "Shaman Hisses You Slide Back into the Night" was created out of her journals, and forms a rich collage of impressions taken during the tour.

The poem is also an example of Waldman's use of "ethnopoetics," a determination to restore poetry to its oral roots and storytelling traditions. As such, "Shaman Hisses" draws on the texts of early civilizations and is built on uncomplicated rhythms. The ending, especially—"a man-woman a shaman a man who makes a song to heal"—makes use of a musical pulse, one that evokes the power of incantation. Throughout, Dylan, as the shaman figure, connects the author's dreams and memories, and is seen as the link to a forgotten oral culture.

Waldman is the author of *Iovis, Vow to Poetry, In the Room of Never Grieve: New and Selected Poems, 1985–2003* and other books; she directs the Jack Kerouac School of Disembodied Poetics at the Naropa Institute in Boulder, Colorado.

THE ROLLING THUNDER REVUE with Bob Dylan at its center was a notable phenomenon, a moving body of artistic individuals, traveling somewhat spontaneously from place to place to perform, interact, and make a movie. I was hired on—with Allen Ginsberg—as a kind of poet-in-residence-witness to contribute ideas to and make a brief appearance in what was to become the epic-length film *Renaldo and Clara*. The public shows were but one aspect, and a powerful one. Dylan on stage in white face, a feather in his hat, mouthing the syllables, surrounded by a host of impressive musicians and guest stars, was catalyst, energy-principle, the word-worker, and "technician of the sacred," i.e., shaman. This poem came out of a journal of the trip and includes a litany-homage to Dylan, overheard phrases, dreams, places, extrapolations, and other humming informations. We were a peripatetic tribe, a merry band of gypsies and a rock-and-roll show. It was a precious time, hard to capture, quintessentially American, a paradigm perhaps of how we'd all like to live—*on the road*, the poet's utopia.

November 11

> *jamming*
> this is about some kind of agreement that doesn't have to work
> you sit down & there you go there you go
> you take a solemn seat
> a room with no personality
> except the music
> something to drink, please
> everybody waiting on shaman
> He lights my Gitane   it breaks up   talking about Amiri Baraka now
> > & Neuwirth singing a touching song
> > > <<don't fall down>>
> for the highwire artist
> > &
> > > <<Please tell Allen Ginsberg to lighten up about the coke.>>
> > > (Roger grinning)

> a man's medley is reaping a benefit   man is medley-prone
> twofold   having two layers   composed of two of the same kind
> composed of 2 different kinds   twice as much   designed for 2
> twofold   in a pair   twice the quantity   twice the fold
> a duplicate & not a double boiler or potboiler so I suspect

(always the sense of a wide-eyed woman)
indefatigable
    Scarlet-The-Shadowy-Who-Saws-Strings (a musician)
    & Gelsey's sister horsing in the stalls
  & Madonna kicking her legs in the air   lets out a scream
    romping in the corridors
        fatigue
            more music
& conversing on the clean lines of Dr. William Carlos Williams

    Allen tossing & turning the night away
I sit inside the dawn
& now I lay me down in motel slumber

Niagara Falls I tell Allen about the thunder myth & how it hurts
we write poem for rock musicians' newsletter & they are suspicious
of a clever woman
so it's strictly thunder & brandy
& singing when we listen
turned & tuned in upon themselves
it's the boyhood I like & the confidence
& I do not place anything on top of this unit
I dream a writer's dream & Pasolini's murder
O the streets of Rome!
arms swinging
always the fault of a competent man
so this is what's happening:
no one to talk to but film crew & I have to talk
it's always talk
it's before I got born

so
it's this
& this is a memory:
many hours through blizzard I stared out super bus Phydeaux

saw Joni's musical fire & caught the air
I wish this in memorable space for the time we spent
we a tribe   no threat   love & assurance
this is not a lament only occasionally when it's lonely

I dream   a man dancing under tremendous rain clouds
I bolt awake in Niagara Hilton ready to face the music
spread it around
a movie gets made   Boston, Connecticut, Maine, Canada

shaman get to bed don't tarry
shaman let's have a miracle
shaman we made for each other?
shaman has it gotta be?
shaman take your hat off
shaman take your necklace off
shaman your mother is talking to you
shaman get behind the wheel
shaman take your watch off
shaman you're showing more interest than anyone
shaman you're tantamount to King
shaman tap your legs again
shaman stop tantalizing us
shaman you're a mischief maker
monkey shaman
shaman give me a souvenir don't yawn
impious shaman
it's implicit shaman
Elizabethan shaman
primitive shaman
no tryst shaman
camaraderie
tropology
& shaman you're too much you're making me pick up the tab
but

shaman's lady is lovely
shaman's lady adorns her body
shaman's lady is wise
shaman's lady sleeps on a bed of twigs
I'll give my words to shaman's lady
& she'll take them down the triple highway
so that

at night may I roam
against the winds may I roam
at night may I roam
when the owl is hooting may I roam

at dawn may I roam
against the winds may I roam
at dawn may I roam
when the first bird is calling may I roam

& into the heart may I roam
& against the dazzle may I roam
& for the music may I roam
when the tribe is calling may I roam

& gaping wide may I roam
& gaping wide may I roam

December

John Cage & Merce Cunningham are performing in a corridor in blue workshirts. I dream their gestures, like seaweed. John has a wand-twig which he attempts to plant on my head & I'm worried about not having enough <<soil>> up there. He then pats me soothingly and gives his marvelous great big glee laugh! Something about <<just keep it watered.>> Dylan comes to call and is made a bit nervous by these gents, they are taller than he is. But everyone is polite and it is understood that Dylan will collaborate and learn to dance by observing their gestures. I say to him <<You ought to write a song about Nijinsky.>>

Dream interrupted by phone ringing—it's Dylan! I'm staying at dance loft of Douglas Dunn on Broadway & Dylan is in the neighborhood & will come to call. He brings as a gift the big gold Nijinsky book with splendid photographs.

Dream: Dylan & <<Don>>

Allen Ginsberg & I go visit Dylan who's living in a series of cabins on a lake on the Lower East Side. He's seemingly in a dark mood for as we enter we find him attempting to climb into his guitar case like a coffin. Soothed by our sudden appearance he gestures toward some color Polaroid snapshots of his kids taken in the woods, which are balancing on the arm of a plush stuffed forest-green chair. We ask him about his work—his <<book>>— & he throws back a gruff laugh. As we go to let in more visitors including Clark Coolidge, Gregory Corso, and a girl desk clerk from the Hotel Boulderado, Dylan slips into one of the back cabins.

I take a walk in the woods and have a pearly white dagger handle thrown at me (which I catch) by a guy named <<Don>> who's standing on an embankment. He explains it is the <<speciality of these woods.>> Then he throws an entire dagger which stabs the ground at my feet & starts the whole place on fire.

Gregory & I have an interchange as the fire is raging. He comments that my leather pants are <<4 feet too long.>>

Everyone is frantic now trying to rescue books and papers & Bob himself who has locked himself into another one of the back cabins which is now in flames. I break the glass in the window & wake up.

mingle	calamity	moist	coda	gaping	adorns
tab	camaraderie	tantamount	gotta	leur	après
freeways	November	powder	patois	bust	weak
drenched	brass	loyal	Douglas	Connecticut	rain
lament	memorable	Phydeaux	Rome	Pasolini	unit
brandy	rock	Niagara	fatigue	indefatigable	prone
Roger	Gitane	seat	Ethan	Journal	shaman

wily   didactic   unshackle   away   deadlock   economy
Brazil   dream   dalliance   scores   chemistry   surly
diction   bleeding   clever   paint   red   multitudes
shadow   humble   river   shaman   yawns   holidays
obscure   tongue   die   ancient   children   horses
moving   tribe   gaping   decrees   urge   ally
river   further   navigating   shadow   imprinting   you
paragraphs   jaguar   chromium   timbrels   snaps   down
cleave   harbor   Chinese   modern   faun   wig
thousand   pains   shaman   ocean   obvious   centripetal
baby   guitar   gruff   compadre   American   meter
feather   brim   struts   kachina   hungry   clocks
Gitane   Rome   eyeballs   gesture   jive   sky
vocalize   vicissitudes   Danbury   coercion   bystander
gaping   kingdom   Egypt   Braille   Dot   meliorism
Byzantine   shaman   flickering   friction   moment   This

a man-woman a shaman a man who makes a song to heal
a woman-man a sha-man a woman makes this song to heal
a mannerism a shaman has a man who plays a drum to heal
a woman singing a woman dancing a woman makes a place a meal
a spinning man a clay a man a shaman takes your song to fuel
a watching woman-man a shaman watches & plans a song to make
     you well.
a showman makes a song so smart to hear it swell
a woman-man a he-she man takes this place to steal the show
a man-woman a shaman woman makes the song appeal
steel man inside shaman gesture in blue
salmon color woman skin make her skin a drum to heal

1976

excerpt from *The Force of Poetry*

CHRISTOPHER RICKS

Over the years, the leading critic of Dylan's lyrics has been Christopher Ricks, a scholar well known for studies of T. S. Eliot, Wordsworth and other poets. By supporting his appreciative view of Dylan with scrupulously close readings, he has given authority to the idea that the songs offer more than just the pleasures of a good line or two—they also reveal much about poetry and the nature of expression. In *The Force of Poetry*, for instance, Ricks examines Dylan's unique use of the English language, and the ways in which his songs help us understand contemporary English and its habits.

The first of these two excerpts is taken from "Clichés." A songwriter, one might think, is immediately placed at a creative disadvantage by singing common or stock phrases. Yet Ricks does not believe that a cliché is always undesirable, and shows how Dylan can alter clichés for the good—to take a familiar phrase and give it a new urgency and resonance. In "American English and the Inherently Transitory," Ricks discusses how the shifting, impermanent quality of language is best conveyed by American poets. Dylan's music is an apt example of this idea. Since many of his songs deal with impermanence—and recognize that there can be no true sense of finality—they often highlight what Ricks calls "the sheer egalitarian width of American English." In both pieces, Dylan is portrayed as a highly idiomatic writer, and one who intuitively understands the evolving contours of language.

Ricks teaches at Boston University and is the author or editor of several books, including *The State of the Language, Milton's Grand Style, Beckett's*

Dying Words and *Reviewery*. *Dylan's Visions of Sin,* his book-length study of Dylan's lyrics, was published in 2003.

BOB DYLAN'S art does not traffic in clichés, but it travels far and near by the vehicle of cliché. For what could a popular song be which scorned or snubbed cliché? Those who wish to disparage the art of Dylan ought to make sure, at least, that they go no further than did William James in his affectionate disparagement of William Shakespeare:

> *He seems to me to have a professional amuser, in the first instance, with a productivity like that of a Dumas, or a Scribe; but possessing what no other amuser has possessed, a lyric splendor added to his rhetorical fluency, which has made people take him for a more essentially serious human being than he was. Neurotically and erotically, he was hyperaesthetic, with a playful graciousness of character never surpassed. He could be profoundly melancholy; but even then was controlled by his audience's needs. . . . Was there ever an author of such emotional importance whose reaction against false conventions of life was such an absolute zero as his?**

FOR SHAKESPEARE, read Dylan? But would it anyway be the best thing for an artist to do with false conventions of life, or of language: to *react against* them?

Dylan has a newly instinctive grasp of the age-old instincts which created a cliché in the first place, and this is manifest on all the occasions when he throws new light on an old cliché, or rotates a cliché so that a facet of it catches a new light. At the same time, like the very unlike Geoffrey Hill, he often grounds his wit, humor, and pathos on an intuition as to how a cliché may incite reflection, and not preclude it, by being self-reflexive.

> *Well, ask me why I'm drunk alla time,*
> *It levels my head and eases my mind.*

---

* To T. S. Perry, 22 May 1910; *The Letters of William James* (1920), ii 336.

I just walk along and stroll and sing,
I see better days and I do better things.
> ("I Shall Be Free")

The phrase "seen better days" has itself seen better days—that would do as the definition of a cliché. But Dylan brings it from its past into his and our present, by turning it into the present tense, "I see better days"; and by marrying it to "and I do better things," he does a far better thing with it than usual. He eases it from a dim past into a bright present. He helps us see it in a better light, so that instead of its ordinary sad backward glance, there is a step forward, the strolling of an unaggressive intoxication which refreshes the flat old phrase. Just an accident? There are too many such happy accidents in Dylan's songs for them not to be felicities. Anyway, Dylan knows perfectly well that the tired phrase "seen better days" is usually imprisoned within its exhausted meaning—you can hear him sing the glum words in someone else's song on a tape from 1961. His own "I Shall Be Free" is free from the clichéness of its clichés, without getting proudly trapped in the illusion that you can free yourself from clichés by having no truck with them.

"I see better days" has its appealingly wide-eyed hopefulness. But Dylan can narrow his eyes, suspicious of too easy a sympathy with those who are dangerously wrong. So take the cliché "see through your eyes." Ordinarily, casually, it means putting yourself in the other man's place, seeing things through his eyes. Far harder to do than the easy saying of it would suggest. Possibly a very misguided thing to do, too. So Dylan wrests the cliché into the more stringent sense which goes with sharp-eyed suspicion: "seeing through things" as knowing their cunning and hypocrisy.

A world war can be won
You want me to believe
But I see through your eyes
And I see through your brain
Like I see through the water
That runs down my drain.
> ("Masters of War")

For the first verse had sung "I just want you to know / I can see through your masks"—the vigilant sense of "see through"—so that when we hear "But I see through your eyes," we see that it doesn't mean the usual blandly magnanimous thing ("from your point of view"), but the stubborn opposite: I see what your eyes are trying to hide. The cliché has been alerted, and we are alerted to its clichéness, seeing the words from a new perspective, a different point of view, and seeing penetratingly through them.

A cliché begins as heartfelt, and then its heart sinks. But no song about lovers and their hearts can afford to turn away from those truths which may never get old but whose turns of phrase have got old and gray and full of sleep. The trouble with a cliché like "take it to heart" is that by now it's almost impossible to take it to heart. Yet genius with words is often a matter, as T. S. Eliot said, of being original with the minimum of alteration, and such is one of the evidences of Dylan's genius.

> *So if you find someone that gives you all of her love*
> *Take it to your heart, don't let it stray . . .*
> ("I Threw It All Away")

"Take it to heart" becomes "take it to your heart," just enough to take it into the heartfelt; *it* stands for "all of her love," and there is the tiny touching swerve from "someone" in the previous line—you'd think it was going to be "So if you find someone that gives you all of her love / Take *her* to your heart," and take her in your arms.

"Make it new," commanded Ezra Pound from the captain's tower. It goes for clichés too. Not one is irredeemable, thanks especially to the grace of that self-reflexiveness, which, so long as it doesn't escalate its claim as if it were the only thing which art were ever preoccupied with, can rightly be valued as a great deal of late-twentieth-century criticism has valued it: as a power for wit, humor, true acknowledgment, thought, and feeling, in the renovation of the state of the language.

THE BEST American poets convey the poignancy of there being nothing final. Bob Dylan, for instance. "It's rapidly rerun all the time." With per-

sonal experience and with American technology in his mind's eye, Dylan
sings, in "If You See Her, Say Hello":

> Sundown, yellow moon
> I replay the past
> I know ev'ry scene by heart
> They all went by so fast.

There is no such thing as a video of the heart; replaying the past does
depend on knowing every scene by heart; but what makes this heartfelt is
the unspoken "And yet" between the lines:

> I know ev'ry scene by heart
> They all went by so fast.

"And yet they all went by so fast"; not "because they all went by so fast."
You'd have been right to expect that it would have been by their having
gone by so slowly that they were known by heart. It isn't that by some
audacity "fast" means "slow" (black English sometimes likes "bad" to
mean "good"); simply that you have to be quick on the uptake as Dylan
kisses the joy as it flies, in both senses of "it flies." Again, in "Is Your Love in
Vain?," he sings: "Are you so fast that you cannot see that I must have solitude?"—where "fast" means slow on the emotional uptake because of
being so determinedly ahead of the game. To say of someone, especially of
a woman, that she was "fast" was itself once a fast (indecorous and sugges-
tive) thing to say; but this sense has faded. The language, sensitive to these
glowings and fadings, is in sympathy with the love-experience which likewise has its glowing and fading.

"No time to think"? That is the title, and the refrain, of a Dylan song.
But in terms of the transitory language, it is not that there is no time to
think, but rather that one of the things that must be promptly thought
about is that there's no time. The refrain in this Dylan song is always "And
there's no time to think"—until the last verse. Then the refrain-line both
expands and contracts: it expands, in that it takes over the whole of the last
verse; it contracts, in that in the final end when it is time for the last

refrain, time so presses ("no time to lose") that instead of "And there's no time to think," the refrain is curtailed to "And no time to think."

> No time to choose when the truth must die
> No time to lose or say goodbye
> No time to prepare for the victim that's there
> No time to suffer or blink
> And no time to think.

The point is not that British English is insensitive to time (no language ever can be); rather that, because it gives a less important role than does American English to the ephemeral or transitory or obsolescent, there are certain effects occluded from it—effects which cannot as clearly be seen and shown from the vantage point of this one form of English as against the other. Effects, for example, of rueful admission; of American English itself conceding that much of it not only is not built to last, but is built not to last. Some love affairs are like that, and a poet or singer is likely to create something worth his and our while when his love affair with his medium, language, is intimate with this sense of what a "while" is (in language and in life) that something should be worth it. Dylan sings, as no English singer quite could,

> You will search, babe,
> At any cost.
> But how long, babe,
> Can you search for what's not lost?
> Ev'rybody will help you,
> Some people are very kind.
> But if I can save you any time,
> Come on, give it to me,
> I'll keep it with mine.
> ("I'll Keep It with Mine")

An English counterpart could have effected the spectral presence there of "keep ... time"; but could not have trusted British English so perfectly to

compact, as American English here does, the smallest social offer and the
largest offer of salvation:

> *But if I can save you any time . . .*
> *But if I can save you   anytime . . .*

It is not only the compacting of the two senses within the one line which
shows the sheer egalitarian width of American English, but the compacting within the second sense—"But if I can save you   anytime"—of the
most serious magnanimity with the casual largesse of conversational
acknowledgment—"any time" in that sense is pure American in the way in
which, socially at ease, it fosters such ease. It can even be printed as one
word in American English; when *sung* by Dylan it is not unmistakably two
words as it is when he prints his words. Within art (and the daily language
too can be used with art), "any time" gets some of its force, breezily fresh,
from the sense that it is not itself a phrase which could have figured in
American society and American English "*any* time."

"No particular word is apt to be final," said Ed Dorn. But *finally* to be
apt, that is a different matter; and the word "final" or "finally" stands differently to experience in American English for this very reason: that a consciousness of how little is final in words or out of them pervades the
saying. There is a gambling song by Dylan, "Rambling, Gambling Willie,"
which has the line: "When the game finally ended up, the whole damn
boat was his." The game didn't just end, it ended up (those verbal phrases
which Eliot deprecated); and it didn't just end up, it finally ended up. ("No
particular word is apt to be final.") There is a mild surprise at its being
possible to say "finally ended up" without sheer tautology; and yet it makes
perfect sense, since a gambling game is always ending and beginning
again, until the last hand, when it finally ends up; in this, the gambling
game is like the song itself, which is always coming to an end with each
verse (ending with the refrain "Wherever you are a-gamblin' now, nobody
really knows"), but does finally end up. Or again, Dylan sings to Ramona:
"You've been fooled into thinking / That the finishin' end is at hand." Not
one of those temporary or tentative ends, but the finishing end. In "All I
Really Want to Do," Dylan sings:

I ain't lookin' to block you up,
Shock or knock or lock you up,
Analyze you, categorize you,
Finalize you, or advertise you.
All I really want to do
Is, baby, be friends with you.

—where "Finalize" gets its pouncing power not just from being a word that was American before English (though Australian before American), but also—given the American sense of how finality fleets away, like an advertisement ("Finalize you or advertise you")—from being such a shrug of a word. And one might (in passing . . .) notice Dylan's dexterity with the phrase which is apocryphally taken as getting the Englishman into trouble, when he asks for an early call in the morning:

I ain't lookin' to block you up,
Shock or knock or lock you up.

The sly propriety tactfully, pregnantly, separates "knock" from "you up" for a couple of words; after all, the preceding "shock" would more suggest "shock you" than "shock you *up*" (though one of the things that Dylan is doing is giving a shake to the phrase "shake you up"). Nobody need feel embarrassed; it all goes by so fast.

The young Dylan in Greenwich Village. (Photo by Ted Russell / Corbis)

Dylan with Pete Seeger at a Mississippi hootenanny sponsored by SNCC in 1963. He is likely singing "Only a Pawn in Their Game," his eulogy for Medgar Evers. (Photo by Danny Lyon / Magnum Photos)

With Suze Rotolo, his first girlfriend in New York City and the subject of such songs as "Boots of Spanish Leather," "Ballad in Plain D," and "Simple Twist of Fate." (Photo by Ted Russell / Corbis)

Dylan performing at Carnegie Hall on October 26, 1963. (Southern Folklife Collection, University of North Carolina)

"Herein is a hell of a poet," Johnny Cash said of Dylan in the 1960s; their friendship was a long and respectful one. When Cash died in 2003, Dylan wrote, "He'll never die or be forgotten, even by persons not born yet—especially those persons—and that is forever." (Photofest)

ABOVE: *After his motorcycle accident in 1966, Dylan lived quietly with his family near Woodstock in upstate New York. (Photo by Elliot Landy / Magnum Photos)*

LEFT: *The 1966 world tour included a stop at Kronborg Castle in Denmark, the basis for Elsinore in Shakespeare's Hamlet. (Bettmann / Corbis)*

LEFT: *Bob Dylan and Muhammad Ali backstage during "Night of the Hurricane"—a benefit for Rubin "Hurricane" Carter held at Madison Square Garden on December 8, 1975, recalled in these pages by Sam Shepard. (Photo by Ken Regan / Camera 5)*

BELOW: *With friends and Beat poets Michael McClure and Allen Ginsberg, North Beach, San Francisco, 1968. (Photograph © Larry Keenan 1995)*

The Rolling Thunder Revue on stage during "Night of the Hurricane." From left: Joni Mitchell, Ritchie Havens, Joan Baez, Ramblin' Jack Elliott, Bob Dylan, and T-Bone Burnett. (Bettmann / Corbis)

In 2001, Dylan received the Academy Award for Best Original Song for "Things Have Changed." He performed the song live from Australia via closed circuit television. (AFP / Getty Images)

RIGHT: *Various collector's items, including a poster, on the left, for the Rolling Thunder Revue and, on the right, for Dylan's first solo concert in New York City, at the Carnegie Recital Hall on November 4, 1961. (Photo by Rick Maiman / Corbis Sygma)*

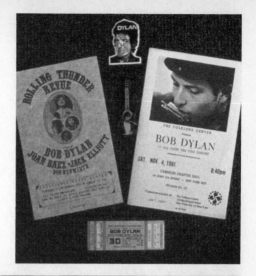

ABOVE: *Receiving a Kennedy Center Honor from President Clinton in 1997, alongside other recipients (from left): Charlton Heston, Edward Villella, Lauren Bacall, and Jessye Norman. (AP / World Wide Photos)*

RIGHT: *"You was the brother I never had," Springsteen said to Dylan upon inducting him into the Rock and Roll Hall of Fame; here, the two perform together in the mid-1990s. (AP / Wide World Photos)*

ABOVE: *Dylan poses for legendary rock photographer Lynn Goldsmith in 1981. (Photo by Lynn Goldsmith / Corbis)*

RIGHT: *Dylan at the age of sixty, during a photo shoot for* Love and Theft. *(Photofest)*

PART THREE

SAVED
(1979–1996)

"Take a harp, go about the city, thou harlot that
hast been forgotten; make sweet melody, sing
many songs, that thou mayest be remembered."

—*Isaiah 23:16*

Dylan: "I Learned That Jesus Is Real and I Wanted That"

ROBERT HILBURN

Dylan refers often to the Bible in his lyrics. Mostly, this is done in literary ways—as a source of imagery or to underscore a theme—that keep the overall tone of a song secular. After converting to Christianity in early 1979, however, Dylan began devoting his music to explicit, faith-inspired messages: "Of every earthly plan that be known to man / He is unconcerned / He's got plans of His own to set up His throne / When He returns." On tour that fall—performing a set comprised exclusively of new Christian songs—he even gave lengthy and hostile sermons to his audience. It might have been the most divisive time of his career, recalling the ambivalence that Newport and other events generated during the 1960s; some applauded Dylan's commitment to Christ, while others walked out of the concerts and ignored the new albums.

These and other matters were discussed when Dylan was interviewed by Robert Hilburn of the *Los Angeles Times* in November 1980. Hilburn has published several important interviews with Dylan since the late 1970s, and he was the first American journalist to speak with him about the conversion. Dylan talks freely about the events that led to his born-again process, including his enrollment in Bible study classes given by the Vineyard Fellowship, a Christian group based near L.A. At one point he interrupts Hilburn when asked about visiting Israel in 1971 to investigate his Jewish heritage. Yet Dylan's religious fervor has in many ways relaxed. These comments return to the idea that belief is a private concern, and he reflects on his attachment to his old songs, admitting that he'll return to nontheological subjects in his writing.

BOB DYLAN has finally confirmed in an interview what he's been saying in his music for eighteen months: He's a born-again Christian.

Dylan said he accepted Jesus Christ in his heart in 1978 after a "vision and feeling" during which the room moved: "There was a presence in the room that couldn't have been anybody but Jesus."

He was initially reluctant to tell his friends or put his feelings into songs but he was so committed to his gospel music by late 1979 that he didn't perform any of his old songs during a tour. He said he feared that they may be "anti-God."

Believing now that the old and new songs are compatible, Dylan sings such stinging rockers as "Like a Rolling Stone" alongside such born-again treatises as "Gotta Serve Somebody" on a tour that includes a stop Wednesday at San Diego's Golden Hall.

Sitting in his San Francisco hotel room before a concert, Dylan, whose family is Jewish, sat on a couch and smoked a cigarette as he discussed his religious experience for the first time in an interview.

"The funny thing is a lot of people think that Jesus comes into a person's life only when they are either down and out or are miserable or just old and withering away. That's not the way it was for me.

"I was doing fine. I had come a long way in just the year we were on the road [in 1978]. I was relatively content, but a very close friend of mine mentioned a couple of things to me and one of them was Jesus.

"Well, the whole idea of Jesus was foreign to me. I said to myself, 'I can't deal with that. Maybe later.' But later it occurred to me that I trusted this person and I had nothing to do for the next couple of days so I called the person back and said I was willing to listen about Jesus."

Through a friend, Dylan met two young pastors.

"I was kind of skeptical, but I was also open. I certainly wasn't cynical. I asked lots of questions, questions like, 'What's the son of God, what's all that mean?' and 'What does it mean—dying for my sins?'"

Slowly, Dylan began to accept that "Jesus is real and I wanted that . . . I knew that He wasn't going to come into my life and make it miserable, so one thing led to another . . . until I had this feeling, this *vision and feeling.*"

Dylan, the most acclaimed songwriter of the rock era, had been unwilling to grant interviews since the release last year of the gospel-dominated *Slow Train Coming* album, suggesting that anyone who wanted to know what he felt could simply listen to that work.

Though the album became one of Dylan's biggest sellers, many of his own fans felt confused, even betrayed: The man who once urged his audience to *question* was suddenly embracing what some felt was the most simplistic of religious sentiments. Furthermore, some critics argued, Dylan's attitudes were smug. Surely, many insisted, this was just another peculiar turn in Dylan's ever-shifting persona.

Even when he returned last spring with another gospel album, the less commercially successful *Saved*, rumors abounded that he had abandoned his born-again beliefs. But his shows here on this tour refuted that speculation. Ten of his seventeen songs on opening night were from the last two albums.

In the interview, too, Dylan stressed that his beliefs are deeply rooted: "It's in my system."

At the same time, Dylan showed that he hasn't lost his questioning spirit.

Asked about the political activism of fundamentalist Christian groups like the Moral Majority, he replied, "I think people have to be careful about all that. . . . It's real dangerous. You can find anything you want in the Bible. You can twist it around any way you want and a lot of people do that. I just don't think you can legislate morality. . . . The basic thing, I feel, is to get in touch with Christ yourself. He will lead you. Any preacher who is a real preacher will tell you that: 'Don't follow me, follow Christ.'"

DYLAN STILL SEEMED uncertain about discussing his religious views when he began the current tour here on November 9, sidestepping questions on the topic at a mini–press conference backstage after the opening show. But once he touched on the subject in the hotel interview, he spoke freely.

The interview centers on his new direction in music because that was the topic I wanted to pursue in the time he had before the show, but it'd be wrong to infer that Dylan has become a "Jesus freak" stereotype, interested only in discussing that subject. During the interview and during other, more informal chats, he spoke with equal zest about various matters, including the decision to do his old material again.

Some people would love you to go on stage and just sing the old songs, like a living "Beatlemania." Isn't there a danger in doing that? That's what Elvis Presley ended up doing.

Elvis changed. The show that people always talk about Elvis was that 1969 TV show, but it's not quite the same as when he did those songs in the beginning. When he did "That's All Right, Mama" in 1955, it was sensitivity and power. In 1969, it was just full-out power. There was nothing other than just force behind that. I've fallen into that trap, too. Take the 1974 tour.

It's a very fine line you have to walk to stay in touch with something once you've created it. . . . Either it holds up for you or it doesn't. A lot of artists say, "I can't sing those old songs anymore," and I can understand it because you're no longer the same person who wrote those songs.

However, you really are still that person some place deep down. You don't really get that out of your system. So, you can still sing them if you can get in touch with the person you were when you wrote the songs. I don't think I could sit down now and write "It's Alright, Ma" again. I wouldn't even know where to begin, but I can still sing it and I'm glad I've written it.

Why didn't you do any of the old songs on the 1979 tour?

I truly had a born-again experience, if you want to call it that. It's an overused term, but it's something that people can relate to. It happened in 1978.

I always knew there was a God or a creator of the universe and a creator of the mountains and the sea and all that kind of thing, but I wasn't conscious of Jesus and what that had to do with the supreme creator.

After you had the vision, I understand you attended a three-month Bible course at a church in Reseda.

At first, I said, "There's no way I can devote three months to this. I've got to be back on the road soon." But I was sleeping one day and I just sat up in bed at seven in the morning and I was compelled to get dressed and drive over to the Bible school. I couldn't believe I was there.

But you had already accepted Jesus in your heart?

Yeah, but I hadn't told anybody about it because I felt they would say, "Aw, come on." Most of the people I know don't believe that Jesus was resurrected, that He is alive. It's like He was just another prophet or something, one of many good people. That's not the way it was any longer for me. I had always read the Bible, but I only looked at it as literature. I was never really instructed in it in a way that was meaningful to me.

I had assumed that these feelings came to you at a crisis point in your life, a time when you were desperately needing something else to believe in.

No. I had gone so far that I didn't even think there was anything left. I thought, "Well, everybody has got their own truth." What works for one man is fine as long as it works for him. I had given up looking and searching for it.

But didn't you go to Israel? You seemed to be searching for some religious. . . .

Not really. If I was searching, it was just to . . . get down to the root reality of the way things really are, to pull the mask off. My thing was always to pull the mask off of whatever was going on. It's like war. People don't look at war as a business. They look at it as an emotional thing.

When you get right down to it, however, war—unless one people need another people's land—is a business. If you look at it that way, you can come to terms with it. There are certain people who make a lot of money off of war the same way people make money off blue jeans. To say it was something else always irritated me.

Did you start telling friends about it when you went to the Bible classes?

No, I didn't want to set myself up. I didn't want to reflect on the Lord at all because if I told people and then I didn't keep going, they'd say, "Oh well, I guess it was just another one of those things that didn't work out." I didn't know myself if I could go for three months. But I did begin telling a few people after a couple of months and a lot of them got angry at me.

Did you have any second thoughts when that happened?

No. By that time, I was into it. When I believe in something, I don't care what anybody else thinks.

Do you have any fear that what you're saying now may come back to haunt you in five years—that you aren't really committed?

I don't think so. If I would have felt anything like that, I think it would have come up to the surface by now.

But we've seen so many rock stars get involve with gurus and maharishis and then move on.

Well, this is no maharishi trip with me. Jesus is definitely not that to me.

When did you start writing the songs for Slow Train Coming?

After about two months. I didn't even want to sing them. I was going to give them to Carolyn [Davis, a singer on the current tour] and have her sing them. I thought maybe I could produce her record.

Why didn't you want to sing them?

I didn't want to step out there yet.

What did you think about some of the hostile reviews to Slow Train Coming?

You can't look at reviews.

Do you see how people could think some of the messages in the album were heavy-handed?

I didn't mean to deliver a hammer blow. It might come out that way, but I'm not trying to kill anybody. You can't put down people who don't believe. Anybody can have the answer I have. I mean, it's free.

What about the decision in 1979 to do only new songs?

I wasn't in touch with those old songs then.

But you're singing them again now.

It's like I said. This show evolved out of that last tour. It's like the songs aren't . . . how can I put it? Those songs weren't anti-God at all. I wasn't sure about that for a while.

Are the early songs still meaningful to you or do you just do them because people want to hear them?

I love those songs, they're still part of me.

Is there any way you can talk about the changes in your life, how the religious experience makes you feel or act differently?

It's in my system. I don't really have enough time to talk about it. If someone really wants to know, I can explain it to them, but there are other people who can do it just as well. I don't feel compelled to do it. I was doing a bit of that last year on the stage. I was saying stuff I figured people needed to know. I thought I was giving people an idea of what was behind the songs. I don't think that's necessary anymore.

When I walk around some of the towns we go to, however, I'm totally convinced people need Jesus. Look at the junkies and the winos and the troubled people. It's all a sickness which can be healed in an instant. The powers that be won't let that happen. The powers that be say it has to be healed politically.

What about some of the new songs? Some seem only remotely religious.

They've evolved. I've made my statement and I don't think I could make it any better than in some of those songs. Once I've said what I need to say in a song, that's it. I don't want to repeat myself.

So you can work from a larger canvas again?

Yeah, but that doesn't mean that I won't keep singing these songs.

Is music still important to you?

Music has given me a purpose. As a kid, there was rock. Later on, there was folk-blues music. It's not something that I just listen to as a passive person. It has always been in my blood and it has never failed me.

Because of that, I'm disconnected from a lot of the pressures of life. It disconnects you from what people think about you. Attitudes don't really make too much difference when you get on stage and play the guitar and sing songs. It's natural for me. I don't know why I was chosen to do it. I'm almost forty now and I'm not tired of it yet.

Love or Confusion?

LESTER BANGS

Dylan's first two Christian albums were perceived very differently—*Slow Train Coming* as one of his best studio efforts, *Saved* as one of the worst. *Shot of Love*, released in August 1981 and completing the Christian trilogy, drew a comparatively moderate response. Lester Bangs calls it "journeyman's work," an album with some high moments but still indicative of Dylan's post-1960s decline. Nevertheless, he takes a sympathetic look at the effects of fame and success on Dylan's career, and praises some aspects of *Shot of Love*, particularly Dylan's singing, even if he doesn't think the songwriting is of exceptional quality.

Bangs was a great and influential music critic whose prose tried to reflect the sounds of rock in some way. He edited *Creem* magazine for several years, wrote for the *Village Voice* and other publications and was performing with his own bands before his death in 1982. Two anthologies of his writing have been released posthumously: *Psychotic Reactions and Carburetor Dung* and *Mainlines, Blood Feasts, and Bad Taste: A Lester Bangs Reader*.

I WAS SITTING in a café on the Lower East Side the other night when I noticed that this bunch of guys at the next table were having a high old time ridiculing Bob Dylan. They'd sing some line from one of his mid-sixties albums in the ludicrous voice heard on the *National Lampoon* parody, which is, after all, not so different from Dylan's itself: "*Take* what you have g*a*thered from co *wa*-in-cidence!" Then they'd all laugh hysterically again.

I certainly have no reason to leap to his defense in 1981, but what struck me was that a lot of the lines they were quoting were *good lines*, probably the same lines they quoted reverently between tokes in college. The lines hadn't changed, but their former guru had, enough to be an outright joke now, so they were gonna have their revenge on prodigal Daddy. Can't say I blame them, having done the same thing myself after a few beers (although I did it to "Changing of the Guards"), besides which this sort of thing probably became inevitable the instant (somewhere around *Bringing It All Back Home*) he was first called a "poet," if not "the best poet" (I said in 1965), if not "the only poet" (my nephew shot back). "The sun's not yellow, it's chicken"???

If people are going to dismiss or at best laugh at Dylan now as automatically as they once genuflected, then nobody is going to know if he ever makes a good album again. They're not listening now, which just might mean they weren't really listening then either. In which case America's greatest troubadour since Hank Williams was never even heard as a songwriter but as a symbol. And given the way he used to talk to interviewers and press conferences, the older or younger onlookers who never really got it anyway might be more than justified in asking, "Yeah, but a symbol of *what*?"

Another thing that might occur to you if you're willing to go this far into cynicism is that, if in the sixties we really were ready to accept absolutely any drivel that dropped out of his mouth—a mercury mouth in the missionary times, say—then if he had released it in 1966 he just might have been able to get away with *Street-Legal*. (Why, symbol of the freedom to get away with things.)

Personally, I always kinda liked *Street-Legal*, certainly thought that it was at least interesting, because it was so muddled, fucked-up, the product of a genuinely tormented confusion which might eventuate in Dylan's actually making a great album again someday. Also, I'm a big fan of meaningless images strung together in rhyme, non sequiturs, that sort of thing. And I had hoped that *Shot of Love* would be either (a) *Street-Legal* redux, (b) a good joke, or (c) complete gibberish.

Now Dylan has confounded my expectations in a way he never did before: he's made a not half-bad LP, a *modest* sort of record, more playable than interesting. Perhaps that's as it should be, except for the fact that there was a certain shell of greatness around the diminished man who made

Street-Legal—in the grandiosity of its ambitions, no matter how grotesque the result, there was a reminder of what this guy once was capable of and, who knows, might still be.

What we have on *Shot of Love* is journeyman's work. But what sort of journeyman cranks out singing as soulful as that on the title cut, "Lenny Bruce," and "Every Grain of Sand"? As for the references to Jesus, implied or explicit, just play *Shot of Love* back to back with *Saved* and the difference in depth of feeling between the two albums, not only by Dylan but his backup singers, is unmistakable. So in his third Born Again album, the one where he begins to move away from Bible thumping, Dylan finally begins to sound like he might have been touched by or be singing to someone or something outside himself.

The trouble is that the material doesn't deserve more than a perfunctory reading. Most of the songs are sufficiently nondescript and inconsequential you'll find yourself sitting around playing the name-that-stolen-riff game. In the best and most deeply felt track, "Lenny Bruce," Dylan typically follows a horrendous line with one whose simple, soulful sincerity touches you if you'll allow yourself to be touched: "They stamped him and they labeled him like they do with pants and shirts / He fought a war on a battle-field where every victory hurts."

The listener's response to this is apt to be as confused as the record itself. It's not enough just to call it transitional, mediocre, hackwork—or just a joke, as some friends already have. *If* you suspend all expectations in any direction, and maybe if you even forget who made it, you can probably just throw *Shot of Love* on and enjoy a nice, bluesy, decidedly minor LP by a medium-level folk-rocker.

Of course, you're not going to be able to forget who made it. I'd still rather listen to *Shot of Love* than Steve Forbert. But there is an oil slick of involuted self-consciousness whose welters run so deep as to have become the man, and which can make even the best songs fairly unpleasant listening. Really, it's a wonder Dylan's not catatonic, and the only hope, which for me was promised by *Street-Legal*, is that someday, maybe four or five albums hence, the sickness and confusion will become so extreme, so hopeless, that he'll finally forget who he is and make a masterpiece.

Infidels

CLINTON HEYLIN

In the mid 1990s, Dylan biographer and rock journalist Clinton Heylin examined the archives at Columbia Records and published *Bob Dylan: The Recording Sessions 1960–1994*, an album-by-album guide to each of Dylan's studio records. A unique portrait of Dylan the recording artist, Heylin's book also noted the drawbacks of Dylan's approach to making albums. He usually cuts a song as informally as possible and is often indifferent toward which take is chosen for release—since, of course, he never views one particular performance as final product.

Specifically, Heylin targets 1983's *Infidels* as the ultimate example of Dylan's uneven studio method and, as such, his true lost masterpiece. He compares the released version of *Infidels* with a much different one that was originally recorded. Oddly, Dylan discarded his laissez-faire approach and repeatedly altered or replaced several of the album's tracks. Heylin calls into question most of these revisions, since they disrupt the thematic power and continuity of the album as first conceived, and offers a probing evaluation of Dylan's working habits.

A popular bootleg of the *Infidels* sessions, *Rough Cuts*, has long been in circulation. Heylin is a leading authority on Dylan, having authored the biography *Behind the Shades* as well as *Bob Dylan: A Life in Stolen Moments* and *Dylan's Daemon Lover*. His other books on pop music include *From the Velvets to the Voidoids* and *Bootleg: The Secret History of the Other Recording Industry*.

IT SEEMS DE RIGUEUR for major rock artists to have their very own "great lost album." The Beatles have their *Get Back,* the Beach Boys have *Smile,* the Who have *Lifehouse,* the Stones have *Black Box,* Richard Thompson has the original *Shoot Out the Lights.* Some, like Neil Young, have had more than their fair share of mightabeens. In Dylan's case, it is only really in the 1980s that his great lost albums begin to stack up. Indeed I'd be hard-pressed to name an album between *Shot of Love* and *Under the Red Sky* where the choice of tracks has not been dubious at best—and I base this only on what I have had the opportunity to appraise.

Never, though, would Dylan deal such a body blow to one of his own works as he did in June 1983, when he returned to Power Station to rework an album he had spent a month recording that spring. If Dylan had released the album Mark Knopfler and he had assembled in May, I don't doubt we would still be calling him to account for the omission of "Someone's Got a Hold of My Heart" (and probably "Tell Me"), and the inclusion of "License to Kill" and "Neighborhood Bully." Yet—I broach no discussion on this point—*Infidels* would have stood as Dylan's one true masterpiece of the eighties. The *Infidels* that was so nearly released comprised nine cuts:

1. Jokerman
2. License to Kill
3. Man of Peace
4. Neighborhood Bully (end of side one)
5. Don't Fall Apart on Me Tonight
6. Blind Willie McTell
7. Sweetheart Like You
8. I and I
9. Foot of Pride

Made in the days when albums came in two parts, the second side of this *Infidels* would have had no more than a half-dozen peers in Dylan's oeuvre (and only one since *John Wesley Harding*). The balance this album achieves would have been something quite different from its released twin. Side one concerns itself wholly with the state of a world on the brink. As false prophets stalk the world, the narrator fears the countdown to

Armageddon has begun. In this context even Dylan's song about a belea-
guered Israel, "Neighborhood Bully," comes across as more than just the
Zionist rant it has been painted as:

> BOB DYLAN: *"You [shouldn't] make it [so] specific . . . to what's going
> on today. What's going on today isn't going to last, you know? The bat-
> tle of Armageddon is specifically spelled out: where it will be fought
> and, if you wanna get technical, when it will be fought."*

On side two Dylan begins to turn his gaze on how individuals might
confront the End times. In the case of "Blind Willie McTell" its narrator
has become commentator, perhaps the last commentator, on human folly.
While Blind Willie McTell sings the world's eulogy, the narrator of "Foot of
Pride" is covered in "the dust of a plague that has left this whole town
afraid."

The other three songs deal with more familiar terrain, the narrator's
"women troubles," even though the backdrop of Revelation remains. In
"Sweetheart Like You," Dylan advises the subject that she should be at
home, "taking care of somebody nice," not in some dive (the Lion's Den?)
where you "gotta crawl across cut glass to make a deal." (There is a similar
sentiment expressed in "Someone's Got a Hold of My Heart," where, in the
face of a storm of biblical proportions—indeed the fall of Babylon revisited—the singer advises his love to "go inside and stay warm.") Deliber-
ately bringing the wrath of the politically correct generation down upon
himself, Dylan chooses to portray the women on *Infidels* as angels of the
hearth ("how sweet she sleeps, how free must be her dreams"; "She just sits
there, as the night grows still").

"I and I," the one song on this side only marginally tampered with on
the released album (though Dylan still took the two electric guitars, previously panned far left/far right, and "centered" them—what is this, Bob,
back to mono?), is the real jewel in this catalog of heartaches. The problems facing the kingdoms of the world are making the narrator feel afraid,
so he rises from his bed, leaving the strange woman who is lying there to
dream her untroubled dreams. The penultimate verse is a masterpiece of
understatement, echoing both a key element of Western folklore (the train
as ————, pick your own motif) and his own holy slow train. Dylan and

the band function as one preassembled unit throughout the song, Sly and Robbie* instinctively knowing exactly when they should be in your face and when they should be in the next room with the door closed.

Indeed Dylan's choice of musicians on *Infidels* was inspired. Alan Clark, alternating between piano and organ, did all that was required of him. Sly and Robbie as a rhythm section were designed to give the whole album "a contemporary feel" without sounding like they had used the dreaded click-track. Mark Knopfler's trademark licks, when dirtied up by Mick Taylor's blues-breaking leads, compounded the album's commerciality, yet were rooted in a sound very different from *Slow Train Coming*.

Unfortunately, this band's finest four minutes—perhaps Dylan's greatest studio recording of the eighties—the electric "Blind Willie McTell," still remains unreleased. As with the New York *Blood on the Tracks* sessions, Mr. Rosen† devoted a generous chunk (twenty-five minutes, no less) of *The Bootleg Series* to the lost *Infidels* tracks. Yet, just like *Blood on the Tracks*, of the five cuts scheduled for the original album (alternates of "Jokerman," "Sweetheart Like You," and "Don't Fall Apart on Me Tonight" plus the electric "Blind Willie McTell" and "Foot of Pride"), just "Foot of Pride" ended up on *The Bootleg Series*.

Which is not to say that the likes of "Tell Me" (a previously unknown take that, for once, is more than equal to its bootlegged counterpart) or "Someone's Got a Hold of My Heart" did not warrant air. Still, I would have thought the logical starting point for a collection of outtakes would be those songs that nearly made it, the songs Dylan pulled at the last minute. And there is no finer example than the electric "Blind Willie McTell."

What I cannot figure out—and maybe Greil Marcus, who finds the electric "Blind Willie McTell" "slick and lifeless," can tell me—is what one gets from the acoustic version on *The Bootleg Series* that one cannot get from the electric take, with interest. What Dylan gained in 1965 by "going electric" was the key element of interplay other musicians could bring to a song. Listening to Dylan play solo might be quite riveting, but the listener is entirely focused on one figure center stage. There is no shock of recogni-

---

* On *Infidels*, Robbie Shakespear plays bass and Sly Dunbar drums. —ED.

† Jeff Rosen, the producer of *The Bootleg Series*. —ED.

tion when a bass line crashes into a guitar riff, which bounces off the vocal that then . . . and so on.

The acoustic "Blind Willie McTell" is exactly the performance you would expect if someone hummed you the melody, read you the lyrics, and said it was a piano/guitar performance. If anyone else gave the same vocal performance, you might wheel out the tour de force plaque. But then, as Paul Cable put it (talking about the Gaslight version of "Moonshine Blues" of all things), "[It] is a reoccurring facet of Dylan [that] he seems to put everything he has into a song on one occasion, then you hear another version on a different tape and by comparison he chucks the whole thing away." Not that Dylan exactly throws the acoustic "Blind Willie McTell" away—it's just that the electric take explodes with surprises that in no way diminish the impact of the lyrics. From Dylan's cough on the second line as his voice strains to hit the note to the tap of (surely Dylan's) a shoe counting the band in on the second verse, the way he sings "can strut" like "instruct," the delightful harmonica interludes, that classic way Dylan has of running the words in the first half of a line together just so he has time to bend the remainder of the line to the beat in his head (an ol' bluesman's trick)—all work together to provide a breathtaking cut. And I ain't even mentioned the way the song builds to a crescendo like only a band can do. Sorry, Greil, you're wrong.

The other mea culpa omissions from the original *Infidels* were certainly "Jokerman" and "Foot of Pride." "Foot of Pride," which at least made *The Bootleg Series,* is a performance today's grunge-merchants would do well to take note of, being almost entirely devoid of a tune or structure beyond a beat. Yet it is everything a Dylan performance should be. There can be few Dylan songs with a vocal more difficult to emulate (good try, Lou, but no laurel), nor more densely packed imagery. To unravel the whole thing would take years—and isn't that the way it should be?

"Jokerman" is equally elusive. Indeed, *Infidels* remains a very wordy album (in either incarnation). The differences between the original "Jokerman" and the released "Jokerman" are far subtler than, say, "Idiot Wind." Yet they shed light on Dylan's recent tendency to overwork the finished article. Although from a literary point of view, it would be hard to fault Dylan's lyrical rewrites on "Jokerman," I've never found anything wrong with the lyrics in the first place (I mean, "no storebought shirt for me on my back, one of the women must sit in the shack and sew one" is a great rhyme scheme). Likewise, in cold isolation, the new vocal Dylan overdubbed in June, after the musicians had gone home (or, in Knopfler and Clark's cases, on tour), sounds perfectly fine, particularly with that great opening line— that is, until you A-B it with the original to contrast passion with artifice, heart and soul versus control.

What happened? Well, after twenty-two years of cutting his albums live, and one month at Power Station with Shakespear, Dunbar, Clark, Knopfler, and Taylor recording every song "as is," Dylan felt dissatisfied by something he couldn't quite put his finger on:

> We put the tracks down and sang most of the stuff live. Only later, when we had so much stuff... [did] I want to fill [the sound] up more. I've never wanted to do that with any other record... Did you ever listen to an Eagles record?... Their songs are good, but every note is predictable. You know exactly what's gonna be before it's even there. And I started to sense some of that on Infidels, and I didn't like it, so we decided to redo some of the vocals.

It wasn't just the vocals that Dylan "decided to redo." In a savage reappraisal of the work to date, Dylan scrapped "Foot of Pride" and "Blind Willie McTell." Despite having seven originals and some fourteen covers (including "This Was My Love," "The Green, Green Grass of Home," "Sultans of Swing," and "Angel Flying Too Close to the Ground") to perm from, Dylan replaced these two important works with just one four-minute "state of the nation" address. "Union Sundown" somehow manages to display the same kind of naïveté in economic matters as Dylan had previously displayed with Hal Lindsey's rabid religious tracts. Yet it seems to have been a song he refused to give up on. An early *Infidels* outtake has Dylan singing "dummy" lyrics over a familiar attack of two guitars and piano. The version Special Rider copyrighted, which presumably postdates this dummy version, has a full set of lyrics (including an astonishing lost verse about a man in a mask in the White House understanding the shape of things to come), but has only the most rudimentary, piano-driven accompaniment, almost suggesting a publisher's demo. Dylan subsequently combined some kind of basic track (cut with Knopfler, Taylor,

Shakespeare, and Dunbar, and possibly Clark) with an entirely new vocal, grafted on at the June mixing sessions.

That Dylan should waste his time on such a piece of tosh when he had the perfect partner for "Sweetheart," "Don't Fall Apart on Me Tonight" and "I and I" in "Someone's Got a Hold of My Heart" may well suggest just how perverse his artistic judgments have become.

"Someone's Got a Hold of My Heart" provides a rare example of Dylan reusing not just various lines but a song's entire sensibility to create a new song a couple of years down the line. Although this has been a popular technique for many fine singer-songwriters—Costello, Springsteen, and Young all spring to mind—Dylan almost never reworks a song he has discarded. The trash can is usually its final resting place, bootlegs notwithstanding. Not so, "Someone's Got a Hold of My Heart," from which Dylan extracted the core of "Tight Connection to My Heart (Has Anybody Seen My Love)" for *Empire Burlesque*. The version of the song on *The Bootleg Series* makes the debt very plain, being almost a prototype arrangement for the latter (the live version of "Tight Connection," performed in 1990, has even more in common with "Someone's Got a Hold of My Heart"). However, this is Holiday Inn land for Dylan and the band, with a vocal that sounds no more than a guide vocal, certainly not a serious attempt to replicate the passion of its bootlegged self (the oft-bootlegged outtake burning with the fever of unconsummated love).

Further evidence, were it needed, that Dylan's perspective on his own work went walkabouts at the end of the *Infidels* sessions (never to return?) can be found on the one cover from these sessions to become Columbia product. Willie Nelson's "Angel Flying Too Close to the Ground," according to a Dylan interview at the end of the June sessions, was actually under consideration for the album. As it happens Dylan decided to hide the song away on the first *Infidels* 45, although again only after a little resculpting had taken place. This time the "touch-ups" did not involve Dylan's (or Clydie King's) vocals, save for bringing them up in the mix. Some serious tampering, though, was done to the rhythm track, losing some great little drum rolls, while Dylan has also dubbed over his original harmonica breaks (both of them) with a couple of atonally inappropriate, not to say skewered, harp solos (the original version appears on the *Rough Cuts* bootleg CD). Dylan also fails to apply the fader early enough, allowing the song to go on a good thirty seconds beyond the point of no return.

In the post-*Infidels* world, Dylan would finally abandon his Luddite ways in the studio. Though he would still refuse to build tracks instrument by instrument, the vocal overdub became a useful way of disguising failing lung power. Ironically, Dylan's determination to cut *Infidels* live had done little to impair the songs. (A fascinating, nay unique, insight into Dylan's approach to recording can be found on a circulating tape of the *Infidels* ensemble working on "Sweetheart Like You" in the studio. On the basis of what sounds like an open-mike tape [sometimes the engineer runs a two-track "log" tape of a session using an open mike in the studio] and the two known outtakes of "Sweetheart," this was a song that, lyrically at least, took shape in the studio.)

If anything a live-in-the-studio album as strong as the original *Infidels* should have vindicated Dylan's previous working methods. Because of the superb unit he had been playing with, and the state-of-the-art twenty-four-track facilities the Power Station offered, Dylan could have easily masked any musical or vocal faux pas without restructuring the entire album. As it is, the reconfigured *Infidels* is a blurred Polaroid snapshot of an original self-portrait.

excerpt from *Song and Dance Man III*

MICHAEL GRAY

Michael Gray was among the earliest researchers of Dylan's art. His book *Song and Dance Man*, first published in the 1970s and updated twice since, was the first scholarly study of Dylan's use of poetic and musical allusion, anticipating the singer's status in the high-art world by some twenty years. By examining Dylan's relationship to rock, blues, folk, the literary tradition and many other subjects, Gray's criticism leaves no aspect of Dylanology ignored.

In *Song and Dance Man III* Gray spends a chapter on the connection between Dylan and the great Georgia bluesman Blind Willie McTell, devoting most of his commentary to "Blind Willie McTell," a song left off *Infidels* but later released on *The Bootleg Series Volume Three* ("perhaps Bob Dylan's greatest work of the 1980s," according to Gray). Gray traces the song back to the English ballad "The Unfortunate Rake" and McTell's "The Dyin' Crapshooter's Blues." A third standard, "St. James Infirmary," is also cited as a precedent to "Blind Willie McTell."

Gray then talks about the thematic similarities and differences between Dylan's song and its folk and blues models. Describing "Blind Willie McTell" as a work of singular emotion and complexity—"a running analogy between Old Testament and New World"—he shows how Dylan preserves many images from the "Rake," while often inverting or altering them to fit the vision of his song. Gray is a learned reader of poetry and draws on a variety of sources to explicate "Blind Willie McTell," revealing the breadth of Dylan's artistic debt while praising the song's originality.

A full text of "The Dyin' Crapshooter's Blues" can be found in *Song and Dance Man III*. Gray liberally footnotes his book; when not explicitly necessary, these notes have been omitted from this excerpt.

FOR ALL HIS EFFORTS, and the extraordinary quality of his talent, Blind Willie McTell's career was doomed. His return to recording in 1949 and 1959, for Atlantic and then for the small Regal label, were his first commercial sessions since his prewar recording career had petered out with a short, unhappy session in 1936 from which nothing had been released (and from which nothing survives). These postwar recordings produced a last small set of 78-rpm releases, but no success or revival of his reputation as an artist. By this time he was fifty-something, and to the extent that he was known at all, it was as an old Atlanta street musician.

McTell does not seem to have become embittered, though he drank, at times heavily, and suffered health problems. Though he still had family and friends in the places he traveled between, many of his friends were dead. Perhaps everything seemed to have come to nothing.

This may explain why McTell, like Dylan, became in his middle years a convert to Christianity, at first so keenly that he experimented with the process of preaching (as Dylan did onstage in the concerts of 1979–80). McTell gave a trial sermon at Mt. Zion Baptist Church on Piedmont Avenue in Atlanta, where he was a member and often played and sang on Sundays, and went so far as to get a license to preach.

He was also a member of the Tabernacle Baptist Church in Statesboro, performing here too—sometimes accompanying gospel quartets—and getting paid from the collection. At the radio station where he cut his 1949 sides for Atlantic Records, WGST in Atlanta, he sang spirituals on the air in the early 1950s, as he did for Radio WERD (then called WEAS) in the Decatur section of town.

His country gospel sides can delight: "Pearly Gates" (Atlantic), "Hide Me in Thy Bosom" and the second take of "Sending Up My Timber" (Regal) make a thrilling trio. McTell was alive with conviction for these performances, whereas the blues sides he was obliged to give Atlantic, and those he threw in for Regal too, tend to be tired reworkings of his old material. Similarly, of course, Dylan's "all-Christian" tour of 1979 showed him remarkably fired-up, while his newfound conviction inspired an explosion of songwriting more prolific than any since the mid-1960s.

McTell's great "Hide Me in Thy Bosom" sounds recorded behind fiberglass, yet at fifty-two he can still make you think of Presley's "That's All Right," his fluid vocal rides and swoops with such unloosed passion. There is also a particular, inspired piece of singing, early on in the track, that one can imagine Dylan coming up with. On repeats of the line later in the song McTell is content with the conventional "feed me, feed me, feed me," which follows the rhythm and gets its excitement from sheer insistent repetition, but the first time around he hits instead a long, sustained, utterly unpredictable "feeeeeeeeeeeeeeeeed me," cutting across the rhythm and holding a note between the expected two. Dylan has done much the same in concert with the chorus of "Knockin' on Heaven's Door," turning "knock knock knocking" into "kno—ckin'," and you can imagine him doing the same in the course of a live performance of something from *Slow Train Coming* or *Saved*.

The themes they share at this point in their lives are evangelically Christian. "Sending Up My Timber" states the "Are You Ready?" theme, performed with the same crusading spirit as the *Saved* sessions generally:

> *It may be morn or night or noon*
> *But I do now know just how soon . . .*

while McTell's Library of Congress session gives us a reminiscence about "those old-fashioned hymns" his parents used to sing around the house before going out to work in the fields, one of which carried the same message:

> *Are you just well to get ready? You got to die, you got to die*
> *Just well to get ready, you got to die*
> *It may be tomorrow, you can't tell the minute or the hour*
> *Just well to get ready, you got to die, you got to die.*

Most interesting here is the switch from the righteous "you" in "Just as Well Get Ready, You Got to Die" to the affecting "I," in "I Got to Cross the River Jordan":

I got to face my dear Saviour,
I got to face Him for myself
There's nobody here can face Him for me
So I got to face Him

And I got to work out my soul salvation . . .
There's nobody here can work it out for me . . .

I got to lie in some old lonesome graveyard
I've got to lie there by myself
There's nobody there can lie there for me
Lord, I got to lie there for myself. *

McTell sings this without melodrama, with great simplicity, such that we feel his faith to be a struggle: a summoning of courage a hairsbreadth from the bereft. It clinches the case of Blind Willie McTell's ability to lament for us—to be the artist on to whose shoulders Bob Dylan can place the weight of his visionary requiem for America's past and everybody's future.

So does "The Dyin' Crapshooter's Blues." This is Blind Willie McTell's personalized version, one among a whole sequence of songs, based on the traditional English ballad "The Unfortunate Rake" and which also becomes the black standard "St. James Infirmary." "The Unfortunate Rake," "St. James Infirmary" and "The Dyin' Crapshooter's Blues" all end up wondrously transmuted into "Blind Willie McTell."

This is the nineteenth-century broadside version of "The Unfortunate Rake," as sung by the distinguished British folk singer and folklorist A. L. Lloyd:

As I was a-walking down by St. James' Hospital
I was a-walking down by there one day
What should I spy but one of my comrades
All wrapped up in flannel though warm was the day

---

* Blind Willie McTell, "Just as Well Get Ready, You Got to Die" and "I Got to Cross the River Jordan," Atlanta, November 5, 1940; issued on *Blind Willie McTell: 1940*, Melodeon.

> *I asked him what ailed him, I asked him what failed him*
> *I asked him the cause of all his complaint*
> *"It's all on account of some handsome young woman*
> *'Tis she that has caused me to weep and lament*
>
> *"And had she but told me before she disordered me*
> *Had she but told me of it in time*
> *I might have got pills and salts of white mercury*
> *But now I'm cut down in the height of my prime*
>
> *"Get six young soldiers to carry my coffin*
> *Six young girls to sing me a song*
> *And each of them carry a bunch of green laurel*
> *So they don't smell me as they bear me along . . ."*
>
> *"Don't muffle your drums and play your fifes merrily*
> *Play a quick march as you carry me along*
> *And fire your bright muskets all over my coffin*
> *Saying: 'There goes an unfortunate lad to his home.'"*

The last verse becomes, in other versions, a chorus repeated between each verse, and its instructions about the fife, drum and march are more usually these, as in the version "The Trooper Cut Down in His Prime" sung by Ewan MacColl:

> *Then beat the drum slowly and play your fife lowly*
> *And sound the Dead March as you carry me along . . .*

(Bob Dylan quotes from this in his *Oh Mercy* song "Where Teardrops Fall":

> *We've banged the drum slowly and played the fife lowly*
> *You know the song in my heart*

so neatly suggesting that the song in his heart is the Dead March, and then, with a faith akin to McTell's in "I Got to Cross the River Jordan," looking beyond death in hope of resurrection:

In the turning of twilight, in the shadows of moonlight
You can show me a new place to start).

The first extant text of "The Unfortunate Rake" wasn't published until 1909, though it dates from 1848, when it was written down in County Cork from the performance of someone who'd learned it in Dublin in 1790. That's one account, anyway; another says that "The earliest text seems to be the eighteenth-century 'Buck's Elegy,' set in Covent Garden."* Either way, it was by oral transmission that this 200-plus-year-old song traveled around Britain and Ireland and to America, where it split into white versions and black.

BY THE TIME Alan Lomax was listening to the Hemphills' fife and drum music in Mississippi, and Blind Willie McTell was singing an early version of "The Dyin' Crapshooter's Blues" to Lomax's father in a hotel room in Georgia in 1940, "St. James Infirmary" had become a standard of sorts, combining its own version of "The Unfortunate Rake" and of that New Orleans post-funeral music. The classic Dixieland version of the song is by Jack Teagarden, from 1941, but such renditions had been popular through most of the 1920s and 1930s: so much so that there was a long period during which, just as all early 1960s British beat-groups had to know "Got My Mojo Working" (we all wondered what a mojo was, but didn't like to ask), so it was more or less obligatory for American jazz bands, black and white, to know "St. James Infirmary."

Blind Willie McTell himself sings it, alongside "The Dyin' Crapshooter's Blues," during his 1956 "Last Session." His performance languishes among the unissued items.

What all these songs do is allow some articulation of a fundamental human problem: how to face death. The use of two narrators allows an interplay, or balancing, between different strategies. In the early versions, the dying hero or heroine is often preoccupied with a sense of shame or

---

* From, respectively, the sleeve notes to the album *The Unfortunate Rake: A Study in the Evolution of a Ballad,* various versions by various artists, compiled and edited by Kenneth Goldstein, Folkways Records (New York, 1960); and from Roy Palmer's *The Oxford Book of Sea Songs* (1986).

unworthiness, while the person who comes upon them is confronting imminent loss, the impermanence of comradeship, the responsibility of bearing witness to death. The later versions mediate between these feelings of tenderness, sorrow and grief for another, and the dying person's own need to banish the fear of death by making light of it. This duality is especially heightened in Blind Willie McTell's "The Dyin' Crapshooter's Blues," which begins with that long and attentive spoken account of caring for the dying friend, of the daily care over a period of weeks, the ambulance ride, the father on hand, the sorting out of practicalities—followed by the reductive mythologizing of those practicalities by the careless victim ("Let a deck of card be my tombstone" . . . "Life been a doggone curse"), and culminates in the first narrator's submission to the second's show of indifference:

> *Throw my buddy Jesse in the hoodoo wagon*
> *Come here mama with that can of booze . . .*
> *With the Dyin' Crapshooter's Blues.*

This is a very similar ending to the conventional one for "St. James Infirmary":

> *Well now you've heard my story*
> *Have another shot of booze*
> *And if anyone should happen to ask you*
> *I got the St. James Infirmary Blues.*

What makes "St. James Infirmary" different is that it almost has three narrators. That is, the first narrator meets not a dying second narrator but a healthy one, who is in turn contemplating death of a third character (his lover). Because death has already arrived in this construction, though only just, the lover doesn't get to speak, but its effect is to make the second narrator meditate upon his own mortality much like the dying second narrators of all the other songs.

THE QUESTION of how many elements of the "Rake" cycle Dylan imports into (it's tempting to say "retains in") "Blind Willie McTell" is only one of its aspects, but it's a starting point: it stresses their shared central purpose. Bob Dylan's rich and complex song, with a melody that winds across the path of the "St. James Infirmary" tune, is also about the problem of how to face death, extended onto the grandest of scales. While implicitly it mourns the death of McTell, it struggles with the problem of how to face, to witness, to confront, the world's death rather than an individual one.

Like the "Rake" songs, there are two narrators, and for the same reason, to summon more than one strategy in the face of death. In the Dylan song we find a first narrator who witnesses and a second who, says the first, could witness better.

> *Seen the arrow on the doorpost*
> *Sayin' this land is condemned*
> *All the way from New Orleans to Jerusalem*

> *I traveled through East Texas*
> *Where many martyrs fell*
> *An' I know no one can sing the blues like Blind Willie McTell.*

> *I heard that hoot-owl singin'*
> *As they were takin' down the tents*
> *The stars above the barren trees was his only audience*

> *Them charcoal gypsy maidens*
> *Can strut their feathers well*
> *But nobody can sing the blues like Blind Willie McTell.*

> *See them big plantations burnin'*
> *Hear the crackin' of the whips*
> *Smell that sweet magnolia bloom and see the ghosts of slavery ships*

> *I can hear them tribes-a-moanin'*
> *Hear that undertaker's bell*
> *Nobody can sing the blues like Blind Willie McTell.*

> *There's a woman by the river*
> *With some fine young handsome man*
> *He's dressed up like a squire, bootleg whiskey in his hand*
>
> *There's a chain gang on the highway*
> *I can hear them rebels yell*
> *And I know no one can sing the blues like Blind Willie McTell.*
>
> *Well God is in His heaven*
> *And we all want what's His*
> *But power and greed and corruptible seed seem to be all that there is*
>
> *I am gazing out the window*
> *Of the St. James Hotel*
> *And I know no one can sing the blues like Blind Willie McTell.*

What a song! And let me say at once that its opening verse parallels the beginning of the "Rake" songs. Where they see a doomed comrade wrapped in white linen and cold as the clay, Dylan sees the same thing on the grand scale: he has

> *. . . seen the arrow on the doorpost*
> *Sayin' this land is condemned*
> *All the way from New Orleans to Jerusalem.*

In the next lines, he pluralizes coming upon "one of my comrades," remembering that "many martyrs fell," and expressing a sympathy with other unwilling recruits whose presence is felt in this pageant of suffering and struggles: the tribes conscripted from Africa as slaves, the chain gangs forced to build the highways, the rebels forced to fight. And between "All the way from New Orleans to Jerusalem" and "I traveled through East Texas" he sets up echoes of "The Streets of Laredo," in which the narrator "born in South East Texas" says "I've trailed from Canadee down to old Mexico." Instead of a crowd round the bedside and people to "sing a song,"

> *I heard that hoot-owl singin'*
> *As they were takin' down the tents*
> *The stars above the barren trees was his only audience.*

In parallel with "the women from Atlanta," "them flash-girls," or "pretty maidens,"

> *Them charcoal gypsy maidens*
> *Can strut their feathers well . . .*

The flowers are here too. The "Rake" songs have "green laurel," "white roses," "red roses," "wild roses," "green roses," and "those sweet-smellin' roses"; they also have, in "The Streets of Laredo," a Southern setting in which "the jimson weed and the lilac does bloom." In "Blind Willie McTell" we see a southern setting in which we "smell that sweet magnolia bloom."

Dylan's

> *With some fine young handsome man*

matches "St. James Hospital's" "with them handsome young ladies" and "The Unfortunate Rake's" "some handsome young woman," and he unites the "Hamilton Hotel" of McTell's narrative with the conventional "St. James Infirmary" in his own, perfectly placed "St. James Hotel." Dylan also uses "the window," from the James Baker/Doc Watson variant. This begins with the window:

> *It was early one morning I passed St. James Hospital*
> *. . . I looked in the window . . .*

and Dylan ends with it. I can't quite be certain, on either of the versions of "Blind Willie McTell" that have circulated, that Dylan sings

> *I am gazin' out the window . . . ,*

which reverses the old Texan version and places Dylan as the dying inmate, quietly appropriate to the theme that we are all facing imminent death; it's always enticingly close to

> *I am gazin' at the window . . . ,*

which would leave it nicely ambivalent as to which side of the glass Dylan is on as he bows his head and cries, while staring at the bleakness of the futureless future.

Dylan can also use the same language as the "Rake" cycle but undermine its meaning. That "fine young handsome man,"

> *He's dressed up like a squire . . .*

which throws a shadow across his fine and handsome aspect: "dressed up like" suggests both the counterfeit, weighted down by that "bootleg whiskey in his hand," and the vain, fluffed up by the resonance of the earlier, matching "strut." Even the "sweet magnolia" sounds quite unlike the "sweet-smellin' roses" of the earlier songs. I don't know why, since Dylan adds nothing more beyond the phrase itself, yet we smell it as overripe and sickly. Where once the flowers were there to cover the smell of corruption, in Dylan's song they give off the smell of corruption themselves.

Falsity, vanity and corruption compound cruelty and pain. Everywhere people are fallen, in chains, under the whip in this maelstrom of history. I say "maelstrom" because though it's been said that "Blind Willie McTell" rolls backward through America's past, in truth it offers no such consistent reverse chronology and its vision is not limited to American terrain, though it returns to it time and again, not least by the device of Blind Willie McTell's omnipresence.

This may disappoint the need for neatness but it is a strength of the song that most of its images evoke more than one era: more than one time *and* place, while pressing upon us, time and again, a running analogy between Old Testament and New World.

It begins at the beginning. The "arrow on the doorpost / Sayin' this land is condemned" flickers with a picture of the marking out of Jewish houses in the pogroms of the 1930s and with the daubing of the doors of plague victims in medieval Europe, but it harks back, as both these later scenes must, to the first occasion to yield such an image: the time of the Passover, when the first-born in Egypt were slain in the night by God, after the people of Moses were instructed to mark a sign on their doorposts in lamb's blood so that death might pass over and spare their children: "take of the blood, and strike it on the two side posts and on the upper door post of the houses," as God instructs Moses in Exodus 12:7.

What's so striking in Bob Dylan's lyric, what gives us the sense that poetry is at work, is that Dylan can use this as the opening of a song that holds out no hope that anyone shall be spared the destruction coming in *our* night. There may be a sign on the doorpost but whose first-born— whose future—is to be spared this time, now that the land has been

> *. . . condemned*
> *All the way from New Orleans to Jerusalem?*

We reach America explicitly enough, of course, when we get to "East Texas, where many martyrs fell." Across the border from New Orleans, Louisiana, it sticks in the memory as a stronghold of the Ku Klux Klan: a place where black victims were untold martyrs and where the same racist attitudes linger still. Yet "martyrs" has other, primarily religious, connotations. The word is thrown in like a spanner, to wobble us off our course of easy assumption about the focus of the song. The word "fell" has a distracting quality here too, somehow calling attention to itself by its declamatory vagueness.

"Takin' down the tents" gives us another glimmer of the Israelites, now on their way out of Egypt, but suggests too the medicine shows, the carnival tents that linger into the twentieth century from an older America. McTell and Bob Dylan both claim a bit of tent-cred in their early days— and for someone whose experience of it was mostly in the mind, Dylan wrote of it in thrillingly energetic detail in "Dusty Old Fairgrounds," where we feel the pitching and dismantling of the tents as a routine, an activity, a part of life, all through the song. He claims a similar intimacy with this life when he discusses his own (now lost) poem "Won't You Buy a Postcard?"

in 1962.* The Hawks had medicine show experience; Elvis's manager, Colonel Parker, was an old carnie trooper. Even as recent a figure as the contemporary blues singer Robert Cray recalls that in the early days he and his musicians hit the road in an old truck and camped overnight in tents as they traveled (roaming the country like "charcoal gypsy maidens"). But "them charcoal gypsy maidens" also conjures up nubile black girls in 1920s cabaret routines, shimmying through the floor shows of smoky nightclubs in black and white movies: the sort in which the blues singers never get a look-in, because "sophisticated" jazz combos deliver slicker, jollier routines more compatible with Hollywood sensibilities.

There is *almost* nothing ambiguous about time or place in the next section of the song, in which time is running backward from *Gone with the Wind* to the roots of *Roots*: yet the word "tribes" arrives strikingly here. It has a rigor that cuts across the assemblage of shorthand images of the Antebellum South. It dislocates the expected chain of words as "martyrs" does earlier.

Aptly, "them tribes" come pouring in across the very center of the song: aptly because the analogy clutched in this double image, the analogy between the twelve tribes of Israel and the African tribes brought over on the slave ships, is the central analogy Dylan draws all through the song. It is, moreover, the classic analogy drawn by the oppressed American blacks themselves, all the way through till at least Blind Willie McTell's generation, as they compensated themselves for the miseries of this life by looking forward to justice in the next and reading the Bible's accounts of the struggles of the Israelites in order to voice their own aspirations. We shall overcome some day. That's why I'm sending up my timber. And I know no one can sing them hymns like Blind Willie McTell.

The "woman by the river" might equally be biblical or Mississippian. She's timeless. The "squire" suggests the seventeenth or eighteenth century, but "dressed up like a squire" adds in all those nineteenth-century Southern landowners striding their estates in high boots and frilly shirts while the blacks, almost invisible, worked the land. The "bootleg whiskey in his hand" can equally smell of the stills in the hills (where they ain't paid

---

* *Folksinger's Choice*, WBAI Radio, New York, probably recorded January 13, 1962, and probably broadcast March 11, 1962.

no whiskey tax since 1792) or of Prohibition Chicago, another milieu the old blues singers lived and worked in. The "chain gang on the highway" must keep us in that recent past but the "rebels," whoever else they must be, insist on yelling to us from the American Civil War.

This multi-layering of the pageant takes its cue from the opening verse: crucially to our whole understanding of the song, "All the way from New Orleans to Jerusalem" must be capable of pitching us both backward and forward—back from the New Orleans of now or of McTell's generation, the New Orleans where you might say black American music found its feet, to the Jerusalem of Bible days; and forward to the new Jerusalem dreamed of but now doomed not to be: dreamed of but "condemned."

One of Dylan's inspired touches here, in that nigh-perfect penultimate stanza, is to underscore his tolling of doomsday by alluding to, and then contorting, those well-known lines of optimism and hope,

> God's in his Heaven—
> All's right with the world.

The twisting of this fresh-faced couplet into the brutish modernism of

> Well God is in His heaven
> And we all want what's His

could hardly be bettered: Dylan uses the mugging energy of the bare greed he describes to give his lines a slashing economy, hitting us with the switch from the lost innocence of the original.

Those lines are by Dylan's old friend Robert Browning—from the first section, "Morning," of the dramatic poem "Pippa Passes"—and Dylan's song takes from the poem more than just this one, expertly handled, crude allusion. To know the context is to see that Dylan snatches away not just the gentleness, nor even primarily the reassuring stasis or apparent permanence of those often-quoted lines, by replacing Browning's contentment with the bleakness of "But power and greed and corruptible seed seem to be all that there is." More especially Dylan contradicts Browning's vision of the world as fresh and pure because *young*, because purged by the coming of spring. This is the context:*

> *The year's at the spring,*
> *And day's at the morn;*
> *Morning's at seven;*
> *The hill-side's dew pearled;*
> *The lark's on the wing;*
> *The snail's on the thorn;*
> *God's in His heaven—*
> *All's right with the world.* *

Dylan's "seed" deftly acknowledges this context, while shriveling it away at once into the biblical rhetoric of "corruptible seed"—a latency that promises only further decay in a world already old and exhausted. Dylan turns morning into mourning, replacing the lark on the wing with the hoot-owl in the barren trees.

While Dylan sounds the undertaker's bell, the song itself never shrivels: it moves but it certainly doesn't depress. It examines the problem of how to face death but it tingles with life. The black girls, in that lovely, eccentric construction, strut their feathers. The song presses a sense of our senses upon us. *Blind* Willie McTell, his other senses heightened, is never far away. Yet true to McTell's uncanny visualizing spirit, *seeing* is insisted upon. In one verse alone we see, hear, smell and see again. The first word of the song is "seen"; the end of the song finds him "gazing." All through, spooky as the plangent, coiling music, Dylan's sixth sense emits its vibrant, probing beam.

Out of death, life arises. Out of bodily pain, the triumph of the spirit (pain sure brings out the best in people, doesn't it?). Out of singing the blues, compensation: even joy. Dylan celebrates, in this song—as Blind Willie McTell does in "The Dyin' Crapshooter's Blues." The work of art, as ever with Bob Dylan, is the recording, not the words on the page: but the words on the page demand from Dylan, and receive, two of his most focused performances: paying tribute to McTell's artistry, he rises to the occasion with the excellence of his own. What a song!, you say when you

---

*"Pippa Passes" (Part I, "Morning"), which formed part of *Bells and Pomegranates*, published in sections, London, 1841–1846.

read the lyric. What a record!, you say when you hear the belatedly issued performance.

This is the spookiest important record since "Heartbreak Hotel," and is built upon the perfect interweaving of guitar, piano, voice and silence—an interweaving that has the space for the lovely clarity of single notes: a guitar string stroking the air here, a piano note pushing back the distance there. And if anything, the still-unreleased performance is even better, for its more original melody (less dependent upon the conventional "St. James Infirmary" structure) and its incandescent vocal, which soars to possess the heights of reverie and inspiration. No one can sing the blues like Blind Willie McTell, but no one can write or sing a blues like "Blind Willie McTell" like Bob Dylan.

A Short Life of Trouble

SAM SHEPARD

In 1987 Sam Shepard, a member of the Rolling Thunder Revue and the co-author, with Dylan, of the song "Brownsville Girl," published a one-act play in *Esquire* featuring two characters named Sam and Bob. Taking place in a single afternoon, the play depicts a loose interview that focuses on Bob's early life as a musician.

Though they discuss several subjects, Sam and Bob's central obsession is the death of actors and musicians, many of whom died prematurely or had their careers blighted by disease. James Dean's car crash is frequently mentioned and recurs throughout the play, like a dire leitmotif. At the end of the piece, the two consider innocence lost and youthful vitality; the play seems to be a kind of rumination, often comic, on the folklore of dead artists, which is particularly relevant since Bob has had a famous death scare of his own.

Whether the play should be read on its own as an interview with Bob Dylan is a separate matter. Certainly, the text and stage directions capture Dylan's restive deportment, manner of speech and wry sense of humor. The most tempting section to read as real life—aside from the passage on visiting Woody Guthrie—is the end, where Bob discusses his motorcycle accident at length. Dylan has always been hesitant to talk about the incident, while here Bob reveals the cause of the accident as well as what he learned during his recovery. Containing, in all likelihood, both fact and fiction, the best answer to the veracity question comes from the play itself: "BOB: Make it up. SAM: Well, there's certain things you can't make up. BOB: Like what? SAM: Certain turns of phrase."

SCENE: *In the dark, a Jimmy Yancey piano solo is heard very softly, floating in the background. Soft, blue, foggy light creeps in, extreme upstage, revealing a large, weathered brick patio bordered by shaggy grass upstage and opening out to a distant view of the Pacific Ocean. The distant rhythmic splashing of waves is heard underneath the piano music and continues throughout the play, always in the background. The only set piece onstage is a round redwood table with a big yellow umbrella stuck in the middle of it and two redwood benches set across from each other at the table. The table and benches are set down left (from the actors' point of view).*

As the light keeps rising, a short, skinny guy named Bob is seen center stage dressed in nothing but a pair of light-green boxer shorts. His arms are clasped across his chest with each hand gripping the opposite shoulder, as though warding off the cold. He turns in a slow circle to his right and then repeats the circle to the left, looking out to the ocean as his gaze passes it. He stops, facing audience, covers his face with both hands, then rubs his eyes and draws his hands slowly down his cheeks to his chin. His mouth drops open and his head slowly drops back on his shoulders to stare at the sky. He holds that position. Piano music stops abruptly. Sam, a tall, skinny guy dressed in jeans and a T-shirt, carrying a tape recorder, several notebooks, a six-pack of beer, enters from right. He stops. Bob drops his hands and stares at Sam. Pause. Sound of distant waves continues.

SAM: Ready?

BOB: Yeah, I just gotta make a couple phone calls first.

[*Bob moves toward stage right, then stops.*]

BOB: Oh, you know where I just was?

SAM: Where?

BOB: Paso Robles. You know, on that highway where James Dean got killed?

SAM: Oh yeah?

BOB: I was there at the spot. On the spot. A windy kinda place.

SAM: They've got a statue or monument to him in that town, don't they?

BOB: Yeah, but I was on the curve where he had the accident. Outsida town. And this place is incredible. I mean the place where he died is as powerful as the place he lived.

SAM: Nebraska?

BOB: Where'd he live?

SAM: He came from the farm, didn't he? Somewhere.

BOB: Yea, Iowa or Indiana. I forget. But this place up there has this kind of aura about it. It's on this kind of broad expanse of land. It's like that place made James Dean who he is. If he hadn't've died there he wouldn't've been James Dean.

SAM: Hm.

[*Bob moves as though to exit stage right again, but stops again.*]

BOB: You know what Elvis said? He said that if James Dean had sang he'd've been Ricky Nelson.

SAM: Is that right?

BOB: Yeah. [*pause*] You need anything?

SAM: Nope.

BOB: You brought some beer?

SAM: Yeah.

BOB: I just gotta make a couple phone calls.

SAM: Good.

[*Bob exits stage right as Sam moves down left toward table. Just as Bob exits, the sound of screeching tires and a loud car crash comes from off right. Sam pays no attention, but goes about setting tape recorder, beer, and notebooks on table. Bob reenters from right but with no reaction to car crash sounds.*]

BOB: Who was playin' that music before?

SAM: What music?

BOB: That piano music.

SAM: I dunno.

BOB: Hm.

SAM: "If James Dean sang he'd've been Ricky Nelson"? Elvis said that?

BOB: Yeah. Poor ol' Ricky. I wish he was here with us today. I wonder if anyone ever told him, when he was alive, how great he was. I mean like the rock-and-roll critics.

SAM: You got me.

BOB: You know, Emilio Fernandez used to shoot the critics that didn't like his movies. At parties.

[*Bob exits stage right. Sam sits on bench facing stage right, pulls out a cassette tape and sticks it in recorder, punches a button, and the same Jimmy Yancey tune is heard coming from the machine itself. Only a snatch is heard before Bob's voice comes from offstage right, speaking on the phone. As soon as Bob's voice is heard, Sam shuts the recorder off and starts leafing through his notebooks, scribbling in them now and then.*]

BOB'S VOICE [*off right*]: Maria? Listen, what's that thing gonna be like tonight? [*pause*] Yeah. There gonna be a lotta people there? [*pause*] Well, that's what I'm tryin' to figure out. [*pause*] Yeah. I don't know. How many people you think there'll be? [*pause*] Okay, well look, I got somebody here so. [*pause*] Yeah, I know. Yeah, well, I seen their act before. Yeah, I seen it. I seen it in St. Louis. Yeah. [*pause*] I dunno—'59 or '60, somethin' like that. [*laughs, pause*] I was around. I been around a long time. I can't count anymore. Okay, look, I'll talk to you later and see what's goin' on. [*pause*] Okay. Bye.

[*Bob hangs up offstage. Sam looks in that direction, then returns to his notebooks, cracks open a can of beer, and drinks.*]

BOB'S VOICE [*off right*]: Sam, what's this thing supposed to be about anyway?

SAM: I dunno.

BOB'S VOICE [*off*]: Are we supposed to have a theme?

SAM: I got a buncha questions here.

BOB'S VOICE [*off*]: You brought questions?

SAM: Yeah.

BOB'S VOICE [*off*]: How many questions?

SAM: Couple.

BOB'S VOICE: What if I don't have the answers?

SAM: Make it up.

BOB'S VOICE: Okay, so ask me a question.

SAM: [*quickly putting a cassette in recorder*] Okay, wait a second. I gotta see if this thing is working.

BOB'S VOICE: You got a tape?

SAM: [*punching RECORD button*] Yeah. Okay. All right. It's rolling.

BOB'S VOICE: Ask me somethin'.

SAM: Right. [*referring to notebooks*] Let's see—okay—let's see now—okay—here we go—Do you have any ideas about angels? Do you ever think about angels?

BOB'S VOICE: That's the first question?

SAM: You want me to start with something else?

BOB'S VOICE [*still off*]: No, that's okay. Angels. Yeah, now, angels now—what is it? [*pause*] Oh—the pope says this about angels—he says they exist.

SAM: Yeah? The pope?

BOB'S VOICE: Yeah. And they're spiritual beings. That's what he says.

SAM: Do you believe it?

BOB'S VOICE: Yeah.

SAM: Have you had any direct experience with angels?

BOB'S VOICE [*off*]: Yeah. Yeah, I have. I just gotta make one more phone call, all right?

SAM: Yeah. [*shuts tape off*]

BOB'S VOICE: You need anything?

SAM: Naw, I'm fine.

[*Sam drinks more beer, scribbles more notes. Pause. Bob's voice is heard again offstage right on phone. Sound of waves continue.*]

BOB'S VOICE [*off right*]: Maria? Hi, it's me again. [*pause, laughs*] Yeah, I just like the sound of your voice. Listen, what's the area code for Tulsa, do you know? [*pause*] Tulsa, yeah. [*pause*] All right. Good. [*pause*] Yeah, that's okay. I don't need it right away. [*pause*] Oh, ya did? [*pause*] Yeah? [*pause*] So, it's just a few people then? What's a few? [*pause*] That's more then a few. [*laughs*] Yeah, but, that's not what you'd call a few. [*pause*] Aw, I dunno. Look, I'll just have to think about it—see how the day goes—then I'll get back to you. [*pause*] Yeah, okay. Bye. [*hangs up*]

SAM: [*after pause*] You want me to come back? I could go out and come back if you want. Have some lunch.

BOB'S VOICE [*off*]: Naw, you're here. Stay. I'm just gettin' some clothes on. I'll be right there. Ask me another question.

SAM: Oh, okay— [*punching recorder on*] uh—let's see— [*referring to notebooks*] okay—What was the first music you can remember listening to? Way back.

BOB'S VOICE [*off*]: First music. First music?

SAM: Yeah.

BOB'S VOICE [*off*]: Live, ya mean? Live?

SAM: Yeah. Live.

BOB'S VOICE [*off*]: First music ever?

SAM: Yeah.

[*pause*]

BOB'S VOICE [*off*]: Polka music.

SAM: Really?

[*Bob enters from right wearing a sleeveless T-shirt, black jeans, and motorcycle boots with brass buckles. He carries a beat-up old acoustic guitar strung around his neck with an old piece of rope. He continually fingers the neck of the guitar and keeps picking out little repetitive melody lines, short blues progressions, gospel chords—whatever comes into his mind. He keeps this up through all the dialogue, even when he's talking, rarely resting into complete silence.*]

BOB [*onstage now*]: Yeah, polka.

SAM: [*drinking beer*] Where? Up in Hibbing?

BOB: Yeah, Hibbing.

SAM: Hibbing's near Duluth, right?

BOB: Right.

SAM: I love Duluth.

BOB: Great town.

SAM: That lake.

BOB: Superior?

SAM: Yeah. Tough town, too.

BOB: [*always moving, picking guitar*] Especially when it freezes over. Indians come out. Fur trappers.

SAM: Beaver.

BOB: Yeah, beaver too. Loons.

SAM: So you heard this polka music in what—dance halls or something?

BOB: Yeah—no—taverns. Beer joints. They played it in all the taverns. You just walk down the street and hear that all the time. People'd come flyin' out into the street doin' the polka. Accordions would come flyin' out.

SAM: Were they fighting or dancing?

BOB: Both, I guess. Mostly just having a good time. People from the old country.

SAM: Polish?

BOB: Some. I guess.

SAM: Were they singing in Polish?

BOB: They were singin' in somethin'. Swedish maybe. Some language. But you know how you don't need to know the language when it's music. You understand the music no matter what language it's in. Like when I went down and heard that Tex-Mex border music—that sounded like the same music to me even though the language was different. It all sounds the same to me.

SAM: Three-quarter time.

BOB: Yeah—waltz. I love to waltz.

SAM: How old were you then?

BOB: Aw. I dunno. Nine—ten.

SAM: Did you feel like you were cut off back then?

BOB: How d'ya mean?

SAM: I mean being up in the Far North like that. In the boondocks.

BOB: Nah, 'cause I didn't know anything else was goin' on. Why, did you?

SAM: Yeah. I still do. [*laughs*]

BOB: [*sings a snatch and plays*]
Down in the boondocks / Down in the boondocks / Lord have mercy on a boy / From down in the boondocks.

SAM: So you didn't have any big burning desire to get to New York or anything?

BOB: Naw. The only reason I wanted to go to New York is 'cause James Dean had been there.

SAM: So you really liked James Dean?

BOB: Oh, yeah. Always did.

SAM: How come?

BOB: Same reason you liked anybody, I guess. You see somethin' of your-self in them.

SAM: Did you dream about music back then?

BOB: I had lotsa dreams. Used to dream about things like Ava Gardner and Wild Bill Hickok. They were playin' cards, chasin' each other, and gettin' around. Sometimes I'd even be there in the dreams myself. Radio-station dreams. You know how, when you're a kid, you stay up late in bed, listening to the radio, and you sort of dream off the radio into sleep. That's how you used to fall asleep. That's when disc jockeys played whatever they felt like.

SAM: I used to fall asleep listening to baseball.

BOB: Yeah. Same thing. Just sorta dream off into the radio. Like you were inside the radio kinda.

SAM: Yeah—I could see the diamond with the lights lit up and the green lawn of the outfield and the pitcher's eyes looking for the catcher's signals.

BOB: But I don't know if you ever dream *about* music. How do you dream *about* music?

SAM: Well, I mean, for instance, a song like "Pledging My Love."

BOB: *Forever my darling.*

SAM: Yeah.

BOB: What about it?

SAM: Well, I used to dream myself into that kind of a song.

BOB: Really? I didn't think you were that romantic.

SAM: Oh yeah, I'm very romantic.

BOB: So, you mean you kinda put yourself into the song when you were listening to it?

SAM: Yeah. Put myself in the place of the singer.

BOB: I see what you mean. [*pause, still moving and picking*] Yeah, I guess I used to dream about music then. You have all different kinda dreams with music, though. I mean, sometimes I'd hear a guy sing a tune and I'd imagine the guy himself. What's the guy himself like? You know? Like Hank Williams or Buddy Holly or John Lee Hooker. You'd hear a line like *black snake moan* or *Mississippi Flood*—you could see yourself waist-high in muddy water.

SAM: Or maybe an image would come up from a line—like, I remember always seeing this image of my algebra teacher's scalp when I heard that Chuck Berry line, *The teacher is teachin' the golden rule*, from "School Day."

BOB: His scalp?

SAM: Yeah, he had one of those Marine-style crew cuts where the scalp shows through on top. I still see his scalp when I hear that line.

BOB: You don't hear that line much these days.

SAM: Nope. [*pause*] So, you'd mainly imagine the singer when you heard the song?

BOB: Yeah. A faceless singer. I'd fill in the face.

SAM: Is that the reason you went to see Woody Guthrie when he was sick? You'd heard his music?

BOB: Yeah. I heard his songs.

SAM: Is there anybody in your life you wished you'd met and didn't?

BOB: [*quick, still playing*] Yeah, Bob Marley.

SAM: Really.

BOB: Yeah. We were playin' in Waco, Texas, one time. And I missed him.

SAM: That was pretty close to miss each other.

BOB: Yeah. I wish I'd met him.

[*rest*]

SAM: So you went to see Guthrie in the hospital.

BOB: Uh-huh.

SAM: And you were there at his death bed?

BOB: Close.

SAM: Were you with him up to where he passed?

[*Long pause. Bob starts playing and thinks hard.*]

BOB: No.

[*Bob immediately jumps back into playing and moving.*]

SAM: You spent a lotta time with him in the hospital?

BOB: Yeah.

SAM: Was he coherent?

BOB: Yeah—no—he was coherent but he had no control over his reflexes. So he'd be . . .

[*pause*]

SAM: What'd you talk about?

BOB: Not too much. I never really did speak too much to him. He would call out the name of a song. A song he wrote that he wanted to hear, and I knew all his songs.

SAM: So you played 'em to him?

BOB: Yeah.

SAM: Did you ask him anything?

BOB: No, I mean there was nothin' to ask him. What're you gonna ask him? He wasn't the kinda guy you asked questions to.

[*pause*]

SAM: So you just kinda sat with him for days.

BOB: Yeah—I'd go out there. You had to leave at 5:00. It was in Greystone—Greypark or Greystone—it's in New Jersey. Out somewhere there. Bus went there. Greyhound bus. From the Forty-second Street terminal. You'd go there and you'd get off and you walked up the hill to the gates. Actually it was a pretty foreboding place.

SAM: How old were you?

[*Bob stops still. Stops picking. Thinks.*]

BOB: How old was I? [*pause*] I don't know. Nineteen, I guess.

SAM: Nineteen. And what kinda stuff were you listening to back then?

BOB: Oh, Bill Monroe, New Lost City Ramblers, Big Mama Thornton. People like that. Peggy Seeger. Jean Ritchie.

SAM: Hank Snow?

BOB: I'd always listened to Hank Snow. "Golden Rocket."

SAM: At that time were you fishin' around for a form?

BOB: Well, you can't catch fish 'les you trow de line, mon.

SAM: This is true.

BOB: Naw, I've always been real content with the old forms. I know my place by now.

SAM: So you feel like you know who you are?

BOB: Well, you always know who you are. I just don't know who I'm gonna become.

[*Pause. Bob keeps moving and picking.*]

BOB: Did we ever see each other back then?

SAM: When?

BOB: When we were nineteen.

SAM: I saw you one time on the corner of Sixth Avenue and Houston Street.

BOB: What year?

SAM: Musta been '66, '67. Somethin' like that. You were wearin' a navy-blue pea jacket and tennis shoes.

BOB: Yeah, that musta been me. Naw, this was earlier than that. I was listenin' to all them records on Stinson label and Folkways.

SAM: Stinson?

BOB: Yeah, Sonny Terry, Brownie McGhee, Almanac Singers.

SAM: Almanac Singers?

BOB: Yeah.

SAM: What about gospel?

BOB: I always listened to gospel music. Dixie Hummingbirds, Highway QC's, Five Blind Boys, and, of course, the Staple Singers.

SAM: What about Skip James or Joseph Spence?

BOB: Yeah. Bahama mama. [*pause*] Skip James. Once there was a Skip James. Elmore James.

SAM: *Rather be buried in some old cypress grove.*

BOB: *So my evil spirit can grab that Greyhound bus and ride.*

SAM: *I'd rather sleep in some old hollow log than have a bad woman you can't control.*

BOB: Now, what was it he died of?

SAM: Skip James?

BOB: Yeah.

SAM: Cancer of the balls.

BOB: What?!

SAM: Yeah. Cancer of the balls. He refused to go to any white doctors 'cause he was afraid they'd cut his nuts off.

BOB: Don't blame him one bit.

[*Phone rings off right. Bob exits off right, leaving Sam alone. Sam turns off tape then rewinds it a short ways and plays it back. Again, the Jimmy Yancey piano music comes from recorder. No voices. As Bob's voice is heard off right on phone, Sam keeps rewinding tape, playing it back in short snatches, trying to find their voices, but all that comes out is the piano music.*]

BOB'S VOICE [*off right*]: Four oh five? Four oh five. You're sure? [*pause*] I dunno. Four oh five sounds like Oklahoma City. I can't remember. [*pause*] All right. [*pause*] Yeah. Four oh five. [*pause*] Naw, I think I'm

gonna pass. [*pause*] I dunno. Sounds like too many record produc-
ers. [*pause*] Yeah. I'll just hang around here probably. [*pause*] Okay.
All right. [*pause*] Yeah.

[*Bob enters again, with guitar, carrying a glass of whiskey on ice. He crosses to
table, sets glass down after taking a sip, then starts picking the guitar again.
Sam is still trying to find their voices on the tape but gets only the piano
music.*]

SAM: [*fooling with tape*] This is incredible.

BOB: What.

SAM: There's nothin' on here but piano music.

BOB: [*laughs, keeps picking*] You mean our voices aren't on there?

SAM: Listen.

[*He lets tape play. Jimmy Yancey rolls out.*]

BOB: [*listens*] That's the same music I was askin' you about.

SAM: When?

BOB: Before. When you first came. That's the music.

SAM: Well, our voices ain't on here.

BOB: Don't matter.

SAM: Well, I can't remember all this stuff. How am I gonna remember all
this stuff?

BOB: Make it up.

SAM: Well, there's certain things you can't make up.

BOB: Like what?

SAM: Certain turns of phrase.

BOB: Try it again. It's gotta be on there. You had it on RECORD, right?

SAM: Yeah.

BOB: So it must be on there somewhere. You just gotta fool around with it.

[*Sam rewinds, then plays tape. Their voices are heard this time, coming out of
recorder.*]

BOB'S VOICE [*from tape*]: "Golden Rocket."

SAM'S VOICE [*from tape*]: At that time were you fishin' around for a form?

BOB'S VOICE [*from tape*]: Well, you can't catch fish 'les you trow de line,
mon.

[*Sam shuts tape off.*]

BOB: There. See. It was just hidin' out. [*laughs*]

SAM: This is amazing. Where'd that music come from?

BOB: Musta been on there already. Is it an old tape?

SAM: No, I just bought it this morning. [*Bob takes a sip of whiskey, sets glass down.*]

BOB: Angels.

[*Sam punches RECORD button. They continue. Bob keeps moving and playing guitar.*]

SAM: Weird.

BOB: Is it on now?

SAM: Yeah. I guess.

BOB: Okay. Fire away.

SAM: Okay. Let's see. [*referring to notebook*] Do you think it's possible to have a pact with someone?

BOB: A pact? Yeah. I know that's possible. I mean you should have a pact with someone. That presents a small problem for me, though—for instance, how many people *can* you have a pact with? And how many at the same time?

SAM: Not too many. How about women?

BOB: Nah, I don't know anything about women.

SAM: How 'bout waitresses?

BOB: Well, it seems to me that waitresses are gettin' younger and younger these days. Some of 'em look like babies.

SAM: So, you don't have much hope for women?

BOB: On the contrary. Women are the *only* hope. I think they're a lot more stable than men. Only trouble with women is they let things go on too long.

SAM: What things?

BOB: The whole Western sense of reality. Sometimes women have a tendency to be too lenient. Like a kid can go down and bust some old man in the head, rob a buncha old ladies, burglarize his brother's joint, and blow up a city block, and his momma will still come down and cry over him.

SAM: Yeah, but that's just nature, isn't it? The nature of being a mother.

BOB: Yeah, I guess so. Nature.

SAM: Have you ever felt like a couple?

BOB: A couple? You mean two? Yeah. All the time. Sometimes I feel like ten couples.

SAM: I mean like you're a part of another person. Like you belong. That other person carries something of you around and visee-versee.

BOB: Visee-versee?

SAM: Yeah.

BOB: Yeah. Sure. A couple. Sure. I've felt like that. Absolutely. Look—listen to this: [*sings and plays*] *You must learn to leave the table when love is no longer being served! Just show them all that you are able! Just get up and leave without saying a word.*

SAM: Who wrote that?

BOB: You got me. Roy Orbison or somebody, dunno.

SAM: Roy Orbison?

BOB: Naw. I dunno. Good lyric.

SAM: Yeah. [*writing a note*] *You must learn to leave the table . . .*

BOB: I mean you gravitate toward people who've got somethin' to give you and maybe you've got somethin' that they need.

SAM: Yeah, right.

BOB: And then maybe one day you wake up and see that they're not givin' it to you anymore. Maybe that's the way it is.

SAM: But maybe you're not, either.

BOB: Yeah. Maybe you haven't been givin' it to 'em for years. Maybe the rhythm's off.

SAM: You know, I've heard this theory that women are rhythmically different from men. By nature.

BOB: Oh yeah? I'll drink to that.

SAM: Yeah. That the female rhythm is a side-to-side, horizontal movement and the male rhythm is vertical—up and down.

BOB: You mean sorta like a flying horse?

SAM: Yeah. Sorta.

BOB: But then the two come together, don't they?

SAM: Right.

BOB: So they become one rhythm then.

SAM: Yeah.

BOB: So there's no such thing as "sides" in the long run. It's all the same.

SAM: It's just a theory.

BOB: Yeah. Well, you can make a theory outta anything, I suppose.

SAM: Do you feel those two different kinds of rhythms in you?

BOB: Yeah, sure. We all do. There's that slinky side-to-side thing and the jerky, up-and-down one. But they're a part of each other. One can't do without the other. Like God and the Devil.

SAM: Did you always feel those two parts?

BOB: Yeah. Always. Like you feel the lie and the truth. At the same time, sometimes. Both, together. Like remember in *Giant*—

SAM: The movie?

BOB: Yeah. That last scene in *Giant*. You know that scene where Jett Rink stumbles all over himself across the table.

SAM: Yeah.

BOB: Well, I never did like that scene. Always felt like there was somethin' phony about it. Didn't quite ring true. Always bothered me. Like there was a lie hiding in there somewhere, but I couldn't quite put my finger on it.

SAM: Yeah, I never did either. You mean where he's drunk and alone in the convention hall or whatever it was?

BOB: Yeah. You know why that was? Why it felt phony?

SAM: The makeup. All that gray in his hair?

BOB: No, no. I wish it was the makeup. Turns out Nick Adams, an actor at that time, who was a friend of James Dean's, he overdubbed that speech because James Dean had died by that time.

SAM: Is that right?

BOB: Yeah. And that makes perfect sense because that don't ring true. The end of that movie. But that's what I mean—the lie and the truth, like that.

[*pause*]

SAM: Well, what happened to his voice?

BOB: Whaddya mean?

SAM: I mean what happened to James Dean's original voice on the track? They must've had his voice track if they had the film on him.

BOB: I dunno. Maybe it was messed up or something.

SAM: Maybe it disappeared.

BOB: Maybe. Just vanished. I dunno.

[*Again, the sound of screeching brakes and car crash off right. Neither of the characters pays any attention. Long pause as Bob moves and picks guitar. Sam makes notes.*]

BOB: Sometimes I wonder why James Dean was great. Because—was he great or was everybody around him great?

SAM: No, he was great.

BOB: You think so?

SAM: Yeah. I mean, remember the scene in *Rebel Without a Cause* with Sal Mineo on the steps of the courthouse? Where he gets shot.

BOB: Plato.

SAM: Yeah, and he's holding Plato in his arms, and in the other hand he's got the bullets.

BOB: Yeah.

SAM: What was it he says? "They're not real bullets" or—no—what was it?

BOB: "I've got the bullets!"

SAM: Right. [*suddenly screaming with his arm outstretched in imitation of James Dean*] "I've got the bullets!" [*back to normal voice*] I mean, that's spectacular acting. Where do you see that kind of acting these days?

BOB: Nowhere. He didn't come up overnight either. I mean he really studied whatever it was he was about.

SAM: I guess.

BOB: Well, why do you suppose—I mean what was it that he did that was so different? For instance, in that scene with the bullets. What made that scene so incredible?

SAM: It was this pure kind of expression.

BOB: Of what?

SAM: Of an emotion. But it went beyond the emotion into another territory. Like most actors in that scene would express nothing but self-pity, but he put across a true remorse.

BOB: Remorse?

SAM: Yeah. For mankind. A pity for us all. This wasted life. This dumb death of an innocent kid. The death of the innocent.

BOB: So he actually did have a cause then?

SAM: I don't know.

BOB: "Rebel *with* a Cause." See, that's the devil's work.

SAM: What?

BOB: Words have lost their meaning. Like "rebel." Like "cause." Like "love." They mean a million different things.

SAM: Like "Hank Williams"?

BOB: Naw, you can never change the meaning of Hank Williams. That's here to stay. Nobody'll ever change that.

SAM: Did you used to listen to him a lot?

BOB: Overload. Who can you listen to if you can't listen to Hank?

SAM: Did he mean the same thing to you as James Dean?

BOB: Yeah, but in different ways. They both told the truth.

SAM: They both died in cars.

BOB: Yeah.

SAM: A Cadillac and a Porsche.

BOB: He was on his way to Ohio, I think. Some gig in Ohio.

SAM: I saw the car he died in. Cadillac coupe, convertible. I looked in the backseat of that car and this overwhelming sense of loneliness seized me by the throat. It was almost unbearable. I couldn't look very long. I had to turn away.

BOB: Maybe you shouldn'ta looked at all.

SAM: Maybe. [*pause*] Are you superstitious?

BOB: Naw.

SAM: You had a crash, right? A motorcycle.

BOB: Oh, yeah. Way back. Triumph 500.

SAM: What happened?

BOB: I couldn't handle it. I was dumbstruck.

SAM: How do you mean?

BOB: I just wasn't ready for it. It was real early in the morning on top of a hill near Woodstock. I can't even remember exactly how it happened. I was blinded by the sun for a second. This big orange sun was comin' up. I was driving right straight into the sun, and I looked up into it even though I remember someone telling me a long time ago when I was a kid never to look straight at the sun 'cause you'll get blinded. I forget who told me that. My dad or an uncle or somebody.

Somebody in the family. I always believed that must be true or else why would an adult tell you something like that. And I never did look directly at the sun when I was a kid, but this time, for some reason, I just happened to look up right smack into the sun with both eyes and, sure enough, I went blind for a second and I kind of panicked or something, I stomped down on the brake and the rear wheel locked up on me and I went flyin'.

SAM: Were you out?

BOB: Yeah. Out cold.

SAM: Who found you?

BOB: Sarah. She was followin' me in a car. She picked me up. Spent a week in the hospital, then they moved me to this doctor's house in town. In his attic. Had a bed up there in the attic with a window lookin' out. Sarah stayed there with me. I just remember how bad I wanted to see my kids. I started thinkin' about the short life of trouble. How short life is. I'd just lay there listenin' to birds chirping. Kids playing in the neighbor's yard or rain falling by the window. I realized how much I'd missed. Then I'd hear the fire engine roar, and I could feel the steady thrust of death that had been constantly looking over its shoulder at me. [*pause*] Then I'd just go back to sleep.

[*Phone rings off right. Bob turns and looks in that direction but doesn't move toward it. He stops playing guitar. Phone keeps ringing. He just stares off right. Lights begin to fade very slowly. Bob stays still, staring off right. Sam stops recorder, then rewinds and punches* PLAY *button. The Jimmy Yancey music fills the room, joining the sound of waves. Lights keep dimming to black. The phone keeps ringing. The waves keep crashing. Jimmy Yancey keeps playing in the dark.*]

excerpt from Liner Notes to *Biograph*

CAMERON CROWE

The liner notes to *Biograph* include a candid essay-interview by former *Rolling Stone* reporter Cameron Crowe, who is also the writer and director of *Jerry Maguire*, *Almost Famous* and other movies. Although Dylan has handled these topics before, this brief excerpt contains an eloquent statement on musical ancestry and what he believes is a singer's ideal achievement.

SITTING ACROSS from Bob Dylan on this afternoon, one could see his influences very clearly. His speech sometimes flecked with the country-isms of his youth, a leather jacket draped on his shoulders, a sharp hand gesture with a cigarette barely holding its ash . . . for all the years of who-is-Bob-Dylan analysis, the answer seemed obvious. He still is, as he always has been, a long figure with a guitar and a point of view.

"Basically, I'm self-taught. What I mean by that actually is that I picked it all up from other people by watching them, by imitating them. . . . The most inspiring type of entertainer for me has always been somebody like Jimmie Rodgers, somebody who could do it alone and was totally original. He was combining elements of blues and hillbilly sounds before anyone else had thought of it. He recorded at the same time as Blind Willie McTell but he wasn't just another white boy singing black. That was his great genius and he was there first. All he had to do was appear with his guitar and a straw hat and he played on the same stage with big bands, girly choruses and follies burlesque and he sang in a plaintive voice and style and he outlasted them all. You don't remember who else was on the bill. I never saw him. I only heard his records. I never saw Woody Guthrie in his prime. I think maybe the greatest of all those I ever saw was Cisco Houston. He was in his last days but you couldn't tell—he looked like Clark Gable and he was absolutely magnificent. . . . I always like to think that there's a real person talking to me, just one voice you know, that's all I can handle— Cliff Carlisle . . . Robert Johnson, for me this is a deep reality, someone who's telling me where he's been that I haven't and what it's like there— somebody whose life I can feel . . . Jimmie Rodgers or even Judy Garland, she was a great singer . . . or Al Jolson . . . God knows there are so few of them, but who knows? Maybe there are just enough."

The Rock and Roll Hall of Fame Speech

BRUCE SPRINGSTEEN

When Dylan became a member of the Rock and Roll Hall of Fame in January 1988, Bruce Springsteen was chosen to give the induction speech. The two met during the Rolling Thunder Revue; Springsteen was then a young artist with three albums to his name and the latest to bear "the next Dylan" moniker ("Hi, I hear you're the new me," Dylan reportedly said when they first shook hands). They have since become good friends, sharing the stage at one point in 1990 and covering each other's songs in concert. Dylan has said in one interview, "Bruce is like a brother to me."

Springsteen talks about the ways Dylan liberated rock-and-roll convention and broadened the idiom's range of expression. His speech is one of the most affectionate and intelligent panegyrics on Dylan, both as a memoir and consideration of musical influence.

One of America's most respected songwriters, Springsteen was inducted into the Rock Hall in 1999 and has recorded several albums, including *Born to Run*, *Darkness on the Edge of Town*, *Live 1975–85*, *The Ghost of Tom Joad* and *The Rising*.

THE FIRST TIME I heard Bob Dylan, I was in the car with my mother listening to WMCA and on came that snare shot that sounded like somebody had kicked open the door to your mind: "Like a Rolling Stone." My mother—she was no stiff with rock and roll, she liked the music—sat there for a minute, then looked at me and said, "That guy can't sing." But I knew she was wrong. I sat there and I didn't say nothing but I knew that I was listening to the toughest voice that I had ever heard. It was lean and it sounded somehow simultaneously young and adult.

I ran out and bought the single and ran home and played it, but they must have made a mistake in the factory because a Lenny Welch song came on. The label was wrong. So I ran back to the store, got the Dylan, and came back and played it. Then I went out and got *Highway 61 Revisited*. That was all I played for weeks, looking at the cover with Bob in that satin blue jacket and the Triumph motorcycle shirt.

When I was a kid, Bob's voice somehow thrilled and scared me, it made me feel kind of irresponsibly innocent—it still does—when it reached down and touched what little worldliness a fifteen-year-old high school kid in New Jersey had in him at the time. Dylan was a revolutionary. Bob freed your mind the way Elvis freed your body. He showed us that just because the music was innately physical did not mean that it was anti-intellectual. He had the vision and the talent to make a pop song that contained the whole world. He invented a new way a pop singer could sound, broke through the limitations of what a recording artist could achieve and changed the face of rock and roll forever.

Without Bob, the Beatles wouldn't have made *Sgt. Pepper,* the Beach Boys wouldn't have made *Pet Sounds,* the Sex Pistols wouldn't have made "God Save the Queen," U2 wouldn't have done "Pride in the Name of Love," Marvin Gaye wouldn't have done *What's Going On?,* the Count Five would not have done "Psychotic Reaction," Grandmaster Flash might not have done "The Message," and there never would have been a group named the Electric Prunes. To this day, wherever great rock music is being made, there is the shadow of Bob Dylan. Bob's own modern work has gone unjustly underappreciated because it's had to stand in that shadow. If there was a young guy out there writing the *Empire Burlesque* album, writing "Every Grain of Sand," they'd be calling him the new Bob Dylan.

About three months ago, I was watching *The Rolling Stones Special* on TV. Bob came on and he was in a real cranky mood. He was kind of bitching and moaning about how his fans come up to him on the street and treat him like a long-lost brother or something, even though they don't know him. Now, speaking as a fan, when I was fifteen and I heard "Like a

Rolling Stone," I heard a guy who had the guts to take on the whole world and who made me feel like I had to too. Maybe some people misunderstood that voice as saying that somehow Bob was going to do the job for them, but, as we grow older, we learn that there isn't anybody out there who can do that job for anybody else. So I'm just here tonight to say thanks, to say that I wouldn't be here without you, to say that there isn't a soul in this room who does not owe you his thanks, and to steal a line from one of your songs—whether you like it or not—"You was the brother that I never had."

Stillborn Again

HOWARD HAMPTON

Dylan's 1989 release *Oh Mercy* is normally considered, alongside *Infidels*, as his most memorable work of the decade. The album contained a few songs now seen as classics—"Most of the Time," "Shooting Star," "Ring Them Bells"—and its modern, layered production, done by U2 producer Daniel Lanois, seemed to herald a new direction in Dylan's music. One person who didn't think highly of it was Howard Hampton of *L.A. Weekly*; the recording, according to him, is of a piece with Dylan's weak output since *The Basement Tapes*. In judging *Oh Mercy* against standards set in the 1960s, Hampton's assessment is guided by familiar, and possibly unfair, criteria. Yet in criticizing the album and its "vague topicality," he acutely identifies many of the songwriting habits that make this era of Dylan's career so problematic.

A longtime contributor to several publications, Hampton is now writing *Badlands: A Psychogeography of the Reagan Era* for Harvard University Press.

> "The sun is going down upon the sacred cow."
> —Bob Dylan

THE STRONGEST performance on *Oh Mercy*, Bob Dylan's latest day pass from oblivion, is "Most of the Time," five minutes of suspended longing and bitterness. The melody is all conspiratorial intimacy, Dylan's voice passing through the delicate instrumental fog like a spy's receding footsteps. He's singing to reclaim a distant present, to convince himself he's escaped the past—a broken past that's more alive to him than the bland contentment of the here and now. "Don't even remember," he asserts, his timbre softly under-cutting him, "what her lips felt like on mine." For an instant, he assumes some of the burden of his own history, to which the last twenty or so years have been little more than a long string of footnotes. This gives "Most of the Time" the tension of a face-to-face standoff, a shot of almost forgotten restiveness. Maybe he'll confront the estrangement and irrelevance of his years as a rock institution; maybe—at long last—something will give.

Before "Most of the Time" is done, the moment has dissipated. Its dissipation is the point of the song: it's the point of his whole post–*Basement Tapes* career. So "Most of the Time" becomes one more exhibit in the museum of Bob. *Oh Mercy* was produced—make that curated—by Daniel Lanois, who gives it the earthy/ethereal sheen he got for the Neville Brothers on *Yellow Moon*, though Dylan no longer has the vocal presence to match with it. Though he sings better than he has in years, his voice still registers as a blur. His timing isn't shot altogether and the tics are nearly under control. But creation isn't just deftly pushing clichés across a shuffleboard.

Of course, practically all his later work is constructed upon that sort of meaning-by-proxy. The words, phrasing, and pressure (on the music, on the singer) that might actually sustain emotion, realize an idea or com-plete an action, have been blunted into mere devices. On "Man in the Long Black Coat," Dylan's fabled diction turns seconds into hours: "Someone / Is / Out there / Beating on / A dead / Horse." The sustaining lie of his career is that of continuity: that he can still make Mr. Ed get up there and talk. This notion serves two ends. It reduces the explosive—and painfully out-of-reach—music he made in the sixties to a manageable tautology, some-thing that refers only to itself and the celebrity and influence of its maker. And it jump-starts Dylan's current material (the real tautology) with the reverence he earned in another time, under separate auspices entirely.

Maintaining this confusionist charade means *Oh Mercy* must be exca-vated from its own insignificance. No problem: any sign that Our Hero is off the respirator and back on semisolid food is cause for rejoicing. What ultimately determines a Dylan record's reception is how easily it can be crowbarred into the ongoing mythic narrative of his life 'n' times. *Oh Mercy* fits the bill because it marks a shift back to quality product after the debacle of *Dylan and the Dead*, thus drawing attention away from the pos-sibility the aforementioned narrative was finished a couple of decades ago.

On close inspection, the distance between *Oh Mercy* and *Dylan and the Dead* isn't much. The singing on the former is less flagrantly arbitrary and a tone of vague topicality prevails, but the arbitrariness of the latter bespeaks an interesting mixture of desperation and indolence. Mud-wrestling with his legacy, as the Grateful Dead fidgit supportively in his corner, he doesn't so much sing stuff like "I Want You" as hurl himself at it. He also has the flat-out masochism to revive "Joey," the De Millean gangster-as-plaster-saint melodrama that epitomizes how far he's fallen. (Its tawdriness is so single-minded it's freakishly compelling.) The litany of corruption that makes up *Oh Mercy*'s "Political World" is snappy and approximates petty conviction, but everything on its laundry list of ills is borrowed. The political world he's describing might as well be Sea World: yet another suburb of the sprawling theme park that is Dylanland. ("Political World? Okay, make a right at the Watchtower, go two more block till you reach the Slow Train crossing....")

Excepting the pious atrocities "What Good Am I?" and "Disease of Conceit," *Oh Mercy* is quite listenable. As necrophilia goes, but then it's always easier to swallow auto-necro-fellatio (the Jagger-Richards, Lydon/Rotten principle) than to witness an interloper performing the dirty deed (the Tom Petty principle). And the record has its small, transitory pleasures, such as the line "People don't live or die, people just float," and the way Dylan understates it. But that's all. This is strictly entertainment, the old pro laying on the sentiment and reassurance.

It is almost inconceivable this is the man who once broke rock—as a form, as a mode of experience—in half. Now he's the dutiful repairman. "Everything is broken," he sings, but promises the pieces can be put back together in his art as assuredly as they cannot be in the world. This is an inversion of what his work once meant, but it is also a continuation of the political world of the past twenty years. Society has structured itself around the suppression of the kinds of demands Dylan's music once made, that it might make such speech unimaginable all over again. To suppose this new record speaks the same language as *Highway 61 Revisited* or the still unreleased "Tell Me Momma," or that those records were but facile entertainments from the beginning, is obscene: selling oneself short transformed on the open market into lust, which Bob Dylan has refined further still into a science.

excerpt from *Songwriters on Songwriting*

PAUL ZOLLO

I n April 1991, while on a short break from tour, Dylan was interviewed by Paul Zollo, a songwriter and the editor of *SongTalk*, the journal of the National Academy of Songwriters. In the course of their discussion, Dylan spoke openly about several topics, including the limits of radio pop, the anxieties of collaboration and what makes the lyrics in his songs so uniquely *his*.

The interview's emphasis on craft is the reason, perhaps, for Dylan's honesty and thoughtfulness; Zollo asks only about the songwriting process and the creative urgings behind specific songs, choosing to ignore Dylan's personal life and political or religious background. Dylan reveals songwriting to be an elusive though capacious medium of expression—"more confessional than professional," he says. In mentioning how songs resist taking on a definitive form, he echoes previous statements, and at times distances himself from his own work. He frequently credits the independent tradition of folk song and the ways in which writing is controlled by unconscious forces.

Excerpted here, the interview appears in Zollo's collection *Songwriters on Songwriting*, recently published in an updated and expanded edition.

Is songwriting for you more a sense of taking something from someplace else?

Well, someplace else is always a heartbeat away. There's no rhyme or reason to it. There's no rule. That's what makes it so *attractive*. There isn't any rule. You can still have your wits about you and do something that gets you off in a multitude of ways. As you very well know, or else you yourself wouldn't be doing it.

Your songs often bring us back to other times, and are filled with mythic, magical images. A song like "Changing of the Guards" seems to take place centuries ago, with lines like "They shaved her head / she was torn between Jupiter and Apollo / a messenger arrived with a black nightingale. . . ." How do you connect with a song like that?

[*Pause*] A song like that, there's no way of knowing, after the fact, unless somebody's there to take it down in chronological order, what the motivation was behind it.

[*Pause*] But on one level, of course, it's no different from anything else of mine. It's the same amount of metric verses like a poem. To me, like a poem.

The melodies in my mind are very simple, they're very simple, they're just based on music we've all heard growing up. And that and music which went beyond that, which went back further, Elizabethan ballads and whatnot. . . .

To me, it's old. [*Laughs*] It's old. It's not something, with my *minimal* amount of talent, if you could call it that, minimum amount. . . . To me somebody coming along now would definitely read what's out there if they're seriously concerned with being an artist who's going to still be an artist when they get to be *Picasso's* age. You're better off learning some music theory. You're just better off, yeah, if you want to write songs. Rather than just take a hillbilly twang, you know, and try to base it all on that. Even country music is more orchestrated that it used to be. You're better off having some feel for music that you don't have to carry in your head, that you can write down.

To me those are the people who . . . are serious about this craft. People who go about it that way. Not people who just want to pour out their insides and they got to get a big idea out and they want to tell the world about *this*, sure, you can do it through a song, you always could. You can use a song for anything, you know.

The world don't need any more songs.

You don't think so?

No. They've got enough. They've got way too many. As a matter of fact, if nobody wrote any songs from this day on, the world ain't gonna suffer for it. Nobody cares. There's enough songs for people to listen to, if they want to listen to songs. For every man, woman and child on earth, they could be sent, probably, each of them, a hundred records, and never be repeated. There's enough songs.

Unless someone's gonna come along with a pure heart and has something to say. That's a different story.

But as far as songwriting, any idiot could do it. If you see me do it, any idiot could do it. [*Laughs*] It's just not that difficult of a thing. Everybody writes a song just like everybody's got that one great novel in them.

"But the enemy I see wears a cloak of decency . . ."

Now don't tell me . . . wait . . . is that "When You Gonna Wake Up?"?

No, that's from "Slow Train."

Oh, wow. Oh, yeah. Wow. There again. That's a song that you could write a song to every line in the song. You could.

Many of your songs are like that.

Well, you know, that's not good either. Not really. In the long run, it could have stood up better by maybe doing just that, maybe taking every line and making a song out of it. If somebody had the willpower.

But that line, there again, is an intellectual line. It's a line, "Well, the enemy I see wears a cloak of decency," that could be a lie. It just could be. Whereas "Standing under your yellow railroad," that's not a lie.

To Woody Guthrie, see, the airwaves were sacred. And when he'd hear something false, it was on airwaves that were sacred to him. His songs weren't false. Now we know the airwaves aren't sacred but to him they were.

So that influenced a lot of people with me coming up. Like, you know, all those songs on the Hit Parade are just a bunch of shit, anyway. It influenced me in the beginning when nobody had heard that. Nobody had heard that. You know, "If I give my heart to you, will you handle it with care?" Or "I'm getting sentimental over you." Who gives a shit? It could be said in a grand way, and the performer could put the song across, but come on, that's because he's a great performer not because it's a great song. Woody was also a performer and songwriter. So a lot of us got caught up in that. There ain't anything good on the radio. It doesn't happen.

Then, of course, the Beatles came along and kind of grabbed everybody by the throat. You were for them or against them. You were for them or you *joined* them, or whatever. Then everybody said, "Oh, popular song ain't so bad," and then everyone *wanted* to get on the radio. [*Laughs*] Before that it didn't matter. My first records were never played on the radio. It was unheard of! Folk records weren't played on the radio. You never heard them on the radio and nobody cared if they were on the radio.

Going on into it farther, the Beatles came out and everybody from England, rock and roll still is an American thing. Folk music is not. Rock and roll is an American thing, it's just all kind of twisted. But the English kind of threw it back, didn't they? And they made everybody respect it once more. So everybody wanted to get on the radio.

Now nobody even knows what radio is anymore. Nobody likes it that you talk to. Nobody listens to it. But, then again, it's bigger than it ever was. But nobody knows how to really respond to it. Nobody can shut it off. [*Laughs*] You know? And people really aren't sure whether they want to be on the radio or whether they don't want to be on the radio. They might want to sell a lot of records, but people always did that. But being a folk performer, having hits, it wasn't important. Whatever that has to do with anything . . . [*laughs*].

Your songs, like Woody's, always have defied being pop entertainment. In your songs, like his, we know a real person is talking, with lines like, "You've got a lot of nerve to say you are my friend."

That's another way of writing a song, of course. Just talking to somebody that ain't there. That's the best way. That's the truest way. Then it just becomes a question of how heroic your speech is. To me, it's something to strive after.

Until you record a song, no matter how heroic it is, it doesn't really exist. Do you ever feel that?

No. If it's there, it exists.

You once said that you only write about what's true, what's been proven to you, that you write about dreams but not fantasies.

My songs really aren't dreams. They're more of a responsive nature. Waking up from a dream is . . . when you write a dream, it's something you try to recollect and you're never quite sure if you're getting it right or not.

You said your songs are responsive. Does life have to be in turmoil for songs to come?

Well, to me, when you need them, they appear. Your life doesn't have to be in turmoil to write a song like that but you need to be outside of it. That's why a lot of people, me myself included, write songs when one form or another of society has rejected you. So that you can truly write about it from the outside. Someone who's never been out there can only imagine it as anything, really.

Outside of life itself?

No. Outside of the situation you find yourself in.

There are different types of songs and they're all called songs. But there are different types of songs just like there are different types of people, you know? There's an infinite amount of different kinds, stemming from a common folk ballad verse to people who have classical training. And with classical training, of course, then you can just apply lyrics to classical training and get things going on in positions where you've never been in before.

Modern twentieth-century ears are the first ears to hear these kinds of Broadway songs. There wasn't anything like this. These are musical songs. These are done by people who know music first. And then lyrics.

To me, Hank Williams is still the best songwriter.

Hank? Better than Woody Guthrie?

That's a good question. Hank Williams never wrote "This Land Is Your Land." But it's not that shocking for me to think of Hank Williams singing

"Pastures of Plenty" or Woody Guthrie singing "Cheatin' Heart." So in a lot of ways those two writers are similar. As writers. But you mustn't forget that both of these people were performers, too. And that's another thing which separates a person who just writes a song . . .

People who don't perform but who are so locked into other people who do that, they can sort of feel what that other person would like to say in a song and be able to write those lyrics. Which is a different thing from a performer who needs a song to play on stage year after year.

And you always wrote your songs for yourself to sing—

My songs were written with me in mind. In those situations, several people might say, "Do you have a song laying around?" The best songs to me—my best songs—are songs which were written very quickly. Yeah, very, very quickly. Just about as much time as it takes to write it down is about as long as it takes to write it. Other than that, there have been a lot of ones that haven't made it. They haven't survived. They *could*. They need to be dragged out, you know, and looked at again, maybe.

You said once that the saddest thing about songwriting is trying to reconnect with an idea you started before, and how hard that is to do.

To me it can't be done. To me, unless I have another writer around who might want to finish it . . . outside of writing with the Traveling Wilburys, my shared experience writing a song with other songwriters is not that great. Of course, unless you find the right person to write with as a partner . . . [*laughs*] . . . you're awfully lucky if you do, but if you don't it's really more trouble than it's worth, trying to write something with somebody.

Your collaborations with Jacques Levy came out pretty great.

We both were pretty much lyricists. Yeah, very panoramic songs because, you know, after one of my lines, one of his lines would come out. Writing with Jacques wasn't difficult. It was trying to just get it down. It just didn't stop. *Lyrically.* Of course, my melodies are very simple anyway so they're very easy to remember.

With a song like "Isis" that the two of your wrote together, did you plot that story out prior to writing the verses?

That was a story that [*laughs*] meant something to him. Yeah. It just seemed to take on a life of its own, [*laughs*] as another view of history [*laughs*]. Which there are so many views that don't get told. Of history, anyway. That wasn't one of them. Ancient history but history nonetheless.

Was that a story you had in mind before the song was written?

No. With this "Isis" thing, it was "Isis" . . . you know, the name sort of rang a bell but not in any kind of vigorous way. So therefore, it was name-that-tune time. It was anything. The name was familiar. Most people would think they knew it if from somewhere. But it seemed like just about any way it wanted to go would have been okay, just as long as it didn't get too close. [*Laughs*]

Too close to what?

[*Laughs*] To close to me *or* him.

People have an idea of your songs freely flowing out from you, but that song and many others of yours are so well-crafted; it has an ABAB rhyme scheme which is like something Byron would do, interlocking every line—

Oh, yeah. Oh, yeah. Oh, sure. If you've heard a lot of free verse, if you've been raised on free verse, William Carlos Williams, e. e. cummings, those kind of people who wrote free verse, your ear is not going to be trained for things to sound that way. Of course, for me it's no secret that all my stuff is rhythmically orientated that way.

Like a Byron line would be something as simple as "What is it you buy so dear / with your pain and with your fear?" Now that's a Byron line, but that could have been one of my lines.

Up until a certain time, maybe in the twenties, that's the way poetry was. It was that way. It was . . . simple and easy to remember. And always in rhythm. It had a rhythm whether the music was there or not.

Is rhyming fun for you?

Well, it can be, but, you know, it's a game. You know, you sit around . . . you know, it's more like, it's mentally . . . mentally . . . it gives you a thrill. It gives you a thrill to rhyme something you might think, well, that's never been rhymed before.

But then again, people have taken rhyming now, it doesn't have to be exact anymore. Nobody's going to care if you rhyme "represent" with "ferment," you know. Nobody's gonna care.

That was a result of a lot of people of your generation for whom the craft elements of songwriting didn't seem to matter as much. But in your songs the craft is always there, along with the poetry and the energy—

My sense of rhyme used to be more involved in my songwriting than it is. . . . Still staying in the unconscious frame of mind, you can pull yourself out and throw up two rhymes first and work it back. You get the rhymes first and work it back and then see if you can make it make sense in another kind of way. You can still stay in the unconscious frame of mind to pull it off, which is the state of mind you have to be in anyway.

So sometimes you will work backwards, like that?

Oh, yeah. Yeah, a lot of times. That's the only way you're going to finish something. That's not uncommon, though.

Do you finish songs even when you feel that maybe they're not keepers?

Keepers or not keepers . . . you keep songs if you think they're any good, and if you don't . . . you can always give them to somebody else. If you've got songs that you're not going to do and you just don't like them . . . show them to other people, if you want.

Then again, it all gets back to the motivation. Why you're doing what you're doing. That's what it is. [*Laughs*] It's confrontation with that . . . goddess of the self.

God of the self or goddess of the self? Somebody told me it was goddess of the self. Somebody told me that the goddess rules over the self. Gods don't concern themselves with such earthly matters. Only goddesses . . . would stoop so low. Or bend down so low.

You mentioned that when you were writing "Every Grain of Sand" that you felt you were in an area where no one had ever been before—

Yeah. In that area where Keats is. Yeah. That's a good poem set to music.

A beautiful melody.

It's a beautiful melody, too, isn't it? It's a folk derivative melody. It's nothing you can put your finger on, but, you know, yeah, those melodies are great. There ain't enough of them, really.

Even a song like that, the simplicity of it can be . . . deceiving. As far as . . . a song like that just may have been written in great turmoil, although you would never sense that. Written but not delivered. Some songs are better written in peace and quiet and delivered in turmoil. Others are best written in turmoil and delivered in a peaceful, quiet way.

It's a magical thing, popular song. Trying to press it down into everyday numbers doesn't quite work. It's not a puzzle. There aren't pieces that fit. It doesn't make a complete picture that's ever been seen.

But, you know, as they say, thank God for songwriters.

Randy Newman said that he writes his songs by going to it every day, like a job—

Tom Paxton told me the same thing. He goes back with me, way back. He told me the same thing. *Every day* he gets up and he writes a song. Well, that's great, you know, you write the song and then take your kids to school? Come home, have some lunch with the wife, you know, maybe go write another song. Then Tom said for recreation, to get himself loose, he rode his horse. And then pick up his child from school, and then go to bed with the wife.

Now to me that sounds like the ideal way to write songs. To me, it couldn't be any better than that.

How do you do it?

Well, my songs aren't written on a schedule like that. In my mind it's never really been seriously a profession. . . . It's been more confessional than professional. . . . Then again, everybody's in it for a different reason.

Do you ever sit down with the intention of writing a song, or do you wait for songs to come to you?

Either or. Both ways. It can come . . . some people are . . . It's possible now for a songwriter to have a recording studio in his house and record a song and make a demo and do a thing. It's like the roles have changed on all that stuff.

Now for me, the environment to write the song is extremely important. The environment has to bring something out in me that wants to be brought out. It's a contemplative, reflective thing. Feelings really aren't my thing. See, I don't write lies.

It's a proven fact: Most people who say I love you don't mean it. Doctors have proved that. So love generates a lot of songs. Probably more so than a lot. Now it's not my intention to have *love* to influence my songs. Any more than it influenced Chuck Berry's songs or Woody Guthrie's or Hank Williams's. Hank Williams, they're not *love* songs. You're degrading them songs calling them *love* songs. Those are songs from the Tree of Life. There's no love on the Tree of Life. Love is on the Tree of Knowledge, the Tree of Good and Evil. So we have a lot of songs in popular music about *love*. Who needs them? Not you, not me.

You can use love in a lot of ways in which it will come back to hurt you. Love is a democratic principle. It's a Greek thing.

A college professor told me that if you read about Greece in the history books, you'll know all about America. Nothing that happens will puzzle you ever again. You read the history of Ancient Greece and when the Romans came in, and nothing will ever bother you about America again. You'll see what America is.

Now, maybe, but there are a lot of other countries in the world besides America . . . [*laughs*]. Two. You can't forget about them. [*Laughter*]

Have you found there are better places in the world than others to write songs?

It's not necessary to take a trip to write a song. What a long, strange trip it's *been*, however. But that part of it's true, too.

Environment is very important. People need peaceful, invigorating environments. Stimulating environments.

In America there's a lot of repression. A lot of people who are *repressed*. They'd like to get out of town, they just don't know how to do it. And so, it holds back creativity. It's like you go somewhere and you can't help but feel it. Or people even *tell* it to you, you know?

What got me into the whole thing in the beginning wasn't songwriting. That's not what got me into it. When "Hound Dog" came across the radio, there was nothing in my mind that said, "Wow, what a great song, I wonder who wrote that?" It didn't really concern me who wrote it. It didn't matter who wrote it. It was just . . . it was just there.

Same way with me now. You hear a good song. Now you think to yourself, maybe, Who wrote it? Why? Because the performer's not as good as the song, maybe. The performer's got to transcend that song. At least come up to it. A good performer can always make a bad song sound good. Record albums are *filled* with good performers singing filler stuff. Everybody can say they've done that. Whether you wrote it or whether somebody else wrote it, it doesn't matter.

What interested me was being a musician. The singer was important and so was the song. But being a musician was always first and foremost in the back of my mind. That's why, while other people were learning . . . whatever they were learning. What were they learning way back then?

"Ride, Sally, Ride"?

Something like that. Or "Run, Rudolph, Run." When the others were doing "Run, Rudolph, Run," my interests were going more to Leadbelly kind of stuff, when he was playing a Stella twelve-string guitar. Like, how does the guy do that? Where can one of these be found, a twelve-string guitar? They didn't have any in *my* town.

My intellect always fell that way. Of the music. Like Paul Whiteman. Paul Whiteman creates a mood. To me, that creates a mood. Bing Crosby's early records. They created a mood, like that Cab Calloway, kind of spooky horn kind of stuff. Violins, when big bands had a sound to them, without the Broadway glitz. Once that Broadway trip got into it, it became all sparkly and Las Vegas, really. But it wasn't always so.

Music created an environment. It doesn't happen anymore. Why? Maybe technology has just booted it out and there's no need for it. Because we have a screen which supposedly is three-dimensional or comes across as three-dimensional. It would like you to believe it's three-dimensional. Well, you know, like old movies and stuff like that that's influenced so many of us who grew up on that stuff.

[*Picks up Peruvian flute.*] Like this old thing here, it's nothing, it's some kind of, what is it? . . . Listen: [*Plays a slow tune on the flute.*] Here, listen to this song. [*Plays more.*] Okay. That's a song. It don't have any words. Why do songs need words? They don't. Songs don't need words. They don't.

Do you feel satisfied with your body of work?

Most everything, yeah.

Do you spend a lot of time writing songs?

Well, did you hear that record that Columbia released last year, *Down in the Groove*? Those songs, they came in pretty easy.

I'd like to mention some of your songs, and see what response you have to them.

Okay.

"One More Cup of Coffee."

[*Pause*] Was that for a coffee commercial? No . . .

It's a gypsy song. That song was written during a gypsy festival in the south of France one summer. Somebody took me there to the gypsy high holy days which coincide with my own particular birthday. So somebody took me to a birthday party there once, and hanging out there for a week probably influenced the writing of that song.

But the "valley below" probably came from someplace else.

My feeling about the song was that the verses came from someplace else. It wasn't about anything, so this "valley below" thing became the fixture to hang it on. But "valley below" could mean anything.

"Precious Angel" [*from* Slow Train Coming].

Yeah. That's another one, it could go on forever. There's too many verses and there's not enough. You know? When people ask me, "How come you don't sing that song anymore?" It's like it's another one of those songs: it's just too much and not enough. A lot of my songs strike me that way. That's the natural thing about them to me.

It's too hard to wonder why about them. To me, they're not worthy of wondering why about them. They're *songs*. They're not written in *stone*. They're on plastic.

To us, though, they are written in stone, because Bob Dylan wrote them. I've been amazed by the way you've changed some of your great songs—

Right. Somebody told me that *Tennyson* often wanted to rewrite his poems once he saw them in print.

"*I and I*" [*from Infidels*].

[*Pause*] That was one of them Caribbean songs. One year a bunch of songs just came to me hanging around down in the islands, and that was one of them.

"*Joey*" [*from* Desire].

To me, that's a great song. Yeah. And it never loses its appeal.

And it has one of the greatest visual endings of any song.

That's a tremendous song. And you'd only know that singing it night after night. You know who got me singing that song? [Jerry] Garcia. Yeah. He got me singing that song again. He said that's one of the best songs ever written. Coming from *him*, it was hard to know which way to take that. [*Laughs*] He got me singing that song again with them [The Grateful Dead].

It was amazing how it would, right from the get-go, it had a life of its own, it just ran out of the gate and it just kept on getting better and better and better and better and it keeps on getting better. It's in its infant stages, as a performance thing. Of course, it's a long song. But, to me, not to blown my horn, but to me the song is like a Homer ballad. Much more so than "A Hard Rain," which is a long song, too. But, to me, "Joey" has a Homeric quality to it that you don't hear every day. Especially in popular music.

"*Ring Them Bells.*"

It stands up when you hear it played by me. But if another performer did it, you might find that it probably wouldn't have as much to do with bells as what the title proclaims.

Somebody once came and sang it in my dressing room. To me [*laughs*]. To try to influence me to sing it that night. [*Laughter*] It could have gone either way, you know.

Which way did it go?

It went right out the door. [*Laughter*] It went out the door and didn't come back. Listening to this song that was on my record, sung by someone who wanted me to sing it . . . There was no way he was going to get me to sing it like that. A great performer, too.

"Idiot Wind."

"Idiot Wind." Yeah, you know, obviously, if you've heard both versions, you realize, of course, that there could be a myriad of verses for the thing. It doesn't *stop*. It wouldn't stop. Where do you end? You could still be writing it, really. It's something that could be a work continually in progress.

Although, on saying that, let me say that my lyrics, to my way of thinking, are better for my songs than anybody else's. People have felt about my songs sometimes the same way as me. And they say to me, your songs are so *opaque* that, people tell me, they have feelings they'd like to express within the same framework. My response, always, is go ahead, do it, if you feel like it. But it never comes off. They're not as good as my lyrics.

There's just something about my lyrics that just have a *gallantry* to them. And that might be all they have going for them. [*Laughs*] However, it's no small thing.

Ode

MICHAEL McCLURE

Michael McClure was among the coterie of San Francisco beat poets who took a great interest in Dylan during the 1960s and 70s, intrigued by the idea of joining poetry to rock and roll: "There was the interest in writing lyrics and perhaps a new way to use rhyme. Rock had mutual attraction for all; a common tribal dancing ground whether we were poets, or printers, or sculptors. . . . Bob Dylan is a poet; whether he has cherubs in his hair and fairy wings, or feet of clay, he is a poet."[*] In *Jaguar Skies*, McClure makes homage to the songwriter, using this kind of expressive and surrealist imagery to signify the ways Dylan's music liberates the imagination.

For Bob Dylan

MY EYES ARE WIDE EXPLOSIONS
in the field of nowhere.
My pocketwatch burns air
and sprouts golden antlers.
I'm
the stand-in
for flaming stars;
my heart murmurs
are electric guitars

---

[*] Michael McClure, "The Poet's Poet," *Rolling Stone*, March 14, 1974: 33.

and
my hair
reflects in rainbows
and in aura glows
that radiate my brow.
The tinsel ice
does melt
beneath my feet—
my words are fleet—
and my songs
are an armada.
I see
the smiles of cherubs float
from the barranca.
The world with all its facets
is a whirling boat
of leopards and of mice
from which I hurl
the radiant dice
of my perceptions.
All conceptions
of boundaries
are lies!

World Gone Wrong Again

TOM PIAZZA

Several writers in this volume—Greil Marcus, Joyce Carol Oates, Christopher Ricks, Greg Tate, Sean Wilentz and others—see Dylan as representing a quintessentially American ethos, whether as an example of reinvention, as generational spokesman or for bringing to life the figures of an oral tradition. It is one of the most fascinating and enduring aspects of his songs.

For Tom Piazza, Dylan is an exemplary American artist because he embodies contradiction. Centering on *Good as I Been to You* and *World Gone Wrong*, the acoustic folk albums recorded in 1992 and '93, his essay discusses the various transformations of Dylan's career, which has accommodated so many roles—protest singer, rocker, evangelist, blues interpreter. Since it has often been remade in this fashion, his music creates certain contradictions, and as Piazza deftly explains, "the containing of those urgent and apparently incompatible claims within one framework is a very American thing." Examining an entire career, "World Gone Wrong Again" is a moving exploration of Dylan's ties to his native culture.

Piazza's books include the novel *My Cold War*, the short-story collection *Blues and Trouble* and *True Adventures with the King of Bluegrass*, a portrait of the country music legend Jimmy Martin. Dylan picked Piazza to write an essay about him for the 1997 Kennedy Center Honors commemorative book. He lives in New Orleans and may be visited at tompiazza.com.

1

"It's so grandiloquent to speak of 'the national character,' "Norman Mailer once remarked, before going on to speak of the national character.

In the centrifuge of the accelerating world, unlike elements once held in solution have separated out. Things go by fast; you have to label them quickly.

America is the incarnation of good; America is the embodiment of evil. Cast your vote; it only takes a second. This is not an essay question; please just mark "yes" or "no."

America. . . . Meaning what, again? Cowboys and Indians? New York City? Hollywood? The Civil War? The CIA? Interstate highways? Main Street? Wal-Mart? John Wayne? John Wayne Gacy? Earl Scruggs? Muhammad Ali? Rosa Parks? Don Rickles? Flaco Jimenez? Edmund Wilson? Redwood forests? Gulf stream waters? Ellis Island? Los Alamos? America wants to include all possibility, hence it takes up, potentially, all the space there is. It expands. Something so internally contradictory is, of course, a target for every kind of projection. The mind has trouble accepting such intense contradictions within the same entity. Their presence creates a profound anxiety. Learning to accept them is a discipline.

Is it because the culture as a whole contains such extremes of good and bad that there is such a pull to identify with only one vein or corner of the culture?

To identify with the culture itself means identifying with a high level of tension among elements. It means identifying with the tension itself.

I don't know. . . . It used to be important to me. Maybe it still is. I'm trying to figure it out.

But the worst elements in the world are either wrapping themselves in the flag or hoping to exorcise their problems by burning it.

2

People like to make generalizations about artists, but you really can't. Generally speaking. Anytime you say something like "artists need freedom," right away you realize that artists also need necessity. If you say they need a tradition, it is also immediately clear that they need to be able to work against a tradition. Or, rather some do. And some don't.

But it is probably true that most people who are artists as we tend to mean that word have very contradictory needs and impulses, and that their work is among other things a way of mediating between opposite forces in their own nature. Melville's poem about art says, "Humility—yet pride and scorn / Instinct and study; love and hate / Audacity—reverence. These must mate . . ." in order to "wrestle with the angel." It is an impulse toward wholeness and balance.

Certainly most significant artists implicitly or explicitly pose questions about the relation between the individual and society. Everybody, of course, leads a dual citizenship as an individual and as a member of a larger group, just as we all live both in the present moment and in a continuum with some past and future. In the United States, these relations are unusually complex, because the society is based not on a fixed grid of social organization against which intelligible individual dramas play out, but on an ideal of fluidity in which identity is nothing if not elastic and individuals can re-create themselves, or try to, by moving down the road, making a fresh start. That's the mythology, at least.

"Significant artists," "American artists" . . . the terms are vaguely embarrassing. Even the word "artist." It is too big a concept. You need to make distinctions among the types. But how useful are the distinctions? Michelangelo, Ravi Shankar, Sarah Vaughan, Akira Kurosawa, Chuck Berry, Beethoven, Sviatoslav Richter, Charley Patton, Emily Dickinson, Romare Bearden, Dock Boggs, Laurence Olivier, William Faulkner, the Notre Dame stone masons, Bessie Smith, an Asmat shield carver, Dante. . . .

Today the distinctions between types of artists seem to be less important than they once were. To some people, of course, it is still vitally important to maintain the distinction between, say, "fine art" and "folk art." Others like to state loudly that there is no difference. But there's a difference. Anytime you can make a terminological distinction there's a difference. But how important is it, and to whom? And—if you are interested in this kind of question—why?

It's easy to be dismissive of the kind of anxiety that fuels a strident emphasis on the setting of boundaries for terms. But the disintegration of a culture, or of an individual personality, often begins when it is no longer possible to pose intelligible questions about boundaries. If there are no locatable boundaries, then there is no locatable center, either. There is a paradox here for any culture or individual that seeks to continue growing. As a paradox, it is inherently insoluble. You have to embrace the paradox itself, perhaps, to keep from being smashed to pieces. Like a gyroscope that has to keep spinning in order to stay upright. A lot of times the struggle results in a religious conversion of some type.

3

Good as I Been to You and *World Gone Wrong*, Bob Dylan's two early-1990s solo recordings, recorded just after he'd hit his fifties and more than a decade after he got Saved, sit like a two-headed sphinx in the middle of Dylan's recorded work. People never talk about them all that much. Two records in a row of Dylan, all by himself, performing only traditional (or at least old) songs from the repertoires of Blind Willie McTell, Frank Hutchison, the Mississippi Sheiks, not one Dylan original among them. Nothing but Dylan; everything but Dylan.

For at least three years before 1992's *Good as I Been to You*, the best parts of a Dylan concert were likely to be his performances of other people's songs, especially traditional songs like "Girl on the Greenbriar Shore," "Roving Gambler," "Barbara Allen," "Golden Vanity," songs he knew from the beginning, back when people didn't mind stepping on him. It was almost as if he was tired of being himself. Whoever that was. Onstage he often seemed lost in the wilderness. The songs, however, had clearly lasted, and were demonstrably true. They had lasted not just outside him, in the culture, but inside him. They could provide a sense of magnetic north, bearings, orientation.

From the beginning, Dylan pieced together a persona, both social and creative, from found elements. That bag of found elements seemed to give him a meaning, or a rationale, a spiritual or psychic exoskeleton, a set of forms in which he could invest his roiling polymorphous energies. But any exoskeleton can become a cage, too. The thing that supports you from outside also constrains the free exercise of the polymorphous imagination. Being labeled—a marketing device for some, a security blanket for anxious listeners—is the ultimate trap. Eventually the id, or whatever you want to call it, will want to bust up the fixed form by which the world has come to know it. "That's not me," the Jokerman inside howls. "Never assume you know who I am." A series of masks or guises, because the inner thing is unknowable itself. Its name is unsayable.

On the evidence, Dylan has been both strongly attracted to absolute claims and yet also extremely wary of them. He apparently operates under an extremely high level of tension. The absolute claim of independence ("Don't follow leaders!"); the absolute need to serve somebody ("Property of Jesus!"). The need to choose moral sides ("It may be the devil or it may be the Lord"); the resistance to shouting "which side are you on?" The containing of those urgent and apparently incompatible claims within one framework is a very American thing.

4

Nobody knows what really goes on for an artist. It's presumptuous to think you can, any more than you can know what really goes on inside somebody else's marriage. Unlike elements are engaged in a constantly evolving dialogue.

"I don't know who I am most of the time," Dylan told David Gates in a 1997 *Newsweek* interview. "It doesn't even matter to me. . . . I find the religiosity and the philosophy in the music. I don't find it anywhere else. . . . I believe the songs." In the interview he was speaking specifically about gospel songs, but it is no stretch to imagine that it also applies to the whole body of folk- and blues-based music that informed his work. The songs gave him a text to go on, a Holy Book containing not an orthodoxy but a kind of anti-orthodoxy in which the most disparate elements were all given space at the table. In the mid-1990s he started appearing onstage dressed like the reincarnation of Hank Williams. It may not be too much to say that his intense reconnection to the traditional material at that point amounted to a kind of small secular conversion, a renewal and realigning of what was of value, what was necessary and what was possible.

Parallel things had happened previously in his career, of course. After arriving in New York City in 1961 as the hobo angel boy from everywhere, performing traditional material and then infusing it with more and more of his own inner light and darkness, the wheels stopped in 1966; he went back to the basics with the material that came to be called the basement tapes and came out with *John Wesley Harding*. The process began again and toward the end of the 1970s the wheels stopped again and he came out with *Slow Train Coming*. One could say that the subsequent *Infidels*, and its outtakes, bears the same relation to *Slow Train* as *Highway 61 Revisited* bore to *The Times They Are A-Changin*—the calculus of doubt and conflict and irony and corrosive anger and livid imagery supplanting the algebra of faith and direct statement. As if Dante had started the *Divine Comedy* in the *Paradiso*, or at least the *Purgatorio*, and ended in the *Inferno*.

Whether there is a causal relation or not, Dylan's performances began pulling together sharply in the year or so after *World Gone Wrong* came out in 1993, and he also began work on the material that would comprise two of the best records he ever made, *Time Out of Mind* and *Love and Theft*.

Dylan cited his sources for the *World Gone Wrong* songs in the disc's booklet; the sources for the *Good as I Been to You* songs have been discussed in print with varying degrees of accuracy. In *Behind the Shades Revisited*, Clinton Heylin quotes Ian Andersen, the editor of something called *Folk Roots*, as writing that there is "no shadow of a doubt" that "the rich old has-been" (that would be Dylan) copied his arrangement of "Frankie and Albert" from Mississippi John Hurt's 1928 recording. Really? You listen to it and tell me. Dylan's vocal approach has a lot more in common with Charley Patton's version of "Frankie and Albert" than with Mississippi John's. Andersen insists that there is "very little doubt" that his arrangement of "Hard Times" comes from De Dannan, but the McGarrigle sisters' version is at least as likely a choice. But, in fact, what is striking about the performances on *Good as I Been* is the extent to which Dylan turns each song to his own expressive purposes. Heylin, with his trademark penchant for broad, definitive, dubious, and eerily hostile statements claims that, of Dylan's performances on *Good as I Been*, only "Tomorrow Night" "had the stamp of originality." I wonder if he knows Blind Boy Fuller's original version of "Step It Up and Go," or Tom Rush's recording of "Diamond Joe," the most likely source for that tune (not to be confused with the song of the same name that Dylan performs in *Masked and Anonymous*, which comes from the Georgia Crackers probably by way of the New Lost City Ramblers . . .). In fact, "Tomorrow Night" may be one of the least original arrangements on the disc, along with "Arthur McBride."

In any case, on both discs Dylan pulls songs from sources as different as English and Irish balladry, the blues, and nineteenth-century parlor songs, and from performers across the range of the folk tradition—as Harry Smith did in compiling his *Anthology of American Folk Music* for Folkways Records—and claims all of the territory as his own.

5

Of course, if you say "American artist," right away a tension is set up. The dual citizenship. Dylan has been one if anyone has. Not by wrapping himself in the term "American," but by being very aware of the culture and place and time in which he has found himself, and trying to make sense of it. Or give an imaginative shape to it. What was "Bob Dylan's 115th Dream" about? Or "Masters of War"? Or "Clean Cut Kid," or "Hurricane," or "John Wesley Harding," or, for that matter, "Foot of Pride"? There is the abiding realization that the fate of the individual and that of the culture as a whole are intertwined. The individual in fact recapitulates his or her sense of the culture within himself.

Possession, demonic or otherwise, implies that one part of an organism has taken control of the whole, putting things out of balance and destroying as much of the organism as possible before someone either exorcises the demon or destroys the host organism from without.

America has always been extremely vulnerable to fears of possession, and it has gone through famous periods of panic over it. The Salem witch trials, populist rhetoric about special interest groups, anti-Communist fever, Eisenhower's warnings against the military-industrial complex. . . . Sometimes the concerns are justified. But the most opportunistic elements in the society usually look for a way to exploit the concern in order to gain greater power. Which in turn fuels greater concern. . . . This tendency toward entropy seems built into the logic of our society, and it is a paradox from which we may not recover.

In the 1970s Dylan could conceive of going out on the road with the Rolling Thunder tour and reclaiming the spirit of America—freedom, possibility, creativity, inclusiveness—from the clutches of the folks who brought us the Vietnam involvement and Watergate. Today we have bigger problems. The spirit itself, the sense of entitlement, is questionable. In the aftermath of 9/11, the oil companies scrambling to enrich themselves, the media full of sentimentality, the rush to jettison constitutionally guaranteed liberties, shopping as a patriotic duty. . . . Is that really what it was all about all the time? Does it really all amount to a big Coke commercial? Who says the greediest and most rapacious bastards in a society get to define what it means? Can a culture get so defiled that its own citizens don't recognize it?

Everybody pieces together their own America in the brain, whether they want to or not. Dylan's career still suggests a way of operating within such painful confusion. In making a harmony of such apparent discord, it reminds us that freedom is a curse and a blessing at exactly the same moment. But that's how you know it's alive.

PART FOUR

WHEN YOU GOT NOTHING, YOU GOT NOTHING TO LOSE (1997–)

"You can always come back, but you can't come back all the way."

—*Bob Dylan, 2001*

Dylan Revisited

F ive months after Dylan suffered a near-fatal heart scare in May 1997, *Time Out of Mind* was released. Perhaps his best collection of blues songs, many critics and fans saw it as his most significant work in decades. In a *Newsweek* feature, David Gates considers the album's relation to Dylan's earlier music, and how it redefines or redeems the public's view of his career. Gates's thoughts on lyrics are particularly keen, and his interview with Dylan contains several revealing quotes. In addition to discussing *Time Out of Mind*, Dylan lets on to the exact origins of his comeback—how and where he alighted upon a renewed sense of purpose—and offers his most sincere answer to the religion question.

Gates is a senior editor at *Newsweek*, where he writes about books and music. He is the author of three works of fiction—*Preston Falls, Jernigan* and *Wonders of the Invisible World*—and is at work on a collection of stories.

AS YOU SIT across from him, his face keeps changing. Sometimes it's that I-see-right-through-you look from the cover of *Highway 61 Revisited*— you barely notice the white hairs among the curls, the two days' worth of stubble and the thirty years' worth of lines. Now he turns his head: there's the profile from *Blood on the Tracks*. Now he thrusts his chin up, and he's the funny, defiant kid who used to wear that Bob Dylan cap. Well, he *is* Bob Dylan. The man who did to popular music what Einstein did to physics. The incarnation of the counterculture. The songwriter of the century. Sitting right there. So what's on his mind?

It turns out that he loves to talk about Merle Haggard and early Elvis. Or Brian Wilson: "That ear—I mean, Jesus, he's got to will that to the Smithsonian." Or Sinatra: "The *tone* of his voice. It's like a cello. Me and Don Was wanted to record him doing Hank Williams songs. I don't know, for some reason or other it never got off the ground." And when it comes to musical arcana, he knows the secret handshakes. Somehow you get talking about the old country duo Johnnie and Jack, and how Jack died in a car crash. "Car crash goin' to *Pasty Cline's funeral*," he chimes in. Bingo.

But you're really here, in an oceanfront hotel in L.A., to talk about the record he's releasing this week, *Time Out of Mind*, completed before his widely reported death scare last spring; it's got that album-of-the-year buzz publicists can help along some but not create. But there's stuff he's put off-limits—where he lives, his children—and stuff you just *know* not to ask. What did those black and white loafers set him back? Is he still in touch with his ex-wife? In fact, he seems near the edge of his comfort zone talking about why he's not talking about one of his most illegible back pages: that conservative, born-again-Christian phase that blindsided his liberal, secular fan base some fifteen years ago. "It's not tangible to me," he says. "I don't think I'm tangible to myself. I mean, I think one thing today and I think another thing tomorrow. I change during the course of a day. I wake and I'm one person, and when I go to sleep I know for certain I'm somebody else. I don't know *who* I am most of the time. It doesn't even matter to me." This cracks him up.

Then he says, "Here's the thing with me and the religious thing. This is the flat-out truth: I find the religiosity and the philosophy in the music. I don't find it anywhere else. Songs like 'Let Me Rest on a Peaceful Mountain' or 'I Saw the Light'—that's my religion. I don't adhere to rabbis, preachers, evangelists, all of that. I've learned more from the songs than I've learned from any of this kind of entity. The songs are my lexicon. I believe the songs."

BOB DYLAN is fifty-six. Last May, when he almost died—of a viral infection in the sac around the heart—Columbia Records got five hundred calls in a single day. Earlier this year Greil Marcus's much-discussed *Invisible Republic*, a study of Dylan's 1967 *Basement Tapes*, rightly ranked his music with "the most intense outbreaks of twentieth-century modernism"; the death scare reminded us that Dylan is a major cultural figure—and that we won't always have him with us. But for Dylan himself, deep thoughts about mortality had to take a backseat. "Mostly I was in a lot of pain. Pain that was intolerable. That's the only way I can put it." By August, though, he was back on tour again, lightheaded from his medication but sounding none the worse for wear.

Last weekend Dylan performed before the Pope, reportedly at John Paul's own request, at a eucharistic conference in Bologna. John Paul listened, eyes closed, to "Knockin' on Heaven's Door" and the apocalyptic "A Hard Rain's A-Gonna Fall"; then Dylan doffed his white Stetson, shook the Pope's hand and sang "Forever Young." In December he will receive a Kennedy Center Honors award, with President Clinton in attendance. Will he have to speak? "No, they say I don't have to do a thing, which is"—he laughs—"perfect for me."

Dylan's been fitfully rebuilding his career for the past decade, after starring in the stillborn 1987 film *Hearts of Fire*, a knockoff of *A Star Is Born*, and releasing such disappointing (though underrated) albums as 1988's *Down in the Groove*. He's had triumphant media moments: his 1988 collaboration with Tom Petty, George Harrison and Roy Orbison as the Traveling Wilburys, his all-star thirtieth-anniversary celebration at Madison Square Garden in 1992, winning over critics in 1993 shows at Manhattan's Supper Club, holding his own with Metallica and Nine Inch Nails at Woodstock '94, his tight, audience-friendly 1994 set for *MTV Unplugged*. But more important are the hundred or so ordinary concerts he plays, year in, year out, on his Never Ending Tour (which he says ended in 1991) and its successors, to which he's given such names as the Why Do You Look at Me So Strangely Tour.

And he's newly famous as the father of the Wallflowers' Jakob Dylan. "I know they've sold a ton of records," says Dylan, who's "superstitious" about discussing family members. "I keep hearing that they're playing arenas or whatever with the Counting the Crows group." Did he try to interest Jakob in old blues and hillbilly music? "Yeah, he's heard the records. He has different likes because he was born at a different time—but sure, if he wants to hear good old-timey records, they're easily available to him." Do we take it he'd rather not comment on the Wallflowers' music? He laughs, either at your discomfiture or his, and—honest to Pete—the phone rings. (He can't help it if he's lucky.) Okay, so has he heard Counting Crows, whose "Mr. Jones" alludes to his "Ballad of a Thin Man" and has the line "I want to be Bob Dylan"? "I *have* heard of them," he says, "but I get them mixed up with somebody else." The few things he catches on the radio anymore sound "weak and hopeless"—and disposable. "The top stars of today, you won't even know their names two years from now. Four, five years from now, they'll be *obliterated*. It's all flaky to me."

This is the marketplace to whose vagaries he's committing *Time Out of Mind*. It's the first collection of his own new songs in six years—some Dylan-watchers feared there might never be another one—and maybe the best since 1975's *Blood on the Tracks*. His last two records, *Good as I Been to You* (1992) and the Grammy-winning *World Gone Wrong* (1993), were solo acoustic versions of blues and folk songs; *Time Out of Mind* should appeal to a wider audience. It's far more accessible than such thorny later master-works as *Infidels* (1983)—though it may also be his darkest record ever.

Producer Daniel Lanois, who also worked on Dylan's 1989 *Oh Mercy*, says he "asked Bob to step into the future" with such technological conveniences as tape-looped rhythm tracks. Dylan hoped to push back the clock. He structured one song around a guitar line in the Memphis Jug Band's 1929 "K.C. Moan," and he wanted his vocals to pack the punch of old recordings. "Bob would say to me, 'Little Richard's voice really cuts.'" (In his 1959 Hibbing, Minnesota, high school yearbook, Robert Zimmerman said his ambition was "to join the band of Little Richard.") Both the forward-looking Lanois and the backward-looking Dylan got their way.

Time Out of Mind is a spare, spooky-sounding album, its lyrics brutally plainspoken instead of "Dylanesque": "My sense of humanity has gone down the drain," he sings in "Not Dark Yet." It's about hopelessly lost love, about endless wandering—its first three songs begin with the singer walk-ing—about an aging man's increasing distance from his world. "I got new eyes / Everything looks far away." The landscape is hot and arid, and though there's no one around, he's "beginning to hear voices" and "listen-ing to every mind-polluting word." Dylan's own voice sounds appropri-ately murky, ravaged, distorted. "We treated the voice almost like a harmonica," says Lanois, "when you overdrive it through a small guitar amplifier."

Hard-core Dylan freaks can be contrary; they may join the crowd and proclaim *Time Out of Mind* the long-awaited best-since-*Blood*, or they may find it *too* accessible. But the last song, the $16\frac{1}{2}$-minute "Highlands," should poleax everybody: it's a Thurber daydream with a Beckett narrator ("talking to myself in a monologue"), a Robert Burns refrain and a hypnotic guitar hook from Charley Patton. In this funny, grim, crepuscular saga, the yearning for human connection gives way, with regret, to a yearning for transcendence. "Nobody knew what to make of it," says Dylan. Lanois, for better or worse, talked him out of a 21-minute version.

"It *is* a spooky record," says Dylan, "because I *feel* spooky. I don't feel in tune with anything." Yet he's proud of having registered his ambivalence and alienation so nakedly. "I don't think it eclipses anything from my earlier period. But I think it might be shocking in its bluntness. There isn't any waste. There's no line that has to be there to get to another line. There's no pointless playing with somebody's brain. I think it's going to reach the people it needs to reach, and the ones it doesn't, maybe they'll come along another day."

SOME THIRTY YEARS AGO, Dylan's work mattered more intensely to more people than anyone's does today. "He not busy being born is busy dying," he sang, and young people yearning for a role model and an imaginary friend hung on every word as he took on and shucked off persona after persona: the new Woody Guthrie, the voice of the Movement, the rock-and-roll Fellini, the poet of the bad trip and the doomed love affair, the minimalist mystic, the back-to-basics country boy. Fans flattered themselves that they were going through the same changes. "I never figured my music to blend into the culture in any kind of way, " Dylan says now. But back then it was hard to tell whether he was mirroring sixties youth culture or actually creating it. He offered ready-to-wear attitudes and ready-to-cherish slogans. "Even the president of the United States sometimes must have to stand naked." "Leave your stepping-stones behind." And—paradoxically—"Don't follow leaders."

Dylan's early political songs—"The Times They Are A-Changin'," "Masters of War"—belong to their era, but the electric music he invented in the mid-sixties is still in our faces. He set modern poetry—confessional, gnomic, comic, denunciatory, prophetic, visionary—to ecstatically dance-able rock and roll. John Lennon said Dylan's music transformed the Beat-les; today, everyone from R.E.M. to Beck to sedulously unlistenable art-metal bands shrieking out Tourettean lyrics over chainsaw guitar is doing what he made thinkable.

Dylan insists he's *not* a poet—"Wordsworth's a poet, Shelley's a poet, Allen Ginsberg's a poet"—and doesn't play rock and roll. Even back when the Beatles and the Rolling Stones were recycling blues and R&B as pop music, he had his doubts about the whole enterprise. "Part of me fell for it, but part of me didn't. The best part of me didn't fall for it at all." These days, he only listens to the old-timers, and he treasures the personal encounters he had. Big Joe Turner "on his last legs," walking with a cane, singing in one more club. Lonnie Johnson—"when he walked into the room, there was an eeriness about him"—showing him guitar fingerings. "I remember all those guys I saw. They live in my head. I can't get rid of them."

If he's adamant these days about seeing himself as their descendant and not a modernist genius for whom they were samples in the mix, who can blame him? Fans imagine the man who wrote "It Ain't Me Babe" *and* "Desolation Row" *and* "Gotta Serve Somebody" as a demigod—or a Mar-tian. "But I'm not the songs," he says. "It's like somebody expecting Shake-speare to be Hamlet, or Goethe to be Faust. If you're not prepared for fame, there's really no way you can imagine what a crippling thing it can be." The will that got him here in the first place has kept him practicing his art—which he insists is simply a "craft" or a "trade"—but he's often about this close from giving it up. "Some days I get up and it just makes me sick that I'm doing what I'm doing. Because basically—I mean, you're one cut above a pimp. That's what everybody who's a performer *is.* I have this voice in my head saying, '*Just be done with it.*'"

But what else would he do? "Oh, *man!*" he cries, and twists around in his chair to look out the window. There's a beach out there. Blue sky. "What *wouldn't* I do?"

TEN YEARS AGO, Dylan says, "I'd kind of reached the end of the line. Whatever I'd started out to do, it wasn't *that.* I was going to pack it in." Onstage, he couldn't do his old songs. "You know, like how do I sing this?

It just *sounds* funny." He goes into an all-too-convincing-imitation of panic: "I—I can't remember what it means, does it mean—is it just a bunch of *words*? Maybe it's like what all these people say, just a bunch of surrealistic nonsense." When the Grateful Dead took him on tour in 1987, Jerry Garcia urged him to try again. "He'd say, 'Come on, man, you know, this is the way it goes, let's play it, it goes like this.' And I'd say, 'Man, he's right, you know? How's he gettin' there and I can't get there?' And I had to go through a lot of red tape in my mind to get back there."

Then, in October 1987, playing Locarno, Switzerland, with Tom Petty's band and the female singers he now says he used to hide behind, Dylan had his breakthrough. It was an outdoor show—he remembers the fog and the wind—and as he stepped to the mike, a line came into his head. "It's almost like I heard it as a voice. It wasn't like it was even me thinking it. *I'm determined to stand, whether God will deliver me or not.* And all of a sudden everything just exploded. It exploded *every* which way. And I noticed that all the people out there—I was used to them looking at the girl singers, they were good-looking girls, you know? And like I say, I had them up there so I wouldn't feel so bad. But when that happened, nobody was looking at the girls anymore. They were looking at the main mike. After that is when I sort of knew: I've got to go out and play these songs. That's just what I must do." He's been at it ever since.

On the beastly hot Labor Day weekend of 1997, he ends his post-hospital tour with an outdoor show in Kansas City, Missouri. It's the usual crowd: sixties geezers, and kids with backwards caps, halter tops or granny dresses, nose studs, faux tattoos, T-shirts advertising a range of loyalties from Beck to Phish. What he sees from up here onstage is a floodlit ocean of faces and bare, swaying arms; he can smell the incense sticks someone in his crew sets burning in buckets of sand. He starts out with "Absolutely Sweet Marie" and moves on to a slinky "It Takes a Lot to Laugh, It Takes a Train to Cry," to the Stanley Brothers' "Stone Walls and Steel Bars," to a stately "Like a Rolling Stone," in which his electric guitar tangles up with countermelodies from guitarist Larry Campbell and pedal-steel player Bucky Baxter in a sweetly chiming, wildly raving choir. When he comes off after the last encore, you congratulate him and touch his shoulder. His jacket's soaked.

He knows what they say about his concerts. " 'Oh, he's massacring the songs, there's no way of knowing what you're going to get when go see a Dylan show, blah blah blah.' It's true, to a certain extent. But okay, so that show wasn't any good. Doesn't matter. There's tomorrow." In fact, he's been reworking his songs in concert since he began touring with the Band in 1966; he calls the familiar recorded versions merely "blueprints." He'll distill a verse of "Mr. Tambourine Man" to just two or three notes, followed up by a couple of choruses on guitar, repeating a single three-note pattern over each of the changing chords. When he's on, there's no place you'd rather be.

True, he's muffed his share of big moments, like his 1985 appearance at Live Aid with Keith Richards, Ron Wood and at least one horribly out-of-tune guitar. He's too self-contained, too inward, to come across on TV or video. But now that every twerp with a stylist wants to be an icon, it's enormously appealing that Dylan doesn't have an act together. Fans affectionately post his curious onstage obiter dicta on the Internet: "On bass guitar tonight, Tony Garnier. I'm not gonna say nothin' about Tony except that he once tried to milk a cow with a monkey wrench." If there's a hint of condescension here—jeez, what a character—it surely beats being Poet of His Generation. "I don't like to think of myself in the highfalutin area," says Dylan. "I'm in the burlesque era."

Huh? *Burlesque*? Oh. Old-timey lowlife entertainment. Standing naked in front of strangers. He's not a poet? Fine. But that's a hell of a word.

The old songsters Dylan reveres are gone now, but their music lives. He can never again be the sweet-faced young man on the cover of *The Freewheelin' Bob Dylan* (1963), walking on a snowy Manhattan street with a sweet-faced girl clinging to his arm. But he's still the man who said, in the notes to that album, "I don't carry myself yet the way that Big Joe Williams, Woody Guthrie, Leadbelly and Lightnin' Hopkins have carried themselves. I hope to be able to someday." Not long ago, he saw a dance performance, to songs he'd cut in the early sixties, and didn't recognize his own voice. "I said, 'What's this? This is incredible.' I thought it was some obscure person. But it wasn't; it was me. I'll have somebody get a copy and send it to you. You'll be amazed." Not at how terrific he was; that's not what he means. He means, *That kid was on to something.* He means, *A lot of water's gone over the dam.*

"We try and we try and we try to be who we were," he says. "That's why everybody who went down went down." Is he talking about the dead-rock-star pantheon he's refused to join? "People we all know," he answers. "Who just—went down. Into the ground. Or scattered in the air, wherever they are. Sooner or later you come to the realization that we're *not* who we were. So then what do we do?" His whole career has been a series of temporary answers. The latest answer's on his new record: you keep putting one foot in front of the other. "I'm walking," the first song begins, "through streets that are dead." It's one of the great Bob Dylan opening lines. *How many roads must a man walk down?* It's the darkest one yet. But the point is, he's walking.

Shadow Play: B-C-D
and Back

ROBERT POLITO

Dylan is the most bootlegged musician in the United States. Unauthorized records, tapes and CDs of studio outtakes and concerts from every point in his career have been widely available since the late 1960s. In this essay, Robert Polito describes the culture of bootlegging and what the unofficial releases suggest about Dylan as an artist. Endorsing the opinion of many collectors and observers, Polito explains how one cannot properly understand Dylan's repertoire or place in American music without hearing the bootlegged oeuvre. The variety of Dylan's studio sessions, his constant touring and the way songs evolve through live performance make this "parallel ghost world" much more than an enthusiast's hobby—as Polito reveals, bootlegs may be the most important Dylan recordings.

Polito directs the Graduate Writing Program at the New School University in New York City. His books include *Doubles* (poems), *A Reader's Guide to James Merrill's The Changing Light at Sandover* and *Savage Art: A Biography of Jim Thompson*, which received the National Book Critics Circle award in biography.

THERE IS THE KICK of the illicit—and the rarer kick of illicit *knowledge*. Bootleg recordings embody both. You tell yourself as you depart the site of purchase, I am not meant to have this; and later as you listen alone in your apartment, I was not meant to hear—overhear?—it. No one would care about the shadow career of Bob Dylan if his official albums weren't so conspicuously innovative and legendary. But **Premise B:** What if Dylan's illicit recordings—bootlegs of live performances, studio outtakes, rehearsals, and unreleased songs—ultimately prove, as now appears likely, his most vital, revelatory, and enduring work?

Since 1962 Dylan has released some forty-plus albums of new music, mainly on the Columbia or Sony/Columbia label, yet on any given afternoon around Greenwich Village there is a variable stock of Dylan bootleg CDs roughly five to ten times the span of his official catalog. Commercial but unlicensed, bootlegs travel an underground though scarcely clandestine economy along the outskirts of fandom. Bootlegs aren't pirate recordings—counterfeit copies of lawful goods—just as bootleg stores aren't really haunts of Bob collectors, a still more crepuscular if arguably "purer" network of swapped cassettes and archival pages of the young Dylan's marginalia in Woody Guthrie's *Bound for Glory*.

Bootlegs once flaunted mimeographed sleeves, and vinyl that visibly degenerated during play. Now the moonshine tops the official releases in style and authority—meticulous annotation, lavish booklets, often stunning sound, and smart titles: *Violence of a Summer's Dream, The Lonely Graveyard of My Mind, After the Crash, Stuck Inside New York,* and *Boots of Spanish Treasure.* Paul Williams vividly refocused Dylan as "foremost a performing artist, as opposed to a composer or songwriter" for three books that venture to map the forty years of live shows that comprise the vast terra incognita of Dylan bootleg CDs. Greil Marcus rooted his plangent vision of the "old, weird America" of Harry Smith, Dock Boggs, and Bob Dylan not in the 1975 Columbia collection of sixteen tracks on *The Basement Tapes* but in a spectacular five-CD bootleg set of 103 songs, *The Genuine Basement Tapes.*

Alongside the popular Dylan legend of masterpieces and betrayals, I wish to posit an entire parallel ghost world of once and future bootlegs. Some shadow releases inevitably circle his catalog like spectral moons, restoring songs and brilliant alternate takes to *The Freewheelin' Bob Dylan* (1963), *Blood on the Tracks (1975), Infidels* (1983), and *Oh Mercy* (1989) or capturing sharper, more decisive concerts from the tours documented on his official live albums. When Sony/Columbia finally issued *Live 1966: The "Royal Albert Hall" Concert,* in 1998, bootleggers matched and raised it—

first in an eight-CD box of coruscating 1966 shows and, then, in a twenty-six-CD box of all extant 1966 concerts from America, Australia, and Europe. Dylan's own generous retrospective compendium of studio and live rarities, *The Bootleg Series Volumes 1–3* (1991), prompted the phantom rival of a trio of three-CD packages, *The Genuine Bootleg Series*—a chronological anthology of 157 additional "lost" performances.

But many imposing Dylan shadows find only faint echo in the official chronicle. The sweeter, tent-show-caravan swing of the 1975 Rolling Thunder Revue can be recovered only on wildcat recordings that catch perhaps Dylan's most resourceful singing. Or the gospel music of 1980 and 1981—again illicit CDs, including a Toronto show recorded by Columbia, yield sole entrée to these nuanced, adventurous performances, and to important songs, such as "Caribbean Wind," "Let's Keep It Between Us," or "Yonder Comes Sin," that never reached his albums.

Recently, *Love and Theft* (2001) offered as a bonus track a 1961 Minneapolis version of an early Dylan original, "I Was Young When I Left Home." But the surest guide to Bob Dylan before *Bob Dylan* (1962) are some fragmentary, surreal boots—starting with a 1958 wire-recorder home tape of the Hollywood Flames' "Buzz, Buzz, Buzz," and Little Richard's "Jenny, Jenny," among other songs and conversation ("When you hear a good rhythm-and-blues song, chills go up your spine," he tells his high school buddy John Bucklen), and continuing on a 1960 tape recorded in a St. Paul apartment that reveals Dylan singing a folk repertoire in a charming lilt reminiscent of Elvis Presley's *Sun Sessions* ("He reminded me of a little choirboy . . . with this beautiful voice," an old friend remembers on an accompanying interview track).

Out of the recesses of hotel, radio, and club recordings, Dylan's early engagement of folk and blues in Minnesota, and soon after in New York, emerges as deeper and more various than even all the death-haunted songs on Dylan's official debut intimate. Traditional tunes frame and ground his live shows into this century. The fearsome *Golden Vanity*, for instance, sweeps up a grievous parade of old ballads culled from late-eighties and early-nineties tours, only one song reappearing on his official folk collections, *Good as I Been to You* (1992) and *World Gone Wrong* (1993). Dylan still tends to open shows with traditional covers—often now of the Stanley Brothers, one of the ghost bands in his ongoing shadow play.

Dylan's current concerts (along the self-styled "Never Ending Tour," nonstop from 1988 through the present at a clip of 115 shows a year) so far lack official documentation. Over the past decade, but particularly on his 2000 British and American tours, Dylan steadily staked his claim to the vast inheritance of American music—not only through traditional covers, but also inside nightly recasting of his old and new songs. Nearly all these shows are retrievable on CDs lifted from vivid source tapes. They are fluid summations sustained by his most versatile and sympathetic backing band ever and his own idiosyncratic lead guitar. Dylan's transformation of his catalog over a single evening can summon American music from the earliest anonymous folk airs through the last century of blues, country, gospel, bluegrass, into rock and roll, punk, even heavy metal (a 1994 "Maggie's Farm" invoked "Smoke on the Water"). Although he rarely rewrites lyrics, his modulations of intonation and phrasing might shift a song's meaning utterly: "The Times They Are A-Changin'," for instance, now conjures the end of the world.

During a recent interview in the *Los Angeles Times,* Dylan remarked that he had experienced a creative resurgence in "the early nineties when I escaped the organized media. They let me be. They considered me irrelevant, which was the best thing that could have happened to me." Dylan probably is more visible now in media culture than at any moment since the late 1960s, but his point is that **Premise C:** once outside his official past, free of the ordeal of generation-spokesman, Dylan could luxuriate in another, more resonant myth—his mastery of all-American music.

Throughout his prior official career, every evolution was a variation on Newport 1965: any fresh move he made, rock, or country, or gospel, marked either a breach of faith ("Judas," as the man shouted at Manchester in 1966) or a return to the fold ("We've got Dylan back again," as *Rolling Stone* intoned in 1970). *That* Dylan was the Byron of his era—yet as an innovator inside a musical tradition, he stands closer to Louis Armstrong, and as a singer inhabiting a lyric, he is nearer Sinatra.

His current shows can converge and reinvent songs from any year: *Slow Train Coming* (1979) and *Nashville Skyline* (1969) alongside *Highway 61 Revisited* (1965), *Blonde on Blonde* (1966), and *Blood on the Tracks* (1975); *Bob Dylan* (1962) and *Freewheelin'* (1963) next to *Infidels* (1984), *Oh Mercy* (1989), and *Time Out of Mind* (1997). His shadow world in that sense is timeless. Released from his chronology and history, his songs are all Dylan songs.

Once there were only his official albums—now the shadows heap them.

SOMETIME during the 1970s I lost touch with Dylan's official career, and even now I am more likely to play a bootleg than one of the Columbia albums, unless that recording appeared after I started listening again in 1991. This indifference followed a conventional fascination with Dylan—conventional, at least, for 1960s school*boys*—and was due to **Counterpremise D:** my own conservatism, although I obsessively tracked new music, Bowie, Roxy Music, punk imports, and read about still more records in the English music weeklies. I marveled at Bryan Ferry's elegant tweaking of Dylan on his theatrical cover of "A Hard Rain's A-Gonna Fall" on *These Foolish Things,* a sly pop art readymade that positioned Dylan alongside Lesley Gore.

Watching the September 1976 NBC broadcast of the Rolling Thunder Revue performing at a rainy Fort Collins stadium, I could lodge only the bewildering differences—in the singing, songwriting, even the gypsy headgear—from the sixties. Not until two decades later when I purchased a bootleg videotape of *Hard Rain,* at a store on Eighth Street, could I recognize the ravishing fury of Dylan's vocal, or the intimations of punk (a few months after the Ramones' debut) particularly in the *Blood on the Tracks* songs: a feral, back-to-the-wall execution of "Idiot Wind."

On occasions when I inadvertently heard Dylan's latest records at parties and dinners, I wouldn't listen also for all the **Counterpremise D:** piety. My graduate-school and young poet friends are readily caricatured; my "Byron of his era" line above is an approximation. But by the 1980s, official Dylan—not so much his songs, but the talk around them, and the gnomic recitation of lyrics—seemed nostalgic, self-congratulatory, middlebrow. Dylan famously introduced literature and art to rock and roll, along with pretension and the notion of the masterpiece, what Manny Farber, writing of film, once tagged "the square, boxed-in shape and gemlike inertia of an old, densely wrought European masterpiece." Yet the masterwork **Premise C:** couldn't be more inimical to his shadow enterprise.

Two events from 1991, only fitfully linked, focused this Dylan ghost world. On February 20 Dylan accepted a lifetime achievement award at the Grammy Awards in New York. This was the eve of the Gulf War. Although pressured to reprise "Blowin' in the Wind" for the troops, he elected instead the sardonic "Masters of War"—except Dylan looked a sodden mess, and he chanted the words in an indistinct blur. He followed the song with a short, halting speech of nearly Napoleonic self-loathing: "My daddy once said to me . . . he said, 'Son . . . it is possible for you to become so defiled in this world that your own mother and father will abandon you . . . and if that happens, God will always believe in your ability to mend your own ways.' . . . Thank you." The moment, as they say, caught your attention, and five weeks later Columbia issued *The Bootleg Series Volumes 1–3*, the collection that started to reconfigure the past Dylan seemed to be running away from, and which was running away with him.

A chronological survey of thirty years of rare and unreleased songs, this imitation black-market CD box charted an alternative recording career for Dylan, salvaging jettisoned wonders, such as "Angelina," "Foot of Pride," and "Blind Willie McTell." There was the hint of a different artist, tentative, experimental, alert to accident, captivated by process, and a hint, too, of all the other missing songs that would soon turn up—are still turning up—on hundreds more shadow CDs. Not long after, I sought out my first bootleg on Thompson Street, a live recording from 1981 titled, prophetically, *Stadiums of the Damned*.

Dylan's official history is haunted by the masterpiece, every strong new record acclaimed his best since (choose one) *Blonde on Blonde, Blood on the Tracks*, or *Oh Mercy*. But ghost collections of studio outtakes impart an interactive spirit to his albums—what if this or that track is restored to, say, *Infidels*—much as concert bootlegs indicate that no song is finished, no take definitive. *Blood on the Tracks* probably is, as Rick Moody suggested at the PEN Town Hall sixtieth-birthday tribute, the most complete and honest account of a love affair ever recorded. Yet the emotional arc is more poignant after you hear the original New York versions of "Idiot Wind," "Tangled Up in Blue," "If You See Her, Say Hello," and "You're a Big Girl Now"—and still more devastating after you listen to Dylan reimagine the songs over twenty-five years of live shows. His hesitations, second-guesses, and revisions enhance the story: a truculent 1976 "Shelter from the Storm" that denies all refuge, and a distant, elegiac 2000 version, tendered like a fable from a previous life.

To my 1980s friends, Dylan was a sage who disguised all the answers—the shadow singer of the bootlegs is nothing but questions.

BOB DYLAN betrays the disconcerting sensation that **Premise B:** He dwells inside a private landscape of the great dead. These posthumous conversations span such monuments as Robert Johnson, Jimmie Rodgers, Hank Williams, Son House, Woody Guthrie, Blind Willie McTell, and Charley Patton, and marginally slighter markers on the order of Sleepy John Estes, Skip James, Rabbit Brown, Mance Lipscomb, Jesse Fuller, John Lee Hooker, Bill and Charlie Monroe, Buell Kazee, Emmett Miller, and Frank Hutchison. "They weren't there to see the end of the traditional people," Dylan once remarked of younger folk musicians. "But I was." Inside this landscape, the occasional live emissary, such as Ralph Stanley, also seems like a revenant.

Beyond a plausible spread of blues, rockabilly, and bluegrass covers, ranging from the Stanleys to Muddy Waters and Elizabeth Cotten, Dylan can direct his band past some inconceivable vistas—Charles Aznavour ("The Times We've Known") and Dean Martin ("Return to Me") among them. At Frank Sinatra's 1995 eightieth-birthday celebration, the strings on Dylan's arrangement of "Restless Farewell" hovered arrestingly between country swing and Nelson Riddle. During recent circuits of the Never Ending Tour he revamped songs from *Time Out of Mind*, layering them with echoes of Hoagy Carmichael and Charlie Christian. *Love and Theft* revisits an instant in the late 1920s when country, blues, jazz, and minstrelsy improbably merged, before resuming discrete paths.

"I find the religiosity and the philosophy in the music," Dylan told David Gates in *Newsweek*. "I don't find it anywhere else. Songs like 'Let Me Rest on a Peaceful Mountain' or 'I Saw the Light'—that's my religion. I don't adhere to rabbis, preachers, evangelists, all of that. I've learned more from the songs than I've learned from any of this kind of entity. **Premise C:** The songs are my lexicon. I believe the songs."

THE FIRST DYLAN (and the first rock) bootleg, the vinyl *Great White Wonder* of 1969, a farrago of basement songs and Minneapolis home sessions, originated in a critique of the songwriter that implied he either had lost his way or no longer could recognize his strongest work. "DYLAN'S BASEMENT TAPE SHOULD BE RELEASED," as the headline ran in *Rolling Stone* for a cover story, "THE MISSING BOB DYLAN ALBUM." He was muddying a once-clear picture with strange new music, and bootleggers knew best. Slipped inside *Great White Wonder* was **Counterpremise D:** a sentimental conjecture (which this Shadow Play cannot fully escape) that somewhere else—back into the past, or on a secret tape—"the real Dylan" endures. Oddly, though, now **Premise D:** the only angle where a reductive search for a truer Dylan vanishes is on the bootlegs: over the sweep and reach of his shadow recordings he is, of course, everywhere, and nowhere.

Dylan's own attitude toward the ghost world is predictably double. Even as in interviews he scolds "those folks out there who are obsessed with finding every scrap of paper I've ever written on, every single outtake . . . It's called stealing," Columbia/Sony teases obsessives with rarities, and his Web site (bobdylan.com) circulates live songs. And every dealer I've ever met tells a story of Dylan exclaiming over some stylish contraband, "Hey, these guys do a better job than my label!"

Just days after I sat down to write, **Counterpremise C:** federal agents raided four stores in Greenwich Village, seizing every bootleg CD on the premises. Past busts tended to interrupt, though not stop, the weekly influx of fresh titles, but so far only legit product sits in the racks. The agents ignored a few smaller outlets that more cleverly and confusingly mix boots among imports; still, the nervous owners relegated the moonshine to the back room.

Then the Twin Towers came down. When lower Manhattan opened again I walked by the raided shops—the grates were up, yet there was nothing for sale you couldn't buy at Tower.

But around the corner, inside a little store they missed, my friend Richard was setting out his stock as before.

"I'm guessing," he said, "that **Premise B:** the FBI has bigger things on its mind right now."

Song for Bob Dylan

NORBERT KRAPF

N orbert Krapf included an ode to Dylan in his book *The Country I Come From* (the title taken from a line in Dylan's "With God on Our Side"). Krapf has said that, like other poets, he sees Dylan as a kind of creative model: "just as poets who rebel against tradition draw nourishment from the tradition they revolt against, Bob Dylan has reformed aspects of American musical tradition. He has been able to breathe life into these traditions just as he has drawn life from them." "Song for Bob Dylan" is a variation on this idea—"one of the things I've always loved about Dylan is that he defies the expectations of his fans. That 'scraping cry' of his, those 'tingling antennae,' and those 'reflecting eyes' are one image, aren't they? My little Midwestern creature 'wings away' to a new rebirth as an artist just as his fans grow comfortable with his last phase. This poem is a fable in miniature."

Krapf has taught at Long Island University and directed the C.W. Post Poetry Center from 1985 to 2004. His twelve poetry collections include the trilogy *Somewhere in Southern Indiana, Blue-Eyed Grass: Poems of Germany* and *Bittersweet Along the Expressway: Poems of Long Island*; he may be visited at krapfpoetry.com

The restless little
Midwestern creature
with reflecting eyes
tingling antennae
& scraping cry

secretes himself in
a new myth for each
winter & then drops
out & wings away
to another tree just
as his followers
begin to wriggle
in the cocoon
that's fallen behind.

Dylan at 60

Dylan's sixtieth birthday, on May 24, 2001, was widely celebrated by the press. Several magazines and newspapers ran commemorative features, and *The New Yorker* and PEN held a festival in his honor at Town Hall in New York. The next month, *Rolling Stone* printed short essays on Dylan by fourteen writers and musicians. Here are four of those tributes, by Bono, Michael Chabon, Jonathan Lethem and Camille Paglia, as well as a piece by Joyce Carol Oates that has not been published before. Together, they speak for all sides of Dylan's appeal—not only as fans, but also the ways, as writers and thinkers, that they have been influenced by the man Oates calls "the exemplary Dionysus figure."

BONO

Bono is the singer for U2—whose albums include *The Joshua Tree*, *Achtung Baby* and *All That You Can't Leave Behind*—as well as a prominent activist working to combat AIDS and poverty. In a conversation with Anthony DeCurtis, he mentions how "Bob is like religion" and repeatedly praises Dylan for resisting the conventions of modern celebrity.

I CAN'T REMEMBER a time when Bob Dylan's voice wasn't in my head, but I first met him when U2 were recording *The Unforgettable Fire* at Slane Castle in Ireland, and he played there. His family was around, and I remember being struck then—as I'm continually struck—by how he seems to have a certain old-fashioned attitude toward his family. For example, he asked me if I'd take a photograph with him, and I was just about to fall backward, when I realized it was so his kids could be in it.

Then one time I interviewed him and Van Morrison for the Irish Maga-zine *Hot Press*, and in the interview I told him, "U2 have no roots." He just said, "Well, you've got to look back, that's the riches in Ireland." He's like this ancient voice that tells you that you need to know where you come from. There was a moment in the sixties when he came off all mod, but he's been combatting the filthy modern tide, as Yeats called it, for a long time.

His words have always had an almost biblical uprightness. No matter where you are in your life, there's a Dylan record that helps you map out the locale. When you're filled with teenage idealism. When you're falling in love. When you've just been divorced. When your kids are growing up. Even when you're facing the shock of illness or a brush with mortality. Bob is like religion: He'll get you one way or the other!

I'm sure he has his demons—the records pay tribute to that. But he's still alive and doing his best work. He started out as a sort of Rimbaud fig-ure, but he just refused to die stupid. There's a lot of mystery about him, but he doesn't turn mystery into melodrama. He's dealt with celebrity with a smirk and a mask of indifference. The same stare he gives the out-side world, he gives himself.

When Dylan played Dublin recently, he walked to the gig! He had his hood up, and he just walked past the punters on the way to see him. I think that's how he wants it. He's lost interest in playing the game, and he's just gotten on with his life as a writer and performer. He's more of the Middle Ages than the New Millenium, the troubadour who will play wherever there's a meal on the table—whether it's Las Vegas or in front of the pope. God bless him.

MICHAEL CHABON

Chabon is the author of two collections of short stories and four novels, including *The Amazing Adventures of Kavalier and Clay*. "Things Have Changed," the song that earned Dylan an Academy Award in 2001, was written for the movie adapted from Chabon's *Wonder Boys*. Here, he mov-ingly revisits a turbulent period of adolescence, when Dylan was both a refuge and an introduction to the powers of narrative.

IN 1976, my mother, recently divorced, broke up painfully and protract-
edly with her first real boyfriend since the collapse of her marriage to my
father. I turned thirteen that May, and her birthday present to me was
Desire. It was my first Dylan album. I had been talking for a while about
this song I'd heard, only once, playing over the speakers in a Washington,
D.C., bookstore sometime during the preceding winter. I stood there in
the aisle, with a copy of *Dune* in my hand, trying to catch the lyric, to guess
the singer, to figure out what the hell was happening in the story. I remembered the song like a promising face, vividly and erroneously, for months
afterward, without hearing it again, until I unwrapped the disc my mother
handed me and put it on the turntable.

I lay down on the rug, between the speakers, with the mysterious
record jacket in my hands. On the front there was a fey Jewish cowboy in
furs and windblown scarves; on the back, tarot cards and a hermetic set of
liner notes shorn of punctuation, in an all but illegible type. As the record
began, I was aglow with the dewy pessimism of adolescence, ready to
extend the limits of my ignorance as far as I possibly could in the hope that
I might receive, as if from the perceived contour of those limits—what?
Some kind of negative confirmation of the path or pattern of my destiny?
A valuable secret about the universe or girls? At thirteen, you put on a
record for the first time with not merely a dire hope but a good possibility
that it is somehow going to alter the course of your life.

It turned out that I had heard the first cut, "Hurricane," on the radio,
several times, without ever associating it with that other elusive tune, the
one about a "mystical child" smiling in the rain and driving a man insane.
Then came the song itself: "Isis." Isis was an Egyptian goddess, the mother
of Horus and wife of Osiris—I knew that story. Isis was also the lead character in a CBS Saturday-morning television show, about a librarian or sci-
entist or other type of bespectacled woman who spun around while saying
"O Mighty Isis" and then was able to stop a Chevy van with her bare hands.
I knew that story, too. But as the story of Isis—Bob Dylan's Isis—began, I
felt, I sensed, or maybe I finally just recognized, that another story was
beginning, one that would take place in a "wild unknown country," in "a
high place of darkness and light." So much has been written about Dylan's
voice—a voice I knew well enough, or thought I did, from the sixties standards, the classic rants and rambles. But this sounded, to me, like a different

man entirely. In the situation he described—a man and a woman united by failure and the memory of happiness, by passion and the memory of bitterness; the pursuit of some unknown treasure through wonder and hardship, to end in futility and a laugh at one's own expense—I thought I recognized, in the ache and the ardor of that windblown, Jewish-cowboy voice, the contours of a world I was just beginning to know.

JONATHAN LETHEM

Lethem has written seven books of fiction, most recently *Motherless Brooklyn* and *The Fortress of Solitude*. His essay, keenly felt and valedictory, considers Dylan's late style and most recent achievements, as well as the songwriter's famously elusive aura.

ABRAHAM LINCOLN grew his beard—the first worn by an American president—between his election and his swearing-in. Things Have Changed, I believe the message was. Similarly, Bob Dylan grew that funny little Clark Gable mustache before being awarded his Oscar but some time since the last time you'd had a good look at his face up close. Only, when was it that you'd had a good look at his face up close? And were you really having one during the Oscars, at that triple remove, peering through your television to watch a crowd of movie stars watching Dylan beamed in like an astronaut from the outback? And yet, for the yearning seemingly beamed back at him by those movie stars—certainly for the yearning and love beamed back at him through screens and across time zones from the room where I sat watching—he was in that moment more present in absence than anyone else in the world.

That face, it was so damn real I wondered if I'd ever seen Bob Dylan before in my life. Who's ever been so universal and spectral, and at once, so sweetly homely and strange as Bob Dylan in 2001? And when was it he drifted into that unassailable, holy-humble twilight stratosphere he now occupies? Somewhere in 1997, probably, when the eerie grace of *Time Out of Mind* persuaded listeners to relinquish can-it-be-as-good-as-I-hope defenses and realized it was better than they'd dared hope. The record achieved its own "I'm here/I'm not" sleight-of-hand, being great in cumulative impact rather than for any particular song. Dylan hid in plain sight in lyrics cobbled from blues sources and his own catalog but capped the album with "Highlands," a laid-back dirge that felt like the unedited Bob's diary he'd never actually delivered before, despite all rumors.

Add his metaphoric brush with death—"BOB DYLAN HEART MYSTERY" was the unforgettable *New York Post* headline—plus the realization that the Never Ending Tour really never did end, that he had vowed to live his remaining days or decades in a nightly communion of gracious, elegant live performances for those who cared and in complete indifference to those who didn't, and it dawned: He'd survived the eighties like a slow-motion motorcycle wreck, and nothing could touch him now. The sublime had secretly appeared in quiet exploration of his folk roots in two acoustic albums, like the face of God discovered in a blown-up photograph of Dock Boggs's banjo. Then he'd built his way back to songwriting for the third? fourth? time, while singing in the elder's voice he'd waited his whole life, and ours, to fully inhabit.

So now the Great Emancipator, the old dinosaur-astronaut, had brought down a single song, ancient lyrics turned glinting into new light: "Things Have Changed." It seemed enough now, one song every couple years, a song so good you were certain he'd written it a dozen times before. Who wouldn't want to give him an Oscar, really? Or a Nobel, or one more cup of coffee for the road, or a big, sloppy hug, if he wanted one, which it's hard not to doubt. The mustache might have been there to help you recall: He's not there, he's gone. And: It ain't him you're looking for. It's you.

JOYCE CAROL OATES

Beginning from a much different time, Oates looks back over Dylan's early career and recalls how radical he seemed in the 1960s, as someone who influenced several idioms while repeatedly changing the focus of his art. Oates is the author of more than forty novels and novellas, including *them, I Lock My Door Upon Myself* and *Blonde*, as well as several volumes of short stories, poetry, plays and literary criticism.

DYLAN! When we first heard this raw, very young, and seemingly untrained voice, frankly nasal, as if sandpaper could sing, the effect was dramatic and electrifying. We—my young husband and I—were classical music lovers for whom the arrival each month of chastely spare, black-on-white Musical Heritage Society albums (does anyone now living remember these?) was an exciting event. Bob Dylan seemed to erupt out of nowhere. The genuine power, originality, and heartrending pathos of "Blowin' in the Wind," "A Hard Rain's a-Gonna Fall," "Masters of War," "Don't Think Twice, It's All Right" were like nothing we'd encountered before.

So long ago in 1962–63 before American history entered its demonic phase—before the Ku Klux Klan bombing of the Sixteenth Street Baptist Church in Birmingham, Alabama, in September 1963, before the assassination of John F. Kennedy in November 1963, before the assassinations of Martin Luther King and Robert Kennedy. Before that pivotal turn in black-white relations in February 1964 when the new young black heavyweight champion Cassius Clay rebaptized himself Muhammad Ali. And before the escalation of the most despised and divisive war in our history. So long ago, it will seem to many now living as a kind of innocent prehistory, there was Bob Dylan.

Dylan, a Tambourine Man for that era, who would both help to define it and characterize it. And finally to influence it, in terms of American and British pop music, for the remainder of the century.

"Dylan" was a self-chosen name in homage to the great, legendarily self-destructive Welsh poet Dylan Thomas, whose lush, lyric, over-the-top poetry presumably influenced many of Bob Dylan's songs. At the time it might have seemed an act of extraordinary chutzpah for a Jewish kid from Duluth, Minnesota, named Bob Zimmerman to anoint himself with the poet's internationally famous name; now, forty years later, Dylan is an American classic whose fame far surpasses that of his namesake, who seems to have entered an eclipse. And even admirers of Dylan Thomas must concede that the brash American Dylan has taken on a far wider range of subjects, idioms, and aesthetic styles than the poet. If, as a poet per se, Dylan is not consistently original or inspired, as a musician-poet he's sui generis.

In the history of American popular music, Dylan is generally credited with the transforming of the folk-revival movement from its reverent fixation upon traditional ballads to the creation of new, socially engaged, and politically provocative music. The composer/songwriter becomes the performer. And what a performer! (Consider the astonishment of the public if Frank Sinatra, Bing Crosby, the Andrews Sisters were to have written their own original songs. And if Elvis Presley, Bill Haley, and Little Richard had aligned themselves with radical activist political causes.)

But hardly had Bob Dylan's raspy voice and aggressive folk style imprinted itself upon the public when, in his brilliant album *Bringing It All Back Home*, he cultivated a more sophisticated musical idiom, synthesizing folk and rock in a way that would seem inevitable in retrospect; yet, at the time, struck folk music purists as disloyal. Dylan clearly anticipated the formal, aesthetic, and tonal limitations of folk music, even as, by way of LSD experimentation, he explored the myriad possibilities of bending music as one bends one's mind, toward the surreal, the fantastic, the phantasmagoric.

When we think of the most charismatic of Dylan's songs, we are likely to think of songs from the era 1964–1970. In this remarkably creative time Dylan wrote such diverse songs as "Gates of Eden," "It's Alright Ma (I'm Only Bleeding)," "Who Killed Davey Moore?", "John Wesley Harding," the tenderly lyric "Visions of Johanna," "Boots of Spanish Leather," and "Farewell Angelina." Perhaps his most haunting song, as it's his most mysterious, is the surreal "It's All Over Now, Baby Blue" (1965), with its air of a fairy tale in which the end of something (a love affair? a life?) is being reiterated in each refrain in the very face of "Strike another match, let's start anew." Like all good poetry, this song of Dylan's can't be paraphrased. Like all good music it is both of its time and timeless.

(My most anthologized short story, "Where Are You Going, Where Have You Been?," written around the time of "Baby Blue," is dedicated to Bob Dylan. A one-sided admiration, clearly! The story was in fact suggested by a real-life incident involving a young teenaged girl and a "charismatic" serial killer in Tuscon, Arizona, and not by Dylan's song. Yet the haunting melody of "Baby Blue" seemed to beautifully approximate the atmosphere of my story, as of that time. Eventually, I would regret the dedication: too many people have asked me, "Why?" Who knows why?)

Dylan has continued in his long, ambitious, ever-evolving public career, through permutations of the self that have left many of his original admirers behind, or unaffected. (Evangelical Christianity? Bob Dylan? Count me out.) My Princeton University students, including musicians, born in the 1980s, very much admire Dylan as a classic, extolling his work of the 1960s and 1970s. In a pop culture of rapid, vertiginous change, when audiences are more fickle and ephemeral than any in history, Bob Dylan yet retains his stature and something of his original mystery. He's the exemplary Dionysus figure: "Hey Mr. Tambourine Man, sing a song for me / I'm not sleepy and there is no place I'm going to."

Most of us have places we are not only going to, but own and must maintain. Dylan's music isn't about us, any more than it's about the sixty-year-old Dylan, but it may be the most purely American music for us.

CAMILLE PAGLIA

Paglia highlights the social and musical trends that surrounded Dylan's 1990s comeback; in discussing her students' changing opinion of Dylan over the years, she offers an astute summary of what draws young people to his music. The author of *Sexual Personae* and *Vamps and Tramps*, Paglia is university professor of humanities and media studies at the University of the Arts in Philadelphia.

BOB DYLAN was a hard sell in 1985, when I first began teaching HU 417, "The Art of Song Lyrics," at Philadelphia's University of the Arts. The Beatles, Rolling Stones, the Doors, the Mamas and the Papas, Simon and Garfunkel, Led Zeppelin—all these groups were respectfully listened to in class by the student musicians for whom I created the course.

But Dylan was another matter. To my shock, young people who had never heard Dylan before found his voice irritating, his lyrics confusing, and his worldview incomprehensible. It was horrifying to realize that so titanic an artist of my own college years in the 1960s could have fallen so completely off the cultural map.

This story has a happy ending. Step by step through the 1990s, students taking that course began to be intrigued, then mesmerized, by Dylan's classic songs. Why the change? First, the grunge movement, whose tragic falling star was Kurt Cobain, revived the image of the suffering, alienated artist and refamiliarized audiences with an abrasive, nasal (and probably white proletarian) vocal style that is half a strangled howl.

Second, the commercial triumph of hip-hop among white teens sparked new interest in socially conscious lyrics after a period in which lyric substance had diminished, thanks to production-heavy recreational disco and operatic heavy metal. Dylan's compassion for the poor and dispossessed (as in the epic "Desolation Row") was back in fashion, and alongside rap, his packed, speed-freak lyrics suddenly made sense. Listening for the first time to "Subterranean Homesick Blues," Dylan's first hit single, students would laugh in amazement as they recognized rap's rhythmic ranting.

But if Dylan's homage to the agrarian "talking blues" helps reveal the artistic ancestry of hip-hop, exposure to his work can partly undermine rap lyrics, which are sometimes formulaic and limited in scope. After twenty flourishing years of that urban genre, surprisingly few rap tag lines have passed into general consciousness or can stand as exempla of their era in the way that dozens of Dylan's axiomatic one-liners have (e.g., "But even the president of the United States / Sometimes must have / To stand naked").

Despite his pose as a Woody Guthrie–type country drifter, Dylan was a total product of Jewish culture, where the word is sacred. In his three surrealistic electric albums of 1965–66 (which remain massive influences on my thinking and writing), Dylan betrayed his wide reading, sensitivity to language, mastery of irony and satire, and acute observation of society. Next to his dazzling achievement, with its witty riffs on mythology and its vast perspective on history (as in "All Along the Watchtower"), the lyrics of too much current popular music look adolescent and parochial.

Dylan is a perfect role model to present to aspiring artists. As a young man, he had blazing vision and tenacity. He rejected creature comforts and lived on pure will and instinct. He catered to no one but preserved his testy eccentricity and defiance. And his best work shows how the creative imagination operates—in a hallucinatory stream of sensations and emotions that perhaps even the embattled artist does not fully understand.

American Recordings: On *Love and Theft* and the Minstrel Boy

SEAN WILENTZ

L *ove and Theft* is a synthesis of American music. It brings together elements of bluegrass, country, rock, folk and blues—a record of Dylan's previous musical obsessions, like a deep and brightly colored stratigraphy that reveals the history of a geological age. And the album's lyrics are among the liveliest in Dylan's catalog, containing a long cast of characters as well as some of his most profound broodings on love and America.

Not long after its release, Sean Wilentz published an essay on Dylan's Web site that examined the album's musical and social roots. Wilentz's knowledge of song literature is vast. He identifies many sources behind Dylan's lyrics, guitar playing and voice articulation, and finds a shrewd contextual model for this kind of writing: minstrelsy, as in a traveling troupe of musicians who imitate the work of others in their own performance. *Love and Theft*, he writes, is Dylan's most traditional and minstrel-like work to date—not derivative in its influence, but rather the apotheosis of a style that bluesmen and folk singers have practiced for centuries.

Wilentz is the Dayton-Stockton Professor of History and director of the program in American studies at Princeton University, and is now "historian-in-residence" at bobdylan.com. He writes widely on American history, politics and culture.

IT IS MAY 24, 1966, and at the Olympia in Paris, also known as "*la salle la plus importante d'Europe*," time slips.

Exactly two years after this night of music, many of the young people who are in the audience will be rioting in the Paris streets, their heads full of ideas that will drive them to proclaim a revolution of the imagination, fight pitched battles with the police and the National Guard, and try to burn down the Paris stock exchange, in what would become known forever in Left Bank lore as "*la nouvelle nuit des barricades*," the most dramatic cataclysm of May '68. Seven hundred and ninety five rioters are arrested, and 456 are injured.

But now it's exactly two years earlier, to the minute, and the rebels-to-be sit expectantly, waiting for the second half of the show, when the curtain parts, and there they see to their horror, attached to the backdrop, the emblem of everything they are coming to hate, the emblem of napalm and Coca-Cola and white racism and colonialism and imagination's death. It is a huge fifty-star American flag.

What's the joke? But it is no joke. They are here to hear the idol, and know full well that the idol now will play electric (after what turned out to be a frustrating-to-all-concerned acoustic set), but this stars-and-stripes stuff turns a musical challenge into an assault, an incitement, as in your face—more so—to the young Left Bank leftists as any Fender Telecaster. In England, the idol had traded insults with the hecklers, but in Paris, on this, his twenty-fifth birthday, he strikes first.

Whether they like it or not, the idol will give them his own version of "America," a place that they have never learned about in books, and, if they have, that they do not comprehend.

Not quite five months after this concert, the French pop singer Johnny Hallyday plays the Olympia. He has two young women backup singers, one wearing a miniskirt, the other, vaguely resembling Marianne Faithfull, dressed in trousers and a vest. He also has a backup band that doubles as his warm-up act, a new group, still in formation and a little rough, that is introduced to the audience as hailing from Seattle, Washington, and that performs, among other numbers, a bent-out-of-shape version of the Troggs' Top 40 summer smash "Wild Thing." There is no flag, and by now the Paris audience has caught up, musically—enough to be amazed, not dismayed, by the Jimi Hendrix Experience, in its fourth public appearance.

Suddenly, it's May '66 again, Hendrix and company have vanished, and the star-spangled banner is back. An organist and a drummer and a bunch of guitarists take the Olympia stage. The organist is the guy from the Sir Douglas Quintet, and the lead guitarist is only ten years old or so, and the headliner, skinny as a fence rail, has swapped his Mod-cut houndstooth suit for a black and silver Nashville number, and he wears a five-gallon hat; and somehow during the intermission he has sprouted a Dapper Dan pencil mustache. Then the kid guitarist turns into a grown-up and the band rips into, not "Tell Me Momma," but a faster version of "From a Buick Six," curling the ears of the rebels-to-be. The headliner rasps the opening lines:

> *Tweedle-dee Dum and Tweedle-dee Dee*
> *They're throwin' knives into the tree.*

Love and theft, Bob Dylan has said, fit together like fingers in a glove. But don't quote somebody when you can steal. The new album's title, people have noticed, is the same as a book by Eric Lott on the origins and character of American blackface minstrelsy. In the 1820s and 1830s, young working-class white men from the North began imitating Southern slaves on stage, blacking up and playing banjoes and tambourines and rat-a-tat bones sets, jumping and singing in a googly-eyed "Yass suh, nooooooo sah" dialect about sex and love and death and just plain nonsense. The minstrels stole from blacks and caricatured them, and often showed racist contempt—but their theft was also an act of envy and desire and love. Bluenoses condemned the shows as vulgar. Aficionados, from Walt Whitman to Abraham Lincoln to Mark Twain, adored the minstrels for their fun, and for much more than that. " 'Nigger' singing with them," Whitman wrote of one blackface troupe in 1846, "is a subject from obscure life in the hands of a divine painter."

Whether Dylan stole his title from Lott is anybody's guess. But there is plenty of theft and love (and divinity) in *Love and Theft*, some of it obvious. One needn't know much more about the songs of Robert Johnson and the rest of the Delta blues players than the versions copped by the Rolling Stones in order to recognize the po' boy prodigal son or the line in "Tweedle Dee and Tweedle Dum" about someone's love being "all in vain." Johnson again, but also the upcountry white pickers Clarence Ashley and

Dock Boggs get plundered on "High Water (for Charley Patton)," the best song on the album. Patton, who is something of the presiding shade of *Love and Theft*, also wrote and recorded a song about the great 1927 flood in Mississippi, "High Water Everywhere." "Lonesome Day Blues" was the title of a song by Blind Willie McTell of Georgia.

Dylan has been committing this kind of theft all of his working life, right down to swiping his own surname. The tune of "Song to Woody," on his very first album, is a direct steal of Guthrie's own "1913 Massacre." Now, as then, Dylan is a minstrel, filching other people's diction and mannerisms and melodies and lyrics and transforming them and making them his own, a form of larceny that is as American as apple pie, and cherry, pumpkin, and plum pie, too. Or as American as Chang and Eng, the original Siamese twins, who, though born in Siam, started touring the United States in proto-carny style in 1829, coming to town right beside the minstrels, before they signed up with P. T. Barnum in 1832, for whom they worked for seven years and then retired to Wilkesboro, North Carolina, became American citizens, married a pair of sisters, and raised two families before showing up on *Love and Theft* for "Honest with Me."

But Dylan is a modern minstrel—a whiteface minstrel. The hard-edged racism taken for granted by the nineteenth-century troupes is of another age. The disguises that Dylan has sported on stage—"I have my Bob Dylan mask on," he told his New York audience, off the cuff, on Halloween night, 1964—are more of himself, his time, and his America. While he has tipped his hat to the old-time minstrels, he has inverted their display, as when he actually whitened his face for the Rolling Thunder Revue.

As a modern minstrel, he has continually updated and widened his ambit, never more so than on *Love and Theft*, lifting what he pleases from the last century's great American songbook. Folk songs, as ever: The wonderful tag line of "Mississippi" comes from an old folk tune called "Rosie." "The Darktown Strutters' Ball" is here, plain as day. But there are also melodies and lyrics reminiscent of songs from the 1930s and 1940s and 1950s, and bits and pieces of the rockabilly "Hopped-Up Mustang" appear on "Summer Days" and "High Water."

(In a disarming little story about three jolly kings that became the liner notes to *John Wesley Harding*, Dylan pokes fun at the Dylanologists who search for the great true meaning in his songs. "Faith is the key!" one king says, "No, froth is the key!" the second says; "You're both wrong," says the third, "the key is Frank!" In the story, the third king is right, sort of—but who would have ever imagined that Frank might turn out to be someone like Sinatra.)

And, of course, among the great old last-century songwriters whom Dylan recycles is himself—and not just from his songs or his adaptations of other people's. In New Orleans, there was a streetcar that had as its destination a street called Desire. Tennessee Williams used it for the title of his play; Dylan appears to have adapted it (or used Williams) for the title of an album. (*Streetcar*, the play, seems to turn up elsewhere in Dylan, as in Blanche DuBois's immortal line about how her family's "epic fornications" led to the loss of its estate on a called-in mortgage: "The four-letter word deprived us of our plantation," Blanche remembers, the word in question being either fuck or love.) Well, "Desire" is back on *Love and Theft*. "Tweedle Dee and Tweedle Dum" and "Honest with Me" and "Cry a While" are all variations of standard twelve-bar blues, but listen hard and I think you'll catch the musicality of "Buick Six" (especially the unreleased version, if you've had the chance to hear it) and of "Leopard-Skin Pill-Box Hat" (like "Song to Woody," a standard number in Dylan's recent live shows) and of "Pledging My Time." (Same thing with the eight-bar blues "Po' Boy" and the eight-bar "Cocaine," yet another recent concert standard.) The opening guitar lick of "High Water" brings my ear back to "Down in the Flood"; and the rest of the song recalls John Lee Hooker's "Tupelo," as rendered on the complete bootleg version of *The Basement Tapes*. Dylan's been singing his own version of "The Coo Coo" at least since his Gaslight days forty years ago.

There's no message to this modern minstrel style. It is a style, a long-evolving style, not a doctrine or an ideology. But that's not to say that Dylan, a craftsman, is unaware of that style, or that we should be either. Several years ago, Johnny Cash released an excellent album of traditional songs that he called *American Recordings*. *Love and Theft* could have the same title, though Dylan's musical reach is even wider than the great Cash's, and his minstrelsy more complicated. He's unfurled that American flag once again.

In keeping with the seemingly miscellaneous but highly structured randomness of the minstrel shows, *Love and Theft* is an album of songs—

greatest hits, except they haven't become hits yet, Dylan has said. And like the shows, the album is funny, maybe the funniest Dylan has produced since he was writing songs like "Outlaw Blues." Some of the jokes, like the minstrels', read flat on the page—"Freddy or not here I come"—but Dylan's delivery of them makes me laugh out loud. Here's another one, a rim-shot pun that could have come right from an old minstrel show—dull to read, but funny when sung:

> *I'm stark naked but I don't care,*
> *I'm going off into the woods, I'm huntin' bare*

When asked who his favorite poets were in 1965, Dylan mentioned a flying-trapeze family from the circus, Smokey Robinson, and W. C. Fields (who through vaudeville had his own connections to minstrelsy); now, in "Lonesome Day Blues," he pays a little homage to Fields's snowbound gag line in *The Fatal Glass of Beer*: "T'aint fit night out for man nor beast!"

Many of the other jokes are high-low literary and operatic. Don Pasquale's 2:00 A.M. booty call in "Cry a While" comes right out of Donizetti's *Don Pasquale*, a farce about an old man's lust for young women, first performed in Paris in 1843—high-minstrel time in America. Then there are the Shakespearean jokes about shivering old Othello and the bad-complexioned Juliet. All of these high-low jokes, too, are in the updated minstrel style, last heard from Dylan in this humorous way on *Highway 61 Revisited*: the blackface companies regularly performed spoofs of grand opera and Shakespeare (*Hamlet* was a particular favorite)—works as familiar to popular American audiences a century and a half ago as *Seinfeld* and Walt Disney are today.

Dylan delivers every joke poker-faced, like someone out of something by the minstrel show patron Twain. And some of the jokes are sinister. To the steel-guitar background in "Moonlight," all is songbirds and flowers in the heavy dusk, when, lightly lilting, the crooner sings:

> *Well, I'm preaching peace and harmony,*
> *The blessings of tranquillity,*
> *Yet I know when the time is right to strike.*
> *I'll take you 'cross the river dear,*

You've no need to linger here;
I know the kinds of things you like . . .

Ah, the silver-tongued devil. Rudy Vallee turns into Robert Mitchum. It's scary, and yet it's hilarious.

And there is plenty more serious and fearful play on *Love and Theft*. More than any old-time minstrel (and more like later bluesmen and "country" singers), Dylan thinks about the cosmos contained in every grain of sand. All of those floods aren't just floods, they're also The Flood. Why else do Charles Darwin and his ultramaterialist friend George Lewes (lover of the great novelist George Eliot) turn up in "High Water," wanted dead or alive by a snarling Mississippi judge? Lewes tells the believers, the Englishman, the Italian, and the Jew (Protestant / Roman Catholic / Hebrew?) that, no, they can't open their minds to just anything, and for that the high sheriff's on his tail. "Some of these bootleggers," Dylan sings on "Sugar Baby," "they make pretty good stuff." Beware of false prophets. (Or maybe Dylan is wryly complimenting the fans who have gone to such extraordinary, surreptitious lengths to record his concerts and release them as bootleg CDs.)

The Lord's messenger is vengeful. Hear what Dylan does with "Coo Coo" in "High Water":

The Cuckoo is a pretty bird, she warbles as she flies
I'm preachin' the Word of God,
I'm puttin' out your eyes

And Jesus isn't any pushover either. Listen to "Bye and Bye," another crooner's tune, and imagine that, alongside Augie Meyers's wickedly goopy organ, the crooner is Christ Himself, in some of the verses anyway, cracking his own minstrel joke while singing lyrics written by the biblical prophet John of Patmos:

Bye and bye, I'm breathin' a lover's sigh
I'm sittin' on my watch so I can be on time
I'm singin' love's praises with sugar-coated rhyme . . .

> *I'm gonna baptize you in fire so you can sin no more*
> *I'm gonna establish my rule through civil war*
> *Gonna make you see just how loyal and true a man can be*

Christ comes with love—and a sword.

There are other seers and magicians here too, the hoo-doo men of the Delta blues—bragging mannish boys with their St. John the Conqueroos who say if you can do it, it ain't bragging.

From "High Water":

> *I can write you poems, make a strong man lose his mind*
> *I'm no pig without a wig*
> *I hope you treat me kind*

"Honest with Me":

> *When I left my home the sky split open wide*

"Cry a While":

> *I don't carry dead weight—I'm no flash in the pan*
> *All right, I'll set you straight, can't you see I'm a union man? . . .*

> *Feel like a fighting rooster — feel better than I ever felt*

And this, from "Lonesome Day Blues":

> *I'm gonna spare the defeated—I'm gonna speak to the crowd*
> *I'm gonna spare the defeated, boys, I'm going to speak to the crowd*
> *I am goin' to teach peace to the conquered*
> *I'm gonna tame the proud*

That last one may just also be a paraphrase from Virgil's *Aeneid*.

Yet some of the supermen on the album turn out not to be so super. Age had caught up with them, but they ungently keep going:

"Summer Days":

Well I'm drivin' in the flats in a Cadillac car
The girls all say, "You're a worn out star"
My pockets are loaded and I'm spending every dime
How can you say you love someone else when you know it's me all the
*   time?*

"Cry a While":

I'm gonna buy me a barrel of whiskey—I'll die before I turn senile
Well, I cried for you—now it's your turn, you can cry a while

And there is a lament for a lost cause in "Honest with Me":

I'm not sorry for nothin' I've done
I'm glad I fought—I only wish we'd won

Aging veterans of the 1960s rebellions—including some of those French '68ers perplexed by Dylan in 1966—might take these lines as a cry of undefeated solidarity, and they might be right. But it should be noted that the second line quotes an old Southern song called, "I Am a Good Old Rebel"—a first-person defiant invective by a racist ex-Confederate soldier who fought for slavery, and who hates equality, the Declaration of Independence, and the United States of America. Rebels can have all sorts of causes. (To add another twist, the song was also one that the young folkie Jerry Garcia played with a bluegrass band in the early 1960s, in the glory days of the civil-rights movement before the birth of the Grateful Dead.)

There is a richness to all of these musical and literary references in *Love and Theft* that was only foreshadowed in "Tombstone Blues," with its mere glimpses of Ma Rainey and Beethoven—just as there is a richness to Dylan's silk-cut voice and to his diction and timing (he has been listening to Sinatra, and maybe Caruso and surely Allen Ginsberg) uncaptured on previous studio recordings. He's mastered so much more, including his own performing style, or at least his recorded performing style. Listen to Dylan's inflection on the breakneck opening lines of "Cry a While"— "didn't havta' wanna' havta' deal with"—then the sudden bluesy downshift; or the killer long-line about repeating the past in "Summer Days";

the pause in Juliet's reply to Romeo; the "High Water" judge's creepy, "Either one, I don't . . . care," the last word dropping and landing with a thud like one of the song's lead-balloon coffins.

And with his expert timing, Dylan shuffles space and time like a deck of playing cards. One moment, it's 1935, high atop some Manhattan hotel, then its 1966 in Paris or 2000 in West Lafayette, Indiana, or this coming November in Terre Haute, then it's 1927, and we're in Mississippi and the water's deeper 'n as it come, then we're thrown back into biblical time, entire epochs melting away, except that we're rolling across the flats in a Cadillac, or maybe it's a Mustang Ford, and that girl tosses off her underwear, high water everywhere. Then it's September 11, 2001, eerily the date this album was released, and we're inside a dive on lower Broadway, and, horribly beyond description, things are blasted and breaking up out there, nothing's standing there. And it's always right now, too, on *Love and Theft*.

Dylan, remember, has been out there a very long time. He spent time with the Reverend Gary Davis, and Robert Johnson's rival Son House, and Dock Boggs, and Clarence Ashley, and all those fellows; he played for Woody Guthrie, and played for and with Victoria Spivey; and Buddy Holly looked right at him at the Duluth Armory less than three days before Holly plane-crashed to his death; and there isn't an inch of American song that he cannot call his own. He steals what he likes and loves what he steals.

POSTSCRIPT: I wrote this essay in August 2001. The maestros at Bob Dylan's official Web site, bobdylan.com, had read some earlier writing of mine about Dylan's work and asked if I'd be interested in writing something new about his forthcoming album. I agreed, on the condition that I could say whatever I wanted and they could take it or leave it. Fine. I got an advance copy of the album and liked what I heard. On the morning of September 11, 2001, album release day, I was working on getting the essay posted, with *Love and Theft* playing in the background. Suddenly, news of the atrocities in New York, Washington, D.C., and Pennsylvania flashed on my computer screen. A few days later, still in shock, I could actually listen to "High Water (for Charley Patton)" again, and was shocked in a different way. It took a while longer before the essay was finally posted, so I was able to add a few words about the connection. (I have since added more about other matters, which appears here for the first time.)

Nearly two years later, a report in *The Wall Street Journal* drew attention to revelations on the Internet that numerous lines in *Love and Theft* looked suspiciously similar to passages in Dr. Junichi Saga's *Confessions of a Yakuza*, a book about the Japanese criminal underworld. Alerted by a friend, I'd already read Dr. Saga's book, and was convinced that I'd only begun to understand the theft and love that went into making *Love and Theft*. The *Journal* report implied that Dylan was a plagiarist, and a predictable little controversy ensued. With a weakness for good fights, I was tempted to put in my two bits. But then I realized I'd already said what I had to say, in this essay.

Intelligence Data

GREG TATE

For many, *Love and Theft* will always be associated with the day it was released—September 11, 2001. A few weeks after the attacks on the Pentagon and World Trade Center, Greg Tate of the *Village Voice* wrote a poignant essay on the link between the tragedy and the album's content, suggesting that Dylan could once again be seen as a public spokesman.

Though he talks about how some of Dylan's lyrics predict national strife, Tate's piece mostly deals with the ways *Love and Theft* (recorded, of course, months before the attacks) depicts and consoles an aggrieved nation. Like Wilentz and other commentators on the album, he also notes its deep debt to various musical traditions. Here Tate's work is very exciting. By taking a post-9/11 interpretation of the lyrics, and remarking how the album's music stretches back over centuries—the future and past as an indelible whole— he presents *Love and Theft* as an archetypally American work of art and, given its relation to current events, a masterful eulogy.

Tate is the author of *Midnight Lightning: Jimi Hendrix and the Black Experience*, as well as the editor of *Everything but the Burden: What White People Are Taking from Black Culture*.

I'm not sorry for nothing I've done.
I'm glad I fought, I only wish we'd won.

PRETTY WRY FOR a spry guy, this Bob Dylan character. The codger's got plenty kick left in him yet. *Feel like a fightin' rooster, felt better than I ever felt, but the Pennsylvania line's in an awful mess, and the Denver road is about to melt.* Plenty parables too. There may be no second acts in American life, but at sixty, Dylan could care less. Like Miles Davis and his shadow, that asshole Pablo Picasso, Dylan has given us one long act to chew on, and one long song: a peerless and exquisite display of craft, nerve, and wit. His riddle-rhyming trail is marked by the silence, exile, and cunning of the hermetic populist—Joyce, Pynchon, Reed, Clinton. Occasional lapses of faith, periods of doubt, self-derision, and personal revival too. Rare among American artists, he shouldered the burden of a great and precocious gift. He crashed but did not burn out after the sixties. Now contemporary evidence, a new release called *Love and Theft*, suggests that the poet of his generation is once again prophet of his age.

The current saber-rattling is probably giving him more than a slight case of déjà vu right about now. This is where he came in, way back when, our freewheelin' troubadour, with his "Talkin' World War III Blues," his "Hard Rain's A-Gonna Fall," his "Masters of War." Before 9-11-01, *Love and Theft* was an abstract expressionist painting Dylan would never have intended to carry a topical frame. Funny what a little moonlight can do: Now poets are bringing us the news. Before that fateful Tuesday, *Love and Theft* could not have been so easily read as Dylan's contribution to the literature of the apocalypse. Now so nakedly he seems revealed, bounding out of the wilderness in high prophetic mode: *I see your lover man coming, across a barren field. He's not a gentleman at all, he's rotten to the core, he's a coward and he's steel. My captain he's decorated, he's very well schooled and he's skilled. He's not sentimental, it don't bother him at all how many of his pals he's killed.* We could have gleaned as much intelligence data from the RZA, the GZA, and the Ol' Dirty BZA, but who besides your Five Percenters and wigga types were paying serious attention to a buncha crypto-alarmist niggas from Shaolin? *Get your shit together before the fuckin' Illuminati hit.* Nostradamus gave advance warning, they tell me, the Book of Revelation, Rastafari. The eons-old Mayan Calendar of Cosmogenesis predicts a cataclysm will reset the world calendar to zero in 2012. The astronomical lore of the pyramids, left behind over 10,000 years ago, informs us that the earth's axis is about to reverse, flipping the planet back to the Stone Age whether we bomb the Taliban there first or not.

This may be the dawning of the age of Aquarius but some of you know we're still in the Age of Pisces—a time of severity and strife, suffering and service, a time whose ruler Neptune is the planet of mystery, illusion, and deception. Four jetliners. Nineteen allegedly surly Middle East passport-carrying muhfukuhs with knives and box cutters breeze past security when your lone black ass can barely make it through with house keys and pocket change. Where was racial profiling when we really needed it? None but the "truly twisted" will find even grim solace in that observation. If there's a hell below we're all gonna go. Curtis Mayfield croons from the wings. The Jamaican family of my man Michael Richards, a brilliant sculptor whose final resting place was his studio on the ninety-second floor of Tower One, can attest to that, as can that of my man, Guyana's Patrick Adams—former proud security presence here at the *Voice* and still missing.

DYLAN'S IMPACT ON a couple generations of visionary black bards has rarely been given its propers—Sam Cooke, Curtis Mayfield, Jimi Hendrix, Otis Redding, Stevie Wonder, Sly Stone, Marvin Gaye, Charles Stepney, Terry Callier, Gil Scott-Heron, Bob Marley, Tracy Chapman. Chocolate Genius would not for a second hesitate to acknowledge coming under his spell. Like Joni Mitchell, Gil Evans, and Charlie Haden, he's left deep, yeti-sized footprints in this thang we call Black Music. It's a matter of record, of sublime and divine social intervention.

Like Miles, Dylan, born May 24, 1941, is a Gemini, the sign ruled by Mercury, messenger of the gods. According to Goldschneider and Ellfers, those born on the day of the magnifier and clarifier also fall under the sway of Venus, but are far more skilled at communicating love than giving it. They tend to favor the dispossessed over the privileged, but must guard against sarcasm and harsh criticism of their friends and also against their own fanaticism and zealotry. *I'm gonna teach peace to the conquered, I'm gonna tame the proud.* Those of Yoruba persuasion might recognize Dylan as an Elegba-Eshu vehicle, those of the Dahomean faith as Legba, devotees of the vodun syncretism as Legba-Pied Cassé. Trickster gods, cosmic jokers who control the crossroads. Dylan ain't just whistling "Dixie" when he pursues archaic, fallen, and decayed American musics. There's souls in them thar hills. And a taste of our cowpoke president's newspeak as well: *George Lewes told the Englishman, the Italian, and the Jew, you can't open up your mind, boys, to every conceivable point of view. They got Charles Darwin trapped out there on Highway 5. Judge says to the High Sheriff, I want him dead or alive, either one I don't care.*

The voice you hear on *Love and Theft* is not that of the cocky young rock star who wrecked folk by simply strapping on an electric guitar, nor is it the vengeful and crotchety man who dripped *Blood on the Tracks*. This Dylan is older, wiser, and grousier, but sweeter, more sanguine if still unsettled too. There's a bitter taste in his mouth, but it's not bile. He might moan but he doesn't bitch, and whether you project the immediacy, and portent in his words that I do, the depth and reach of songcraft remains monumental and omnivorous. *Love and Theft* presents an assured master working with a cornucopia of tuneful frames, all set out on leisurely, laconic display. There are blues forms and jazz forms here, gypsy-jazz folk forms, Tin Pan Alley and rockabilly, boxcar rounds, campfire sing-alongs and sea chanteys, cowboy songs, madrigals, and various alchemical mixtures as they're needed. His current band speaks his language, being connoisseurs of antiquity too, and are as adaptable, supple, and blissfully out of touch as any he's ever had. They understand how to support and navigate his juke-joint rhythms and cascading, sometimes colliding, cadences. Even at its most foreboding, this is good-time music. The overall impression it leaves is that of bodies in motion and bodies at rest, sometimes at breakneck speeds and sometimes arrested, of folks flying forward and folk stopped dead in their tracks, having finally looked back to see what's been gaining on them. There is an economy, transparency, and conviviality that complement the newfound humility, civility, and camaraderie of our city—a place that, achingly, feels so much smaller in scale without our twin megalopolis-marking towers of money and babble, traded in now for a massive laying-on of hands.

So many prescient, portentous lyrics beg the question: What did Dylan know and when did he know it? Some up-to-the-minute somebody at the Federal Bureau of Immigration, very few Angolans, and no Haitians at all will surely wish to inquire about the former Mr. Zimmerman's connection to Osama bin Laden: *Tweedle Dum and Tweedle Dee they're throwing knives into the tree. Two big bags of dead man's bones, got their noses to the grindstone. Living in the land of Nod, trusting their fate to the hands of God.* "Bye and Bye"'s breezy B-3 lounge jazz skates beneath lines I hear as fair appraisal of the conduct of our mayor and wartime consigliere, who will waltz out of office on a heroic grace note: *Bye and bye, on you I'm casting my eye. I'm painting the town, swinging my partner around. I know who I can depend on, I know who to trust. I'm watching the roads, I'm reading the dust . . . The future for me is already a thing of the past. You were my first love and you will be my last.* The national psyche, the national moment, the nightly jingoistic appeals to revive the national resolve, avenge the national honor, and spill the national blood can strangely, spookily be heard sounding their retort in this music Dylan wrote who knows how many months ago: *I'm gonna baptize you in fire, so you can sin no more. I'm gonna establish my rule through civil war, make you see just how loyal and true a man can be.* Dylan's sleeping giant is more wary, weary, and diplomatic than the one who rose out of Pearl Harbor, but just as ready to applaud good old American know-how and the desire to just get the job done.

There are also intimations of the humpy-throated suspense we're all held in now, waiting for the proverbial shoe to drop, the proverbial ax to fall, and what comes next, our collective jumpiness as it were: *Last night the wind was whispering, I was trying to make out what it was. I tell myself something's coming, but it never does.* In this Dylan you can hear the banjo-strumming wagon-train ghosts of America past riding shotgun with our after-the-innocence future shock, but because it's Dylan you also hear this place where the personal and apocalyptic mesh. *You don't understand it, my feeling for you. You'd be honest with me if only you knew . . . I'm here to create the new imperial empire. I'm going to do whatever circumstances require.*

"Po' Boy" is what hip-hop would be if it told the tale of all those players doomed to lives of quiet desperation—*Po' boy need the stars that shine, washing them dishes, feeding them swine.* But it is in "Sugar Baby," the album's swan song, a final address to a tearful, fearful nation, that this record's kinder, gentler, crustier, creakier Dylan quietly dons his gold lamé glittersuit one last time and goes for the jugular with run-down, melancholic glee: *Every moment of existence seems like some dirty trick. Happiness can come suddenly and leave just as quick. Any minute of the day that bubble could burst. Trying to make things better for someone sometimes you just end up making it a thousand times worse. Your charms have broken many a heart and mine is surely one. You've got a way of tearing a world apart, Love see what you've done.* Whether he's speaking as Dylan the martyred lover or as some kind of Jesus, the message appears abundantly clear: These may be the last days, but not even armageddon is going to save us from growing up, and our learning curve remains steep.

Constant Time for Bob Dylan

BARRY HANNAH

In an essay written especially for this collection, Barry Hannah describes his profound and long-held admiration for Dylan. Hannah calls him "a master of spiritual geography," recalling how *Slow Train Coming* brought him closer to Christ and reprieved his religious faith. The medicinal properties of song, Dylan as a distant friend: these are ideas that are common among Dylan's audience though not, perhaps, expressed often enough in this book. And when it comes to artists he respects, Hannah denies the value of personal contact or critical study. So while discussing Dylan's impact on his life and times, he evokes the pleasures and significance of solitary listening, unaided by anything except music's basic emotive powers.

Hannah is the author of many books, including the novels *Yonder Stands Your Orphan* and *Ray* as well as the story collections *Airships* and *Bats Out of Hell*.

I WILL ALWAYS ENVY good musicians. A fiction writer can spend two hours and move no further ahead than straightening his CD collection. A true artist like Bob Dylan can have a masterpiece within the hour. "The Gettysburg Address" written on a napkin or whatever's handy in a moving coach and ready to sing. Poets, in other words. Words beyond words. Music. Nothing between the ear of the soul and the singer. Hearts and minds will follow. Nothing written will ever touch song, and we folks of the page, driven ahead at the pace of zombies in mud even at our best, will always eat our hearts out, gnash our teeth, and curse fate for leaving us gifted with nothing better than mere literature.

I've been way high on Dylan since 1966 and thank God he went electric when he did or I'd have forgotten him quickly. Folk music has always irritated me from the word go. I was on a beautiful literary mountaintop in Vermont in '71 so overrun by gentle poets of the meadow and their horrible acoustic guitars they forced me into my first morning bloody marys and two decades of alcoholism. For one thing, I worked too hard to be a hippie. I was against the war, but Christ, who wasn't? It was electric hippie musicians I loved—Dylan, Hendrix, Clapton, the Stones, the Beatles, Joplin. No surprises for a person my age. Miles Davis anyway he came, but especially electric.

Dylan couldn't sing, but I loved the struggle to sing in his voice. This has nothing to do with the horror of garage-band and rap democracy that has afflicted radio bands the last twenty years. Many fine musicians can't really sing, but Dylan's voice was absolutely distinct. When he quit cigarettes a while and *did* sing well on *Nashville Skyline*, you were a little shocked but it was a voice always there in the roughest earlier work. He damn well knew the *notes*, in other words, and his voice has always had a more interesting distance from the note then most rock singers have. My wife casually despises Dylan. When I told her "Lay, Lady, Lay" was both written and sung by him, she called me a liar. Then she adored him, briefly.

Dylan has been such a private experience for me, close to religious faith—I never had much interest in seeing him live. I saw him once when he came to my town, Oxford, Mississippi, thirteen years ago. He performed with a band who, except for a studly blond long-haired lead guitarist, wore Hassidic fedoras. They performed in a small basketball coliseum at Ole Miss—at a volume meant for the Super Dome in New Orleans. I don't know who the band was but it was a mistake. Dylan had absolutely no interest in anything but screaming songs as rapidly as possible for an hour and a half. The attendance was poor, mainly people my age from the faculty, a few neohippies and always-hippies, hip frat boys and sorority gals, who were there to hear him yell "Oxford Town" or "Mississippi" in any fashion.

He was like a small vigorous corpse. I feared for his health, was dismayed by his frailty. I gave him months to live. Still, his *stamina* impressed me, although I wrote it off to cocaine, or even better performance drugs. His disease I instantly identified as alcoholism. My late pal Larry Debord, a Dylan and George Jones fanatic, had bought us second-row seats. Maybe I'd just never been that close to any rocker my age before. It had been ages since I'd been that close to *speakers* of that magnitude. The night was an ear-, sight- and heart-ache.

But shortly thereafter I heard he gave happy performances in Tupelo and Memphis, and was laughing with a girl who jumped on stage wanting to dance with him, one of her arms full of old Dylan vinyls. Dylan was probably happier in the towns of Elvis, whom he loves.

I live an hour from the Mississippi Delta. Everybody knows what Dylan and all rock and roll got from those shack towns. Never a blues purist, try as I might, I do at last enjoy reading the history of blues and the history of Dylan and just a few others. The thereness, the itness, of music is the supreme joy. Its lore is a supreme bore, unless you love the man. Music criticism is the death of joy as we know it, only slightly better than modern lit crit, which is worse than a funeral because the dead are talking. Dylan, I feel, is the best poet of our days when you know how to listen. His recent reported theft wholesale from a Japanese author seems so lazy and unstealthy it could be a bad movie, another one from a prince of disguises even beyond Miles Davis, who looked eighteen when he died.

You might best beware of knowing too much about an idol. When I was in a room with Johnny Cash for an hour in Austin, working for *Spin* magazine, I was shocked he was not that *tall* anymore, and rushed the interview because I loved him so deeply, not wanting to waste this hero's time. He was completely cordial, articulate, and meek ("Why don't you have any bodyguards?" I asked him. Cash's reply: "Who'd want to mess with an old body like mine?"). But the main issue was I *feared* knowing too much about him. Dylan has done an uptown job of making this condition impossible. Hats off.

Cameron Crowe's booklet in the *Biograph* CD set is all you really need to read about Dylan. You won't get Dylan as honest about himself in as short a space anywhere else I've looked, and music is all about short space anyway, unless you're an opera fanatic. Dylan is just as articulate as Cash about his history and influences and loves. When the two met in Nashville,

Cash took him fishing on his lake near Franklin. Dylan fished and said not a word for two hours, Cash told me. I'd give what's in my wallet right now right now for a picture of Dylan fishing. I can't even imagine it. A cane pole and enormous Tom Mix hat? What? I just looked in my wallet. Seventy-four bucks. Okay, five. I'd give a fin for the picture mailed directly to my house. Cash's place is apparently some kind of farm zoo too. Cash was knocked out by an ostrich there and went into such suffering he got back on pills briefly. Ten bucks for a picture of the ostrich in the background bearing down on Bob fishing. Please, I wish no harm to Bob. A close miss of the bird's giant nasty foot and Dylan oblivious, perhaps. Reminds me that Johnny Cash has recently lost his wife, June, and we should pray for him, who has suffered all number of ills in his golden years. I don't have to imagine Dylan praying for Cash. I'm pretty dead certain he is.

Which brings me to spiritual states and how well Dylan has stated them throughout his work. Personally, I'm still "Stuck inside of Mobile with the Memphis blues again," along with Dylan. He is a master of spiritual geography, has stood playing the guitar in Mississippi for black civil rights in the days when you could get shot for it—the sixties—and has absorbed place-names as expressions of the condition of the soul much like Hemingway, who found exact street and city nouns the only trustworthy, hard-edged map of the soul after World War I. Dylan also knew enough Rimbaud to write the unforgettable couplet in "It's All Over Now, Baby Blue": "Yonder stands your orphan with his gun / Crying like a fire in the sun." Those lines stayed in my head for almost four decades until I wrote a book with orphans in it and stole (or honored Dylan, more) the first line for a title. The echo was that intense. "Crying like a fire in the sun" is a condition so, well, metareal, how can anybody doubt that Dylan reaches the soul, and has always done so, better than "soul music" itself. His choice of mate has been black Christian women for a long time (according to Howard Sounes's biography of Dylan). Dylan is both Christian and Jewish, as I read him.

I never knew *Slow Train Coming* went platinum until three days ago. This album made a deep impression on me in the seventies, but all I recall about its acceptance was grumbling and dismay about his being "born-again" from music critics, some of them Jewish, who felt betrayed, or that he was acting in serious error. Never far from Christ, this writer was not committed and deep in drink when I heard it. But I played it over and over. It brought me closer to both Dylan and Christ, as did some of the album *Saved*. I wonder if Cash had anything to do with Dylan's conversion. Fans and critics in Tuscaloosa and even in Oxford, Mississippi, it seemed to me, would rather he'd made a public announcement that he was a desperate heroin addict. But I stayed quiet and harkened to Christ as more than just a hero and prophet. Finally I quit drink, and now try to live with Christ as closely as possible, though God knows faith is a rough, rough thing for a twentieth-century mind. You sometimes wish the world were run by a gentle atheist king, and for me that would be Christ Himself. Being a son of the deity, He doesn't have to believe in God, any more than you'd have to believe in your own father. He just *is* father, no belief required.

I apologize for the mild Christian rant, not because I am ashamed of it but because this whole piece of mine has been almost nothing but the personal. It's all I've got to add on Dylan. I remain a small man (although taller than Dylan, ha) and shortsighted. The best I can do as a writer is just get intense on my own backyard. From the bottom of my heart, however, I want to thank Bob Dylan for his poetry, his music, his soul. He's made life, sometimes a desperate crawl through a vicious universe, clearer, cleaner, and quieter for me, even when he was at his noisiest. I hope never to meet him. This meeting would involve very little. A handshake. He's already shaken my hand.

Good God, thank you, Bobby Zimmerman.

Bob Dylan the Singer: Who's Gonna Throw That Minstrel Boy a Coin?

GARY GIDDINS

Dylan's voice has always been a subject of contention—uniquely melodious for some, an atonal rasp for others. Gary Giddins, in this unique essay, considers the origin and implications of the debate, claiming Dylan's singing as one of the underappreciated aspects of his art. With an understanding of how a lyric's meaning can be strengthened by vocal nuance, Giddins evaluates Dylan's early albums and finds an "exceptional ability to concoct a fresh attack that exactly suited his material." Giddins's fresh look at *Bob Dylan* merits highlighting, as does his discussion, near the end, of the songwriter's affinity with Rodgers and Hart.

Giddins wrote the *Village Voice*'s "Weather Bird" column for many years. He is the author of the biographies *Satchmo* and *Bing Crosby: The Early Years*, as well as several collections of essays on jazz and culture, including *Riding on a Blue Note*, *Rhythm-a-ning* and *Visions of Jazz*.

IT WAS DISCONCERTING to flip the channels in August 2003, and come upon the brusque, croaky "Love Sick" in an ad for Victoria's Secret. Bob Dylan's brain was wired: He walked the dead city, the clouds weeping amid thunderous silence, sick of love but ready to give everything for . . . frilly lingerie? The commercial was almost as surprising as his humble gratitude in accepting an Academy Award a few years back for "Things Have Changed." I don't fault him for taking the easy payday or succumbing to

Hollywood's fantasia; nor would I suggest that either inclination signals decline—not after *Love and Theft*, my favorite Dylan album since *Highway 61 Revisited*. Yet I miss the conceit of the young scruffy outsider who shuns the glitter, though I recognize it was never really his conceit. Dylan has always been a climber, dreaming of Liz Taylor, hungering for admittance to a motley of restricted organizations—the Folk Music and Protest Association, the Rock & Roll & Racquet Club, the Nashville Chamber of Commerce, not to mention high-lit, movies, Christianity, Judaism, and the mafia. He was so much older then; he's older now.

TV ads are only marginally lower on the devolutionary scale of capitalist compromise than indentured servitude to the record industry, and Dylan is nothing if not marketable. Still, a measure of his genius is the ability to sustain, withal, the promise of the eternal unrepentant underground man—a troubadour with an attitude, a Céline with a song in his heart. His originality continues unambiguously in the infinitely analyzed Torah of his collected lyrics, defining his role as a prophet, satirist, social critic, and phrasemaker unrivaled since Johnny Mercer, if not Kipling. But Dylan's assault on musical conventions precedes his words and music; it begins with his delivery. His voice (or voices) and the way he uses it (them) generate the first visceral responses of attraction or revulsion.

In the 1960s, his singing was often found so repellent that his admirers readily apologized for it. Forget the voice, they said, listen to the words—an argument that found its logical outcome as well as box-office support in covers by Peter, Paul and Mary and the Byrds. Yet it was Dylan's unmistakable antistylish stylish singing that made him irresistible and unique to those very admirers. His singing was so innovative they praised it chiefly for what it wasn't: smooth, which is to say commercial. Approbation, such as it was, centered on his rough-hewn timbre, Woody-like naturalness, road-tested coarseness, conversational ease. Detractors who claimed that he was unintelligible simply weren't listening—Dylan's early elocution was crystal. They were too much put off by the snarling, chortling, demonic voice that implied "fuck you" even while insisting, "All I really want to do is, baby, be friends with you."

They never got far enough to worry about the things that roiled Dylan fans: his politics, women, rhythms, rhymes, melodies, drug use, hair, liner note jive, sallow color, and harmonica playing, let alone the relative merits of acoustic versus electric music. The voice was challenge enough: In song, the messenger precedes the message. The musical divide between coarse and smooth is far wider than that between acoustic and electric or between folk and pop. Early admirers of Louis Armstrong's singing frequently advised unsophisticated listeners to get beyond the grainy, guttural inflections to the notes, until it became evident that those inflections were attracting rubes by the millions. When Ornette Coleman first recorded, not a few pundits paid lip service to his talents as a composer while complaining that his saxophone sound was too raw to do justice to the melodies it produced.

The idea that Dylan was one of the most dynamic singers to emerge in the sixties is now beyond cavil. He was an American original—as distinctive and decisive as Guthrie or, for that matter, Al Jolson, Louis Armstrong, Bing Crosby, Jimmy Rushing, Jimmie Rodgers, Leadbelly, Blind Willie Johnson, Frank Sinatra, Hank Williams, Elvis Presley, and James Brown. Whatever he may have lacked in relative range, control, and interpretive diversity, he shared with a select few the exceptional ability to concoct a fresh attack that exactly suited his material. His vocal approach telegraphed his meaning, fixed his attitude, and sold his viewpoint. You couldn't ask for a better illustration of Dylan in full theatrical mode than his corrosive rendering of "Like a Rolling Stone"—especially as compared with the flatter live version on *Self Portrait*, performed without the sting of callow vengeance. Yet commentators continue to ignore his singing qua singing, preferring to invoke Rimbaud, Whitman, Blake, Milton, and Dante.

His singing is what made his first album worth hearing, and overcame the puerile excesses of the second. He never sounds like he's trying to be someone else, or paying homage to classic repertory, or instructing us in the wonders of old-time music. In a period when white blues singers were offering precise carbons of black blues classics, memorializing cotton-picking or sentimentally growling the party songs of juke joints, *Bob Dylan* was too self-conscious and enthusiastic to bother with respectful imitation. Listening to his versions of "Fixin' to Die" and "In My Time of Dyin'," one can almost forget their origins and imagine them as Dylan tunes; he treats them as songs worth singing and not as artifacts for study. From the beginning, he was fishing for style. If the most acute changes in Dylan's vocal mask would unfold between the pugnacious hilarity of

Blonde on Blonde (1966) and the phlegmatic remoteness of *John Wesley Harding* (1967) and the strange, hollow crooning of *Nashville Skyline* (1969), the chameleon was already evident on the twenty-year-old's 1961 debut. He switches from the dark bluster of Delta blues to the hearty openness of "Man of Constant Sorrow" and yet both approaches are certifiably Dylanesque.

And where was he fishing? Not solely in the approved texts of, say, Harry Smith's *Anthology of American Folk Music,* but also—as the liner notes to *Bob Dylan* make clear—in the territory of Elvis and the Everlys. No one wanted to believe him, certainly not then. Adulators preferred Robert Shelton's *New York Times* assessment (also printed in the notes) of a Dylan who captured "the rude beauty of a Southern field hand musing in melody on his porch." The Elvis-thing was provisionally mooted with the arrival of the prophetic Dylan of "A Hard Rain's Gonna Fall," "The Times They Are A-Changin'," and other jeremiads, conveyed with a dauntless, saber-rattling authority unparalleled in America's secular music and intrinsically different from the parallels in black gospel and blues. Those songs are so definitively *sung* that, unlike the numbers in his catalog that inspire sundry covers (memorable jazz takes include Bob Dorough's "Don't Thing Twice, It's All Right," Abbey Lincoln's "Mr. Tambourine Man," and Cassandra Wilson's "Shelter from the Storm"), they practically defy secondary interpretations, as numerous attempts—see dylancoveral bums.com for the farcical details—prove.

To the national vocal mask as it existed in 1963, Dylan added the divinatory insight (no mean accomplishment in itself), bitter retaliation, adolescent giggle, and generational sneer—songster poses as old as minstrelsy, but dormant so long they were all but forgotten. His emphatic nuances underscored the asymmetrical phrases and resonant repetitions of his melodies and suffused his lyrics with a persona that might exude contempt but rarely sacrificed intonation. Rock and roll heightened his assurance. His fervor spiraled to a new plain, at once lighter and darker, in "Ballad of a Thin Man" and the matchless "Desolation Row"; his appetite for the absurd hit full throttle on *Blonde on Blonde.*

But rock also required a greater obeisance to Tin Pan Alley formalism. As country blues singers of the 1920s learned when they joined urban jazz bands, you can stretch a blues chorus to thirteen and a half bars by yourself and hardly anyone will notice; a band needs to begin and end at the same time. The transitional LP was the much-undervalued *Another Side of Bob Dylan* (1964). "All I Really Want to Do" displayed Dylan's interior rhyming dictionary (a Tin Pan Alley necessity); "Black Crow Blues" and "Motorpsycho Nitemare" were R&B dry runs for the rock breakthrough of the next year's *Bringing It All Back Home* (the restored *g*, deleted from *Freewheelin'* and *Changin'*, seemed notable, a renouncement of the cosmetically folksy); "Spanish Harlem Incident" stretched his range while the more Españolish "To Ramona" employed subtle chords and discreet melisma in a melody that might have served the 1940s hit parade; and the self-pitying cruelty of "Ballad in Plain D" prefigured the sniping rage of "Like a Rolling Stone."

After *Blonde on Blonde*, Dylan's voice proved more chameleonic than ever. His stylistic gambits ranged from deliberate unintelligibility to gentle articulation, offering something to disenchant everyone at one time or another. For me the breaking point was the high, arid whimper heard in *Nashville Skyline* entries like "Lay, Lady, Lay" and "Tonight I'll Be Staying Here with You." The anger and excesses and rampaging id were gone, and *Self Portrait* affirmed where they'd gone to—the sea of Elvis, whose crooning influence found intermittent traction on "I Forget More Than You'll Ever Know" (a touch of Blind Willie McTell there, too), "Let It Be Me," "Take Me as I Am," and—in what suggested a possible accord with mainstream songwriting traditions—"Blue Moon," which his biographer Robert Shelton disdainfully and wrongly described as "à la Bing Crosby." It was, of course, Elvis who recorded it, not Bing.

"Why had he recorded 'Blue Moon'?" Shelton asks Dylan in *No Direction Home*, clearly unsatisfied with his explanation that it "was an expression," part of a middle-of-the-road jaunt in the mode of Presley and the Everly Brothers. He would have done better to ask him about the truly incomprehensible "All the Tired Horses" or "Wigwam." Because Lorenz Hart, with his ingenious internal rhymes and caustic outlook, was Dylan's kind of lyricist: The insistent consonants of "alone" and "own" and the quadruple rhyme and near rhyme of "there for," "prayer for," "care for," and "appeared before" were right down his alley. How much Dylan admired Richard Rodgers's melody became clear when he sponged the song's main four-bar hook for "Bye and Bye" on *Love and Theft*, a gusher of Americana subsuming minstrelsy, pop, folk, blues, rhythm-and-blues, rock and roll, and jazz.

By then the throaty rasp that had always been a part of his vocal makeup ("Watching the River Flow" trailed "Lay, Lady, Lay" by only two years) had taken over. It added weight, in 1978, to "Little Pony" on *Street-Legal*, a reminder of his country blues affinities; and grit, in 1983, to *Infidels* ("Jokerman" has an intricate rhyming grid worthy of Hart); and it consumes *Oh Mercy*, in 1989, the sandpapery timbre eradicating the early range and mannerisms while producing the color-blind gospel of "Ring Them Bells." The idea that Dylan might tackle Tin Pan Alley was put to rest by his disastrous rendering of "Tomorrow Night," on 1992's intrepid but uneven solo stint, *Good as I Been to You*. But *Time Out of Mind*, in 1997, a tour de force from "Love Sick" through the magisterial "Highlands," suggested his renewed comfort zone as a singer, a coming to grips with the not-unpleasant huskiness that achieved greater satisfaction four years on in *Love and Theft*, for which he proceeded to invent his own Tin Pan Alley. He'll be hard-pressed to match it, though no more so than when he traveled from *Highway 61 Revisited* to *Blonde on Blonde*. Dylan's never really had to compete with anyone but himself. In the meantime, there's always black satin and lace.

The Wanderer

ALEX ROSS

First published in *The New Yorker* in May 1999, "The Wanderer" by Alex Ross is one of the best essays yet written on Dylan. Labeling him as a "composer and performer at once," Ross believes that the songs and live performances point back not to the counterculture or the songwriter's own garbled biography, but to the broader traditions of Western music. To research the piece, Ross followed Dylan on tour and interviewed several authors along the way (the theory on lyrics that he quotes from a talk with Christopher Ricks is of especial interest). Once immersed in this culture of fandom, Ross aptly describes the disparity between the two wings of Dylanology, pop culture and academe.

But the most edifying aspect of "The Wanderer" is its musical analysis. Ross, a meticulously close listener, studies the vocal line and chord structure of several songs. He names a wide variety of influences on Dylan's music, from disciplines that may have originally seemed incongruent. Finding Franz Schubert and Hank Williams in the same performance, Ross captures the depth and complexity of Dylan's songwriting more precisely than any other critic.

Toward the end of the essay, he praises the way Dylan "withdraws his personality from the scene"—an unmistakable, if unconscious, echo of the *Little Sandy Review* editors asking Dylan to do the same thirty-six years earlier. These days, as Ross and other writers in the anthology have suggested, there can be little doubt that the tradition is the music's true subject.

Ross has been the music critic of *The New Yorker* since 1996. His history of twentieth-century music, *The Rest Is Noise*, is forthcoming from Farrar, Straus and Giroux.

IF YOU LOOK through what has been written about Bob Dylan in the past thirty-odd years, you notice a desire for him to die off, so that his younger self can assume its mythic place. When he had his famous motorcycle mishap in 1966, at the age of twenty-five, it was presumed that his career had come to a sudden end: rumors had him killed or maimed, like James Dean or Montgomery Clift. In 1978, after the fiasco of *Renaldo and Clara*, Dylan's four-hour art film, Mark Jacobson wrote in the *Village Voice*, "I wish Bob Dylan died. Then Channel 5 would piece together an instant documentary on his life and times. . . . Just the immutable facts." James Wolcott was unhappy to find him still kicking in 1985: "My God, he sounds as if he could go on grinding out this crap *forever*." When Dylan was hospitalized with a chest infection in 1997, newspapers ran practice obituaries: "Bob Dylan, who helped transform pop music more than thirty years ago when he electrified folk music . . ."; "Bob Dylan, whose bittersweet love songs and politically tinged folk anthems made him an emblem of the 1960s counterculture . . ."

PUYALLUP, WASHINGTON. I'm at the 1998 Puyallup Fair, in this agricultural suburb of Tacoma, and among the attractions are Elmer, a twenty-four-hundred-pound Red Holstein cow; a miniature haunted house ingeniously mounted on the back of a truck; bingo with Hoovers for prizes; and Bob Dylan. He is announced, with cheesy gusto, as "Columbia recording artist Bob Dylan!" He saunters out from shadows in the back of the stage, indistinguishable at first from the rest of the band (a well-honed group consisting of Tony Garnier, Larry Campbell, Bucky Baxter, and David Kemper). He is dressed in a gray-and-black Nashville getup and looks like a lopsided owl. As the show gets under way, he tries a few cautious strutting and dancing moves, Chuck Berry style. He plays five numbers from his most recent album, *Time Out of Mind*; several hits, among them "Don't Think Twice, It's All Right" and "Masters of War"; and something more unexpected from his five-hundred-song back catalog—"You Ain't Goin' Nowhere." He ends with "Forever Young." The crowd goes wild.

When I told people that I was going to follow Dylan on the road, I got various bemused reactions. Some were surprised to hear that he still played in public at all. It's easier, perhaps, to picture him in *Citizen Kane*–like seclusion, glowering at the Bible and listening to the collected works of Blind Willie McTell. Maybe he does, but he also plays more than a hundred shows a year. Last year, he appeared in Buenos Aires, Nuremberg, Brisbane, Saskatoon, and Bristol, Tennessee, among other places. Starting in June, he will pass through thirty American cities, with Paul Simon in tow. As of this writing, he is in Slovenia.

What are these shows like? How are they different from the classic-rock nostalgia acts that clutter summer stages? I've been to ten Dylan concerts in the past year, including a six-day, six-show stretch that took three thousand miles off the life of a rental car. The crowds were more diverse than I'd expected: young urban record-collector types, grizzled weirdos, well-dressed ex-hippies, and enthusiastic kids in Grateful Dead T-shirts. Deadheads are a big part of Dylan's audience, and they created odd scenes as they descended on each venue: in Reno, they streamed in a tie-dyed river through the Hilton casino. I asked some of the younger fans how they had become interested in Dylan, since he is not exactly omnipresent on MTV. Most had discovered him, they said, while browsing through their parents' old LPs. One kid, who had been listening to a 45-rpm single of "Hurricane," thought that he should come and check out the man behind it. The younger fans didn't seem to be bothered by the fact that Dylan was three times their age. A literate teenager asked me, "Do you have to be from Elizabethan England to appreciate Shakespeare?"

Before each show, for some reason, minor-key sonatas and concertos by Mozart were played over the P.A. system. Male Dylanologists explained lyrics to their girlfriends. "Every Dylan song contains *eight questions,*" I heard one saying. A boozy group who sat in front of me at a show in Minnesota seemed to have the Dylan songbook pretty well memorized. The rowdiest of them was shouting out first lines of the songs at the top of his voice, and once, in his excitement, he crashed into the hard plastic seats. He got up again, blood dripping down his chin, and bellowed in my face, "*Once upon a time you dressed so fine! God said to Abraham, 'Kill me a son!'*" Other fans took a cooler view. Before a show in Portland, I chatted with a levelheaded twenty-something guy who plays in a progressive funk group. "Last time I saw him, in '90, it was *brutal,*" he told me. "I hope he doesn't fuck up the songs again. I hear he's better. Even when he's awful, he's sort of great—he's never just *mediocre*." In Dylan's vicinity, I noticed, everyone italicizes.

Many people had told me that Dylan makes a mess of the songs. He does change them, and fans who come to hear live-action reenactments of the favorite records of their youth tend to be disappointed. Dylan sometimes writes new melodies for old songs and he sometimes transposes one set of lyrics into the tune of another. He writes a little more every night; I kept hearing fresh bluesy bits of tunes in "Tangled Up in Blue," which was at the center of every set. As a performer, he is erratic: his voice sometimes thins into a bleat, he occasionally drops or jumbles lines, and every so often his guitar yelps wrong notes. But he has a saturnine ease onstage; even from a hundred feet away, his squinting stare can give you a start. And he is musically in control. The band's pacing of each song—the unpredictable scampering to and fro over a loosely felt beat, the watch-and-wait atmosphere, the sudden knowing emphasis on one line or one note—is much the same as when Dylan plays solo. You can hear him thinking through the music bar by bar: he has a way of tracing out his chords in winding one-note patterns and bringing them alive. And the basic structures of the songs are unshakable. There are wrong notes, but there is never a wrong chord.

IN THE VERBAL JUNGLE of rock criticism, Dylan is seldom talked about in musical terms. His work is analyzed instead as poetry, punditry, or mystification. A new book, entitled *The Bob Dylan Companion*, goes so far as to call him "one of the least talented singers and guitarists around." But to hear Dylan live is to realize that he *is* a musician—of an eccentric and mesmerizing kind. It's hard to pin down what he does: he is a composer and a performer at once, and his shows cause his songs to mutate, so that no definitive or ideal version exists. Dylan's legacy will be the sum of thousands of performances, over many decades. The achievement is so large and so confusing that the impulse to ignore all that came after his near death and disappearance in 1966 is understandable. It's simpler that way—and cheaper. You need only seven discs, instead of forty-three. But Columbia Records, after years of putting out bungled live recordings, is finally beginning to illustrate, in its *Bootleg Series*, the entire sweep of Dylan's performing career.

Don DeLillo, in his novel *Great Jones Street*, imagined a Dylanesque rock star and said of him, "Even if half-mad he is absorbed into the public's total madness; even if fully rational, a bureaucrat in hell, a secret genius of survival, he is sure to be destroyed by the public's contempt for survivors." But Dylan has survived without becoming a "survivor"—a professional star acting out the role of himself. He has a curious, sub-rosa place in pop culture, seeming to be everywhere and nowhere at once. He is historical enough to be the subject of university seminars, yet he wanders the land playing to beery crowds. The Dylan that people thought they knew—"the voice of a generation"—is going away. So I went searching for whatever might be taking its place. I went to the shows; I listened to the records; I patronized dusty Greenwich Village stores in search of bootlegs; I sought out the Dylanologists who are arguing over his legacy in print. Strange to say, Dylan himself may explain his songs best, just by singing them.

CONCORD, CALIFORNIA. The crowd is dominated by ex- and neo-hippies from Berkeley, twenty miles to the west. Dylan threatens to dampen their enthusiasm by opening with "Gotta Serve Somebody," the snarling gospel single with which he had horrified the counterculture in 1979. But he works his way back to the sing-along anthem "Blowin' in the Wind." I was sitting near a teenage girl who had first heard Dylan in a class on the sixties and was there with her teacher.

Dylan's looming presence in the politics and culture of the sixties is for many a point in his favor: he wrote songs that "mattered," he "made a difference." For others, particularly for those of us who grew up in later, less delirious decades, the sixties connection is a stumbling block. Until a few years ago, when I started listening to Dylan in earnest, I had mentally shelved him as the archetypal radical leftover, reeking of politics and marijuana. I'd read a story that went something like this. He was born in Minnesota. He went to Greenwich Village. He wrote protest songs. He stopped writing protest songs. He took drugs, "went electric." He was booed. He fell off his motorcycle. He disappeared into a basement. He reappeared and sang country. He got divorced. He converted to Christianity. He converted back to something else. He croaked somewhere behind Stevie Wonder in "We Are the World." And so on. If you're not in the right age group, the collected bulletins of Dylan's progress read like alumni notes from a school you didn't attend.

The challenge for anyone who thinks Dylan is more than a lifestyle trendsetter is to define those qualities that have outlasted his boisterous term as the voice of a generation. So far, the informal discipline of Dylanology—founded around 1970, by a creep named A. J. Weberman as he fished through Dylan's trash on MacDougal Street—has reached no consensus on the matter. At the moment, there are about a half-dozen luminaries in the field. Greil Marcus, the most formidable of rock critics, connects Dylan with a homegrown, folk-and-blues surrealism that he calls "the old, weird America." Paul Williams, who founded the rock magazine *Crawdaddy!* in the sixties, celebrates Dylan as a tireless, generous performer who rewrites his songs at every show. The Dylan biographer Clinton Heylin lavishes attention on the gospel period and the apocalyptic rants that followed in the eighties. Christopher Ricks, a renowned scholar of Milton, Tennyson, Eliot, and Beckett at Boston University, supplies a formalist reading—of Dylan as a pure poet, who thrives on word choice, rhythm, and structured rhyme. In the same spirit, Gordon Ball, a professor of English at the Virginia Military Institute, has nominated Dylan for a Nobel Prize in Literature.

Below the main authorities are the amateur Dylanologists: enthusiasts, cranks, editors of fanzines, caretakers of gigantically detailed Internet sites. There is no end to their production. *The Cracked Bells*, for instance, is an unreadable book-length guide to Dylan's unreadable book-length poem *Tarantula*. The author, Robin Witting, writes, "*Tarantula* has six main themes: America, Viet Nam, Aretha, Mexico, Maria, and—the great panacea—Music." I didn't find much about music, but I enjoyed a note on geraniums: "Do geraniums stand for coolness? Insouciance? Moreover, the odour of death?" Aidan Day's *Jokerman*, a book on Dylan's lyrics, analyzes some lines from "Visions of Johanna," in *Blonde on Blonde*, and finds in them "a reduction of form to primal elements as—in an image that itself displaces Marcel Duchamp's rendering of the Mona Lisa in the painting *LHOOQ* (1919)—even gender difference becomes confused and human contour a feature are erased." The text in question is "See the primitive wallflower freeze / When the jelly-faced women all sneeze / Hear the one with the mustache say, 'Jeeze / I can't find my knees.' "

Despite everything that has been written about Dylan, not a great deal is known about him for certain. Heylin's chronology of Dylan's life, for example, is an archly self-canceling document, in that every piece of information points to a larger lack of information. Here are three consecutive entries for the year 1974:

> *Late April. Dylan attends a concert by Buffy St. Marie at the Bottom Line in New York. He is so impressed he returns the following two nights, and tells her he'd like to record her composition, "Until It's Time for You to Go."*
>
> *May 6. Dylan runs into Phil Ochs in front of the Chelsea Hotel and they decide to go for a drink together.*
>
> *May 7. Dylan visits Ochs at his apartment and agrees to perform at the "Friends of Chile" benefit.*

What happened during the rest of the first week of May? Where *was* he going when he ran into Phil Ochs? Dylan's life story sometimes feels as if it has been pieced together from centuries-old manuscripts that were charred in a monastery fire. "Between January and June 1972 there is no evidence that he was in New York at all," Heylin writes in his attempt at a full-scale biography, *Dylan: Behind the Shades.* Heylin, a skeptical Englishman who is known for a history of American punk, is at least willing to admit what he doesn't know, and his book is the most readable and reliable of four biographies.

THE ACCUMULATED files of Dylanology, despite their gaps, give a rough sense of the personality behind the enigma. A thumbnail sketch from a classic 1967 essay by Ellen Willis holds up well: "Friends describe [him] as shy and defensive, hyped up, careless of his health, a bit scared by fame, unmaterialistic but shrewd about money, a professional absorbed in his craft." Stubborn persistence is his main characteristic: although he has often vanished in a funk brought on by the vagaries of his career, he never fails to trudge back with some new twist on his obsessions. He is at odds with the modern world in many ways. "There's enough of everything," he said in a 1991 interview. "There was too much of it with *electricity*, maybe, some people said that. Some people said the *light bulb* was going too far." His eccentricity has an everyday quality—he's the weird neighbor you can never figure out. I heard an excellent Dylan anecdote from a friend who played on a Little League team with Dylan's kids in the late seventies, during the singer's gospel period. When a dog ran onto the field, my friend yelled, "Get that goddamn dog off the field!" A familiar voice rasped from the parents' bench, "Ahhh, that was *what* kind of a dog?"

Dylan's rise was fabulously odd. He was famous before he was twenty-one. World fame—not just celebrity but intellectual fame, with plaudits from Allen Ginsberg, Frank O'Hara, and Philip Larkin—came to him by the age of twenty-five. The speed of his ascent required some luck, but it was mostly a function of his energy. He skipped heedlessly from one genre to another: folk, blues, country, spirituals. He played at being an activist, but his sharpest polemics, such as "The Lonesome Death of Hattie Carroll," were the character-driven ones. His early vocal style incorporated pieces of Woody Guthrie, Mississippi John Hurt, Hank Williams, and not to be forgotten, Johnnie Ray, the flaky fifties crooner who smacked his consonants with unnerving ferocity. In the early sixties, Dylan sought to play rock and roll and electric blues alongside his acoustic material: he had hammered the piano, Little Richard style, in high school, and he longed to resume that kind of noisemaking. He originally planned to have his second album, *The Freewheelin' Bob Dylan*, be part electric and part acoustic, like the later *Bringing It All Back Home*. He signaled his intentions by covering "That's All Right, Mama," Elvis's debut single, at his first electric session, in October 1962. He was trying frantically to say everything at once.

But he soon discovered that you can be famous for one thing at a time. The record business and the music press wanted a narrower genius. The electric songs from 1962 didn't fit the image that Columbia wanted to create—Dylan as folk prophet. He was gaining notoriety chiefly for his civil-rights and antiwar material, and Columbia advertised him accordingly:

Bob Dylan has walked down many roads. For most of his 22 years he "rode freight trains for kicks and got beat up for laughs, cut grass for quarters and sang songs for dimes." . . . Bob does what a true folk singer is supposed to do—sing about the important ideas and events of the times. . . . His new best-selling album (the first was Bob Dylan) is The Freewheelin' Bob Dylan. It features ten of Bob's own compositions, including the sensational hit, "Blowin' in the Wind." Also, songs on subjects ranging from love ("Girl from the North Country") to atomic fall-out ("A Hard Rain's A-Gonna Fall"). Hear it and you'll know why Bob Dylan is the voice of the times.

This ingenious ad copy, complete with Dylan's tall tales about his past, infiltrated the press coverage. Dylan soon became annoyed at the generalizations, and found himself fighting his own publicity; he denied, for example, that "Hard Rain" depicted a nuclear winter. Even so, he played along with the spirit of marketing: he later claimed that the song had been a general reaction to the dread of the nuclear age, and to the atmosphere of the Cuban missile crisis in particular. In a widely quoted statement, he said, "I wrote that when I didn't figure I'd have enough time left in life." "Hard Rain" had actually been written at least a month before the Cuban crisis began. Before long, he learned not to talk about his songs at all.

"Hard Rain" was a breakthrough in Dylan's writing, but for a different reason. It's a small epic, lasting seven minutes, and yet it lacks the sort of blow-by-blow storytelling that sustains the picaresque ballads of folk literature. How does Dylan keep us interested? One way is through repetition; another is through changes that occur between the first repetition and the last. Almost all of Dylan's songs have a structure of verse-refrain, verse-refrain, and the refrain is almost always a simple-seeming, folkish phrase that tolls like a bell: "Tangled up in blue," "You gotta serve somebody," "It's not dark yet, but it's getting there," "It's a hard rain's a-gonna fall." In "Hard Rain," the first lines—"Oh, where have you been, my blue-eyed son? And where have you been, my darling young one?"—are a nod to the old ballad "Lord Randal," which begins, "Oh, where ha' you been, Lord Randal, my son? Oh, where ha' you been, my handsome young man?" Dylan breaks the symmetrical call-and-response pattern of the original: his blue-eyed son answers not with two lines but with five. The images—"twelve misty mountains," "six crooked highways," and so forth—carry the flavor of the Book of Revelation, with its insistence on exact numbers of bizarre objects ("I saw seven golden candlesticks"). The song hangs on a musical trick of suspension: E and A chords seesaw hypnotically as the number of answering phrases increases from five to seven and eventually to twelve. In the chorus—"And it's a hard, and it's a hard . . ."—Dylan grasps for and finally gets the resolution, which in each verse has moved a little farther out of reach. Coming down the mountain of the song, he starts to sound like a prophet.

Many myths of Dylan's sixties career don't hold up under the evidence gathered in Heylin's books and other Dylanological tomes. Dylan's songwriting is said to have been transformed by a plunge into the drug culture, but he had been using drugs on and off since his Minnesota days. He was said to have been inspired by the Beatles to "go electric," but he had sketched out his folk-rock sound as early as 1962. The first electric shows reportedly provoked universal booing, but on the tape of his famous appearance at the Newport Folk Festival, in 1965, it's difficult to hear boos amid the applause. D. A. Pennebaker, who filmed Dylan's 1966 tour with the Hawks, doesn't recall many confrontations; he says that if there were such incidents the ringleader didn't appear to be greatly bothered by them. "Dylan was having the best time of his life," he said at a recent symposium on Dylan's tour movie *Eat the Document*, at the Museum of Television and Radio in New York. "He was like a cricket jumping around onstage."

Greil Marcus describes the 1965–66 tours differently—as a war against dark reactionary forces. He quotes Al Kooper's reason for not wanting to follow the tour into Texas: "Look what they did to JFK down there." Marcus finds special significance in an exchange that took place between Dylan and the audience in Manchester, England, in May 1966. In his book *Invisible Republic*, Marcus renders this moment as Dylan's ultimate, shattering encounter with the collected forces of Them:

> As if he had been waiting . . . a person rises and shouts what he has been silently rehearsing to himself all night. As over and over he has imagined himself doing, he stands up, and stops time. He stops the show:
> "JUDAS!"
> Dylan stiffens against the flinch of his own body. "I don't believe you," Dylan says, and the contempt in his voice is absolute. As one listens it turns the echo of the shouter's curse sour, you begin to hear the

falseness in it, that loving rehearsal—and yet that same echo has already driven Dylan back. "You're a liar!" he screams hysterically.

When Columbia finally released a CD of the show, last year—it had circulated for thirty years on bootlegs—neophytes may have skipped to the end in order to hear the renowned "Judas!" dialogue. They were probably disappointed. What you hear first is an ordinary lull, during which Dylan tunes his guitar. When the shout of "Judas!" comes, the crowd variously laughs, groans, and applauds. The voice from back yammers unintelligibly, and others join in. When Dylan responds, he is not screaming hysterically, or, indeed, screaming at all. It's as if he couldn't understand what the lads in the back were hollering and therefore supplied the kind of all-purpose non sequitur that he liked to dish out at press conferences.

Marcus implies that there was a conspiracy among folk purists to silence Dylan: the heckler is said to have been "well informed as to the precise order in which Dylan played his songs." But C. P. Lee, a minor Dylanologist, recently took the trouble to write an entire book about the Manchester show, and after its publication a great discovery was made: the "Judas" shouter was no Pete Seeger–like elder statesman of folk but a confused twenty-year-old university student named Keith Butler. "It was not a premeditated thing," Butler told the English press after coming forward. (He now works at a bank in Toronto.) "I was swept along by the mood, which was chaotic. I was feeling disappointed and angry." In other words, two disparate youth cultures—rock-and-rollers and folkies—were jockeying for control of a spokesman who was declining to give a clear message to either of them. Thirteen years later, after all, the rock generation in turn would feel betrayed by Dylan's gospel songs, and shouts of "Judas!" and "Traitor!" would be thrown at him again. The gospel shows were sometimes no less electrifying than the 1966 concerts, but they happened not to fit the story of a generation.

As Dylan's tour passed through California, I went to see Marcus, who lives in the Berkeley hills. "The funny thing is that I'm not a *Dylan person*," he told me. "Many years went by when I didn't care about him at all." For Marcus, as for many of the original followers, Dylan disappeared in the seventies and eighties, expect for brief comebacks. Marcus's *Rolling Stone* review of the 1970 *Self Portrait* began with the words "What is this shit?"

Only when Dylan started recording folk and blues covers in the nineties was he restored to Marcus's favor. In *Invisible Republic*, which deals with Dylan's basement tapes, Marcus makes compelling side trips into older American music—the shrapnel-voiced Dock Boggs and other comical-sinister back-country singers who had been collected in Harry Smith's celebrated 1952 *Anthology of American Folk Music*. In the eighties, the critic asked to hear "more Dock Boggs" in the singer's aging voice, and that alchemy more or less happened. Marcus seems to have got inside his subject's mind, and Dylan indicated as much by providing a blurb for the paperback of *Invisible Republic*.

But there has to be something missing in a reading of Dylan that skips twenty years of his career. What if, as some think, he reached his peak not with the put-ons and put-downs of the sixties but with the chaotic love songs of the seventies? And what if, as Clinton Heylin suggests, he went even further in the eighties, when he fused the personal and the apocalyptic—"Love-sick Blues" with the Book of Revelation? Lester Bangs wrote in 1981, "If people are going to dismiss or at best laugh at Dylan now as automatically as they once genuflected, then nobody is going to know if he ever makes a good album again. They're not listening now, which just might mean they weren't really listening then either."

I WAS READY to give up on Dylanology until I had tea with Christopher Ricks, a legendary close reader of canonical English poetry. We met in his decorous sitting room, in Cambridge, Massachusetts. Although he speaks in the clipped tones of a modern English don, he has a way of plunging into the passive-aggressive dynamic of Dylan's emotions. "The words constitute an *axis*," he said to me. "They do not point in one direction." Dylan says one thing and may mean the opposite. This may seem like irony, but I don't think it is; irony, strictly speaking, requires a reversal of meaning. Dylan can obtain ambiguity simply by repeating a phrase. "Think of 'Don't Think Twice, It's All Right,' " Ricks continued, intoning the refrain, "How many times can you tell somebody not to think twice? You can say 'It's all right' over and over. That's comforting—but not 'Don't think twice.' I'd start to think."

I was reminded of some similarly hazy lines from "Meet Me in the Morning," circa 1974:

> *Look at the sun, sinking like a ship*
> *Look at the sun, sinking like a ship*
> *Ain't that just like my heart, babe*
> *When you kissed my lips?*

This tangled metaphor—the sun like a ship, the heart like the sun—can spin in any direction. Is the heart glowing like a sunset? Or is it sinking out of sight? And is the ship going over the horizon, or is it just sinking? The less happy implication is that it is in the nature of ships, and of hearts, to sink.

When others have tried to read Dylan line by line, they have usually chased after outside references. ("He mentioned the bomb! T. S. Eliot! Joan Baez!") Talking about "The Lonesome Death of Hattie Carroll," Ricks begins not with the case of William Zantzinger—a wealthy young farmer who caused the death of a black barmaid at a Baltimore ball and got off with a six-month sentence—but with the rhythm of Zantzinger's name: a strong beat followed by a weak one. The whole song, he says, is dominated by that loping, tapering rhythm of the name, from which Dylan removed an unsingable "t":

> *William Zanzinger killed poor Hattie Carroll*
> *With a cane that he twirled round his diamond ring finger*
> *At a Baltimore hotel society gathering.*

It produces a feeling of helplessness, the way each line ends in a weak beat, and this seems to be the point: cry all you want, the gentle suffer. The dominant emotion is not political rage but a quavering sympathy for Hattie Carroll, whose race is never mentioned. This song certainly doesn't raise hopes for judicial reform, and it has not gone out of date, like the cardboard protest anthems of its era. (In 1991, William Zantizinger was found to have collected rent from tenants who had been living in extreme squalor in houses that he didn't own. This time, the judge handed down sternly an eighteen-month sentence, in a work-release program.)

"Now's the time for your tears," Dylan sings at the end. Ricks said to me, "He doesn't underscore it—say, 'Now *is* the time.' He doesn't exhort you. Maybe you should have cried before, when Hattie died." (Paul Williams thinks the refrain for the preceding verses, "Now ain't the time for your tears," is actually sarcastic, and that Dylan is saying, "You can't cry because you're a leftist do-gooder who cares only about the legal ramifications." Another axial moment.) Ricks went on to criticize some of Dylan's more recent performances of "Hattie Carroll," in which he pushes the last line a little: "He doesn't let it speak for itself. He sentimentalizes it, I'm afraid." Here I began to wonder whether the close reader had zoomed in too close. Ricks seemed to be fetishizing the details of a recording, and denying the musician license to expand his songs in performance. I had just seen Dylan sing "Hattie Carroll," in Portland, and it was the best performance that I heard him give. He turned the accompaniment into a steady, sad acoustic waltz, and he played a lullabylike solo at the center. You were reminded that the "hotel society gathering" was a Spinsters' Ball, whose dance went on before, during, and after the fatal attack on Hattie Carroll. This was an eerie twist on the meaning of the song, and not a sentimental one.

Still, Ricks's writing on Dylan is the best there is. Unlike most rock critics—forty-year-olds talking to ten-year-olds, Dylan has called them—he writes for adults. But he has been slow to publish. He has produced only one major essay, for *The Threepenny Review*, and he has been mulling for years over a book-length Dylan study. "I don't teach Dylan," he told me. "It's just an *obsession*." And he writes, half jokingly, "I need to show that I'm not besotted with the man." Ricks, like Marcus, might not want to be called a "Dylan person." Academics who write about Dylan are labeled eccentrics at best. Academe, which is usually so eager to splash around in the pop culture pool, rejects Dylan because he's an old white male.

Dylan himself declines the highbrow treatment—though you get the sense that he wouldn't mind picking up a Nobel Prize. Even in the sixties, he said of those who called him a poet, "Genius is a terrible word, a word they think will make me like them." He seems to prefer an audience of teenage Deadheads in a basketball arena. He may occasionally surprise the kids with moody masterpieces, like "Hattie Carroll," "Visions of Johanna," and "Not Dark Yet," or he may teach them a Stanley Brothers bluegrass hymn, but more often he gets them to jump up and down to "Tangled Up in Blue." This way, he packs in the crowds, and he also makes sure that he cannot be pinned down. Every night, whether he is in good or bad form, he says, in effect, "Think again."

DULUTH, MINNESOTA. Dylan was born here, in 1941, before moving with his family to the iron-ore town of Hibbing. He has never played Duluth before. The city is moderately excited for his return. He is front-page news for two days running in the Duluth *News-Tribune*. Storefronts downtown are adorned with "Welcome Home, Bob" signs. Duluthans are hoping that he will have something to say to the city; he did, after all, mention Duluth when he accepted the 1998 Grammy for Album of the Year. (WOW! DYLAN SAID "DULUTH!" ran a local headline.) At the show, a fan tosses onto the stage a paper airplane on which he has written, "Please speak." It lands upside down. Dylan does not speak. The silence is a little chilly; a few words would have made the audience ecstatic. Dylan's defense for this kind of criticism is that public speeches are a no-win situation. If he speaks a few words, people will say he hasn't said enough. If he speaks at length, people think he's lost his mind. In the end, Minnesotans don't seem too miffed by the episode. I ask one local resident the following day whether he's disappointed. "A little," he replies. "But in the paper it said he smiled a lot."

Discussions of Dylan often boil down to that: "Please speak. Tell us what it means." But does he need to? He had already given something away, during the ritual acoustic performance of "Tangled Up in Blue." This dense tale, which may be about two couples, one couple, or one couple plus an interloper, seems autobiographical; it's easy to guess what Dylan might be thinking about when he sings, "When it all came crashing down, I became withdrawn / The only thing I knew how to do was to keep on keeping on / Like a bird that flew . . ." See any number of ridiculous spectacles in Dylan's life. But the lines that he shouted out with extra emphasis came at the end:

> Me, I'm still on the road, heading for another joint
> We always did feel the same, we just saw it from a different point
> Of view
> Tangled up in blue.

Suddenly the romance in question seemed to be the long, stormy one between Dylan and his audience. There's a Ricksian detail that locates this shift in meaning: used as rhyme, "point" cuts the phrase "point of view" in half, so that the "you" and the "I" are literally looking from different points in space—Dylan being over there and the rest of us over here. And what is the "it" that we're seeing? The thing that comes between him and us—the music. Still, he says, "We always did feel the same." Interpretations are different, feelings are the same. That's a major concession from a man who seems so distant.

Why, night after night, did "Tangled Up in Blue" prove to be the song that brought the audience to life, as if Dylan had dived in and given everyone a hug? You could argue that those generous closing lines did the trick. But from the outset Dylan established an intimacy with the audience: the music did the emotional work for him. The current version of "Tangled Up in Blue" begins, like the original one on *Blood on the Tracks*, with chiming major chords, but the onstage Dylan soon slips into a different scale—into the blues. Dismantling and rebuilding his own song, piece by piece, he bends notes down, inverts the melody, spreads out the pitches of the chords, leans on a single note while the chords change around it, stresses the offbeats, lays a triple rhythm on double ones. As the rest of the band holds on to straitlaced harmony and a one-two beat, the song tenses up: opposing scales meet in bittersweet clashes, opposing pulses overlap in a danceable bounce. At some point, the classic radio staple becomes a new animal. By the end, Dylan may be speaking right at you, but you're probably too caught up in the music to notice.

As I went through my collection of Dylan records and tapes, I realized that in many cases I was only half listening to the lyrics—that the music was giving the words their poetic aura. Often, Dylan's strongest verbal images occur toward the beginning of a song, and it falls to his musical sense to make something of the rest. In "Sad-Eyed Lady of the Lowlands," the eleven-minute ballad that closes *Blonde on Blonde*, Dylan fashions some majestic metaphors to capture the object of his affection—"your eyes like smoke and your prayers like rhymes"—and then, in the second-to-last verse, he clouds over: "They wished you'd accepted the blame for the farm." What farm? What happened to it? Why would she be to blame for it? "Phony false alarm" is the rhyme in the next line, and it doesn't clear things up. The refrain makes another appearance—"My warehouse eyes, my Arabian drums / Should I leave them by your gate, / Or, sad-eyed lady, should I wait?"—and by this time you ought to be losing patience with it. What are "warehouse eyes," and how can one leave them? Dylanologists beat their heads against such questions. But the music makes you forget them. The melody of the refrain—a rising and descending scale, as in "Danny Boy"—is grand to begin with, but in the fifth verse Dylan makes it grander. As the band keeps playing the scale, he skates back up to the top D with each syllable. He sings on one note as the rest of the harmony moves around him: it's as if he's surveying the music from a summit. This is a trick as old as music. In Purcell's *Dido and Aeneas* the soprano catches our hearts in the same way as she sings, "Remember me, remember me."

Like Schubert, Cole Porter, and Hank Williams before him, Dylan sharpens the meaning of the lyrics in the mechanics of the music. Take "Mama, You Been on My Mind," which was long associated with Joan Baez and finally appeared in Dylan's own voice on the boxed set *The Bootleg Series, Vols. 1–3*. The song begins with a crabbed, somewhat indecipherable image:

> *Perhaps it's the color of the sun cut flat*
> *And covering the crossroads I'm standing at . . .*

The harmony under these words moves from an E-major chord to a G-sharp seventh and on to C-sharp minor and an F-sharp seventh. It's an awkward series of changes which matches the baroque images on the page. Our eyes and ears go "Huh?" Then the singer seems to shrug off, with a self-deprecating grin, the attempt to poeticize his emotion—"Or maybe it's the weather or something like that / But Mama, you been on my mind"—and the harmony gets easier, too, swaying gently from E major to C-sharp minor and back to E. The meaning changes as the chords change.

Dozens of Dylan songs work in the same way. The disturbing gospel number "In the Garden" shows the agony of Jesus in Gethsemane by wandering through ten different chords, each one like a betrayal. "Idiot Wind," the centerpiece of *Blood on the Tracks*, channels its universal rage—"Someone's got it in for me, they're planting stories in the press"—into a single harmonic convulsion: each verse of the G-major song begins with grinding C minor, which is like a slap to the ear. More often, the chords are mesmerizingly simple. In "Knockin' on Heaven's Door," there are just four of them, but they occur in an unresolved, drooping sequence—a picture of the "long black cloud" that comes down on Billy the Kid.

This is not to say that the music is everything. Dylan does have an original command of the English language. The neat click of the rhymes keeps you interested across all leaps of sense and changes of scene. John Lennon, not long before he died, satirized Dylan as a cynic who rhymed out of a lexicon, but I don't know of a dictionary that would have generated this couplet:

> *What can I say about Claudette? Ain't seen her since January.*
> *She could be respectably married or running a whorehouse in*
>   *Buenos Aires.*

Dylan also has a knack for tricky enjambments—lines that seem complete in themselves but are subverted by what follows. These are effects for the ear, not for the eye, and Dylan sells them in performance. There's a tape of him singing "Simple Twist of Fate" in San Francisco in 1980, in which the meaning twirls almost word by word. It's a heavily rewritten version of the *Blood on the Tracks* song, and the last verse starts this way:

> *People tell me it's a crime*
> *To remember her for too long a time*
> *She should have caught me in my prime*
> *She would have stayed with me*
> *Instead of going back off to sea*
> *And leaving me*

Dylan slows down, and we may think that the sentence is at an end. But it's not.

> *To med-i-tate . . .*

A grin now creeps into the voice, which had been appropriately wistful before. Dylan's stress on "meditate" tells us that the title refrain is coming around for its final rhyme, but we can't guess how he'll make the leap. His voice fills with pride—pride is one of the great emotions that he can convey—and the tempo picks up again: "*Upon! A! Simple! Twist! Of! Fate!*"

THE PECULIAR SOLIDITY of Dylan's lyrics comes in their easy give-and-take with older songs. He has said that the old traditions of folk, blues, spirituals, and popular ballads are his real religion and his habit of crossing genres may explain his habit of crossing religions. A few years ago, he said, "I believe in Hank Williams singing 'I Saw the Light.'" Dylan has a viselike memory for lyrics of all sorts, and his favorite method is to take a line from an old song and add one or a dozen lines of his own. "As I went out one morning," an old lyric says. "To breathe the air around Tom Paine's," Dylan adds. *Time Out of Mind* is thrillingly Dylanish, because he has returned with a vengeance to the magpie mode of writing. Old song: "She wrote me a letter and she wrote it so kind, / And in this letter these words you can find." Dylan rewrites the second line: "She put down in writing what was in her mind." Old song: "This train don't pull no gambles, / Neither don't pull no midnight ramblers." Dylan says, "Some trains don't pull no gambles, / No midnight ramblers, like they did before." There are a dozen or more borrowings in "Tryin' to Get to Heaven"—most of them from the "Spirituals" chapters of Alan Lomax's *Folk Songs of North America*. These buried quotations may be a bit of a joke at the expense of rock critics, who listen to Dylan for news of his love life, mental health, and commercial viability. What happens to their diagnoses of Dylan's misanthropy when it turns out that the lines they quoted come from black spirituals?

Time Out of Mind is the first Dylan record in a while which has reached a mass public, but it has confused the diehard fans. Clinton Heylin, for one, rejects it as mere atmosphere; it promises, he says, "depths that aren't there." True, Dylan no longer seems to be writing individual songs: lots of phrases could be moved from one track to another, and everything goes under one dreamy, archaic mood. The album manages to skip the twentieth century: people ride in buggies, there's no air-conditioning ("It's too hot to sleep"), church bells ring, "gay" means "happy", the time of day is measured by the sun, lamps apparently run on gas (and are turned "down low"), and, most of the time, the singer is walking. The wistfulness is intense. The singer is in love with a musical past that's gone forever. You picture him leaning late over his favorite records and songbooks, listening, reading, writing. These are songs about the loneliness of listening: you could add to them "Blind Willie McTell," which was recorded in 1983 and appeared in the *Bootleg* boxed set as a kind of fanfare to *Time Out of Mind.* "I'm gazing out the window of the St. James Hotel," he sang. "And I know no one can sing the blues like Blind Willie McTell."

The melancholy could become crushing, but Dylan doesn't let it. The best of the new songs are inexplicably funny: There's a wicked glee in the performance as Dylan manipulates the tatters of his voice, the scattered-ness of his inspiration, the paralysis that might arise from his obsession with the past, the prevailing image of himself as a mumbling curmud-geon. And in one song—"Not Dark Yet"—all the flourishes of his song-writing art come together: slow, stately chords, swinging like a pendulum between major and minor; creative tweakings of the past ("There's room enough in the heavens" becomes "There's not even room enough to be *anywhere*"); prickly aphorisms ("I can't even remember what it was I came here to get away from"); and glints of biblical revelation, not to mention what one Internet expert has identified as a reference to the Talmud ("I was born here and I'll die here against my will"). If he can't sing some low notes, he gestures toward them with a slide, so that you feel them. As he did in "Sad-Eyed Lady," he finds a way to intensify the refrain "It's not dark yet, but it's getting there." The line keeps creeping up, note by note, in the singer's now limited range. Like Skip James, the cracked genius among Delta-blues singers, Dylan gives a circular form a dire sense of direction.

The sense of arrival in "Not Dark Yet" is enormous. Once again, as Ricks would point out, words turn on their axis and encompass their opposite. The song ends, "I don't even hear a murmur of a prayer / It's not dark yet, but it's getting there." This couldn't be bleaker, could it? Bob Dylan stares into the face of death and decay. But as he sings "murmur of a prayer" he lifts the tune yet another step and does a graceful little turn at the top, creating an altogether new melody. And he slips in a triplet—a slight dancing rhythm that someone else picks up on guitar. As the song winds down, it's not the darkness that lingers but the freshly swaying motion in the music, and that theoretical possibility of a "murmur of a prayer." The man who worships Hank Williams is looking back at "I Saw the Light"—a would-be uplifting gospel number that was really filled with terror. "I saw the light, I saw the light, / no more darkness, no more night," Hank insisted, in a melody that fell, and you didn't believe him. Bob declares, with a gallant upward turn, "I don't even hear a murmur of a prayer." You don't believe him, either.

MINNEAPOLIS. Dylan has just played in Target Center, downtown. Toward midnight, walking away from the arena, I see a bus and a truck parked by a curb. A group of techies are loading equipment. There is bright electric light from somewhere—the spotlight of a handheld TV camera, it turns out. People are standing around, smiling sheepishly, as they do in the presence of someone famous. My heart begins to beat a little faster. A man with thick, tangled hair is standing next to the bus, looking awkward as he signs autographs. It's Lyle Lovett, who has just finished playing on the stage around the corner. I walk back to my hotel.

This episode pointed up for me the embarrassment of fandom. I hadn't expected to meet Dylan, but for a moment I thought I was about to see him up close. I felt the bubbling excitement of a fan. I'd been a fan, I suppose, since Dylan's music really hit me, a few years ago, while I was staying in a friend's apartment in Berlin. *Highway 61 Revisited* was one of the few records my friend owned, and after a couple of days I'd fallen for it: the fiercely funny lyrics, the music that was both common and grand, the whole proud, angry, backward take on life. I've since found that my belated conversion to Dylan matches up all too well with the latest research into rock fandom: Daniel Cavicchi, in a disquieting new study; divides fans into categories out of William James's *Varieties of Religious Experience*, noting that one kind of fan undergoes a sudden conversion or "self-surrender," often in a state of isolation or in a foreign land.

Is fandom as foolish as it feels? Or is it the respect owed to the sort of artist who used to be called "great"? Americans have always distrusted the concept of greatness, with its clammy Germanic air. Stardom, the cult of youth and wealth, long ago took its place. Dylan may be many things, but he is not a star: he can't control his image in the public eye. At the same time, he doesn't look, act, or sound like any great man that history records.

He presents himself as a traveling musical salesman, like B. B. King or Ralph Stanley or Willie Nelson. He is generally unavailable to the media, but he is in no way a recluse, and reclusiveness is traditionally the zone in which American geniuses reside.

America is no country for old men. Pop culture is a pedophile's delight. What to do with a middle-aged, well-worn songwriter who gravitates toward the melancholy and the absurd? An "artist," by contemporary definition, is one who displays himself in art, who shares "felt" emotion and "lived" experience, who meets and greets the audience. Art becomes Method acting; art, in various senses, becomes pathetic. With Dylan, the emotion has certainly been felt, at one time or another, but it wells up spontaneously in the songs themselves, in the tangle of words and music. Even at his most confessional, he withdraws his personality from the scene—usually by becoming beautifully vague—and lets the music rise. The highest emotion hits late, in the wordless windups of his greatest songs—from "Sad-Eyed Lady" to "Not Dark Yet"—when the band plays through the verse one more time and language sinks into silence.

BIBLIOGRAPHY

Biographies

Heylin, Clinton. *Behind the Shades Revisited.* New York: William Morrow, 2001.

Scaduto, Anthony. *Bob Dylan.* London: Helter Skelter, 2001.

Shelton, Robert. *No Direction Home: The Life and Music of Bob Dylan.* New York: William Morrow, 1986.

Sounes, Howard. *Down the Highway: A Life of Bob Dylan.* New York: Grove Press, 2001.

Spitz, Bob. *Dylan: A Biography.* New York: W. W. Norton, 1989.

Anthologies

Bauldie, John, ed. *Wanted Man.* London: Black Spring Press, 1990.

Benson, Carl, ed. *The Bob Dylan Companion.* New York: Schirmer Books, 1998.

Corcoran, Neil, ed. *Do You, Mr. Jones?: Dylan with the Professors and Poets.* London: Chatto and Windus, 2002.

McGregor, Craig, ed. *Bob Dylan: A Retrospective.* New York: William Morrow, 1972.

Thomson, Elizabeth M., ed. *Conclusions on the Wall: New Essays on Bob Dylan.* Manchester, Eng.: Thin Man Press, 1980.

Thomson, Elizabeth, and David Gutman, eds. *The Dylan Companion.* New York: Da Capo Press, 2001.

Other Books

Baez, Joan. *And A Voice to Sing With.* New York: Summit Books, 1987.

Bowden, Betsy. *Performed Literature: Words and Music by Bob Dylan.* 2nd ed. Lanham, Md.: University Press of America, 2001.

Doggett, Peter. *Are You Ready for the Country? Elvis, Dylan, Parsons and the Roots of Country Rock.* New York: Penguin, 2001.

Dylan, Bob. *Lyrics 1962–1985.* New York: Alfred A. Knopf, 1985.

____. *Tarantula.* New York: Macmillan, 1966.

Ellison, James. *Younger Than That Now: The Collected Interviews with Bob Dylan.* New York: Thunder's Mouth Press, 2004.

Feinstein, Barry, Daniel Kramer, and Jim Marshall. *Early Dylan*. Boston: Bullfinch, 1999.

Garman, Bryan K. *A Race of Singers: Whitman's Working-Class Hero from Guthrie to Springsteen*. Chapel Hill: University of North Carolina Press, 2000.

Goodman, Fred. *The Mansion on the Hill*. London: Jonathan Cape, 1997.

Gray, Michael. *Song and Dance Man III*. New York and London: Continuum, 2001.

Hajdu, David. *Positively 4th Street: The Lives and Times of Joan Baez, Bob Dylan, Mimi Baez Fariña and Richard Fariña*. New York: Farrar, Straus and Giroux, 2001.

Heylin, Clinton. *Bob Dylan: A Life in Stolen Moments*. New York: Schirmer Books, 1996.

___. *Bob Dylan: The Recording Sessions, 1960–1994*. New York: St. Martin's, 1995.

___. *Dylan's Daemon Lover: The Tangled Tale of a 450-Year Old Pop Ballad*. London: Helter Skelter, 1999.

Kooper, Al. *Backstage Passes and Backstabbing Bastards*. New York: Billboard Books, 1998.

Kramer, Daniel. *Bob Dylan: A Portrait of the Artist's Early Years*. London: Plexus, 1991.

Krogsgaard, Michael. *Positively Bob Dylan: A Thirty-Year Discography, Concert and Recording Session Guide, 1960–1991*. Ann Arbor, Mich.: Popular Culture, Ink., 1991.

Larkin, Philip. *All What Jazz*. New York: Farrar, Straus and Giroux, 1985.

Lee, C. P. *Like a Bullet of Night: The Films of Bob Dylan*. London: Helter Skelter, 2000.

Marcus, Greil. *Invisible Republic: Bob Dylan's Basement Tapes*. New York: Henry Holt, 1997.

Marqusee, Mike. *Chimes of Freedom: The Politics of Bob Dylan's Art*. New York: New Press, 2003.

Marshall, Scott, and Marcia Ford. *Restless Pilgrim: The Spiritual Journey of Bob Dylan*. Lake Mary, Fla.: Relevant Books, 2002.

Ricks, Christopher. *Dylan's Visions of Sin*. New York: Ecco, 2004.

Riley, Tim. *Hard Rain: A Dylan Commentary*. New York: Alfred A. Knopf, 1992.

Shepard, Sam. *Rolling Thunder Logbook*. New York: Penguin, 1977.

Sloman, Larry. *On the Road with Bob Dylan*. New York: Three Rivers Press, 2002.

Smith, Larry David. *Bob Dylan, Bruce Springsteen, and American Song*. Westport, Conn.: Praeger, 2002.

Williams, Paul. *Bob Dylan: Watching the River Flow; Observations on His Art in Progress, 1966–1996*. New York: Omnibus, 1996.

Reviews, Essays, Poems and Interviews

Many of the books listed above—particularly Behind the Shades Revisited, Song and Dance Man III *and* The Bob Dylan Companion—*include extensive bibliographies; with some exceptions, articles cited or reprinted in those works are not included here. This is a highly selective list emphasizing recent articles on Dylan as well as other pieces that are perhaps not known to the scholar or casual listener.*

Bono. "Foreword." *Q,* October 2000: 1.

Carroll, Jim. "Dylan and the KGB." In *Forced Entries: The Downtown Diaries, 1971–1973,* 65–70. New York: Penguin, 1987.

Christgau, Robert. "Dylan Back: World Goes On." Review of *Under the Red Sky. Village Voice,* October 30, 1990: 84.

Costello, Elvis. "Unafraid." Review of *Time Out of Mind. Mojo,* February 1998: 65.

Creeley, Robert. "In London." In *Selected Poems,* 170–177. Berkeley: University of California Press, 1991.

Davis, Francis. "Napoleon in Rags." *The Atlantic,* May 1999: 108.

"Did Bob Dylan Lift Lines from Dr. Saga? Author Is Flattered." *Wall Street Journal,* July 9, 2003.

Fariña, Richard. "Baez and Dylan: A Generation Singing Out." *Mademoiselle,* August 1964: 242.

Ferlinghetti, Lawrence. "Jack of Hearts." In *These Are My Rivers: New and Selected Poems, 1955–1993,* 181. New York: New Directions, 1994.

Fricke, David. "Blood on the Tracks." Review of *Live 1966. Rolling Stone,* October 29, 1998: 74.

Gilmore, Mikal. "Bob Dylan: The *Rolling Stone* Interview." *Rolling Stone,* November 22, 2001: 56.

Greenman, Ben. "Dylan! The Special." *The New Yorker,* July 17, 2000: 36.

Holborn, Mark. "His Various Selves." *Granta* 76 (Winter 2001): 181.

Jacobson, Mark. "Tangled Up in Bob." *Rolling Stone,* April 12, 2001: 65.

___. "Tangled Up in Gray." Review of *Renaldo and Clara. Village Voice,* January 30, 1978: 25.

James, Clive. "Don't Think Twice." Review of *Writings and Drawings* by Bob Dylan. *Guardian,* July 26, 1973.

Kermode, Frank, and Stephen Spender. "Bob Dylan: The Metaphor at the End of the Funnel." *Esquire,* May 1972: 110.

Komunyakaa, Yusef. "Gift Horse." In *I Apologize for the Eyes in My Head,* 20. Middletown, Conn.: Wesleyan University Press, 1986.

Kozinn, Allan. "Singing Dylan's Words to a Different Tune." *The New York Times,* March 12, 2000.

Marcus, Greil. "Comeback Time Again." Review of *Empire Burlesque. Village Voice,* August 13, 1985: 63.

___. "Sometimes He Talks Crazy, Crazy Like A Song." Review of *Love and Theft. The New York Times,* September 3, 2001.

___. "Where Is Desolation Row?" *The Threepenny Review,* Spring 2000: 28.

Marquart, Debra. "Dylan's Lost Years." In *Sudden Stories: The Mammoth Book of Miniscule Fiction,* edited by Dinty W. Moore, 52. Dubois, Pa.: Mammoth Books, 2003.

Motion, Andrew. "Masked and Anonymous." *Masked and Anonymous* official Web site. www. sonyclassics.com/masked/andrew-motion-essay.html.

Perna, Alan di. "Mind Control." *Guitar World*, April 1998: 199.

Piazza, Tom. "Bob Dylan's Unswerving Road Back to Newport." *The New York Times*, July 28, 2002.

Ricks, Christopher. "Bob Dylan." In *Hiding in Plain Sight*, edited by Wendy Lesser, 145–58. San Francisco: Mercury House, 1993.

Selvin, Joel. "Bob Dylan's God-Awful Gospel." Review of concert at Warfield Theater. *San Francisco Chronicle*, November 3, 1979.

Sterritt, David. "Dylan's First Film Unconventional." Review of *Renaldo and Clara*. *Christian Science Monitor*, January 26, 1978.

Waldman, Anne. "Hard Rain." In *Vow to Poetry*, 255–57. Minneapolis: Coffee House Press, 2001.

Wright, Charles. "When You're Lost in Juarez, in the Rain, and It's Eastertime Too." In *Appalachia*, 46. New York: Farrar, Straus and Giroux, 1998.

Ybarra, Michael J. "Tennyson, Milton and Bob Dylan?" *Los Angeles Times*, January 21, 1998.

ACKNOWLEDGMENTS

Grateful acknowledgment is given for permission to reprint lyrics from the following songs by Bob Dylan:

"All I Really Want to Do": copyright © 1964 by Warner Bros., renewed 1992 by Special Rider Music. All rights reserved. International copyright secured. Used by permission.

"Blind Willie McTell": copyright © 1983 by Special Rider Music. All rights reserved. International copyright secured. Used by permission.

"Bye and Bye": copyright © 2001 by Special Rider Music. All rights reserved. International copyright secured. Used by permission.

"Cry a While": copyright © 2001 by Special Rider Music. All rights reserved. International copyright secured. Used by permission.

"High Water": copyright © 2001 by Special Rider Music. All rights reserved. International copyright secured. Used by permission.

"Honest with Me": copyright © 2001 by Special Rider Music. All rights reserved. International copyright secured. Used by permission.

"If You See Her, Say Hello": by Ram's Horn Music. All rights reserved. International copyright secured. Used by permission.

"I'll Keep It with Mine": copyright © 1963 by Warner Bros., renewed 1991 by Special Rider Music. All rights reserved. International copyright secured. Used by permission.

"I Shall Be Free": copyright © 1963 by Warner Bros., renewed 1991 by Special Rider Music. All rights reserved. International copyright secured. Used by permission.

"I Threw It All Away": copyright © 1969 by Big Sky Music. All rights reserved. International copyright secured. Used by permission.

"Lonesome Day Blues": copyright © 2001 by Special Rider Music. All rights reserved. International copyright secured. Used by permission.

"Masters of War": copyright © 1963 by Warner Bros., renewed 1991 by Special Rider Music. All rights reserved. International copyright secured. Used by permission.

"Moonlight": copyright © 2001 by Special Rider Music. All rights reserved. International copyright secured. Used by permission.

"The Wanderer" by Alex Ross, originally published in *The New Yorker,* May 10, 1999. Copyright © 1999 by Alex Ross. Used by permission of the author.

Every effort has been made to contact copyright holders of original material contained in this volume.

In addition to the sources cited above, I would like to thank, most of all, Maribeth Payne for accepting the book and being a motivating—though encouraging and sympathetic—editor in every way. Allison Benter and Courtney Fitch at Norton were most helpful when it came to all sorts of tasks. Greil Marcus generously commented on an early draft of the contents and suggested new entries. For reading the introduction and offering a helpful critique, I thank Alex Ross. Robert Polito also helped out in many ways, and opened the door for several contacts that I might not otherwise have found. Thanks to Norbert Krapf for showing me his poem and being a good friend. Clinton Heylin was always available for advice, and his books on Dylan greatly aided my research. David Gates made a lot of helpful suggestions; Tom Piazza answered the phone every time, and always had a good story about Bob or one more blues source for *Love and Theft.* And Mitch Blank's archive remains the best resource for any fan's research and appreciation of Dylan.

For accepting my offers to write original essays, I thank Gary Giddins, Barry Hannah and Tom Piazza, as well as Rick Moody and Joyce Carol Oates for granting permission for works previously unpublished. Gratitude is also owed to Bob Bettendorf, Bono, Nadja Coyne, William Heyen, Neil Hoos, Daniel Kramer, Rose Robinson, Jeff Rosen, Augustin Sedgewick, Sam Shepard, Lynne Okin Sheridan, Howard Sounes, Anne Waldman, Michael Waters, Sean Wilentz and Paul Zollo.

Kate, thank you for your editorial help, patience and love.

To my mind, I first heard a Dylan song at Eagle's Nest Camp—so thanks to the creators of that songbook, who took the time to arrange all the glorious folk music therein.

INDEX